India and Pakistan

D0103704

A half century ago, the independence of India and
beginning of the end of Western colonialism and the emergence of new
nation-states in much of Asia and Africa. The year 1997, the fiftieth
anniversary of independence, offered an excellent milestone for considering the progress, problems, and prospects of the two countries. For
this purpose, ten well-known specialists presented papers at a conference
at the Woodrow Wilson International Center for Scholars in Washington, D.C., assessing Indian and Pakistani domestic political developments, economic development, social trends, and foreign and security
policies, as well as U.S. relations with India and Pakistan. The papers
have been collected in *India and Pakistan: The First Fifty Years,* and the
editors, themselves well-known experts on South Asia, have added a
sizable introduction. The result is a comprehensive review of how the
two countries, home to one-fifth of the world's population, have fared.

This book is the first serious effort to examine and compare trends in
the two countries during their first fifty years. Although the authors are
specialists, they have targeted their texts for lay readers as well as scholars. The book should be of use for supplemental readings on South Asia
in university courses and as background for anyone seeking to do business in South Asia. It is the only work of its kind currently available.

Selig S. Harrison has been an Associated Press correspondent in New
Delhi, South Asia Bureau Chief for the *Washington Post,* Senior Fellow
in charge of Asian Studies at the Brookings Institution, and Senior Fellow of the Carnegie Endowment for International Peace. He is the author of *India: The Most Dangerous Decade* and *India and the United
States.* He is currently a Senior Scholar at the Woodrow Wilson International Center for Scholars and an adjunct professor of Asian Studies
at George Washington University.

Paul H. Kreisberg, formerly a U.S. diplomat based in India and Pakistan,
has moderated a series of fifteen diplomatic dialogues among Indians
and Pakistanis since 1991. He is a Senior Scholar at the Woodrow Wilson International Center for Scholars.

Dennis Kux, formerly in the U.S. Foreign Service, specializing in South
Asia, served as Country Director for India, Deputy Assistant Secretary
of State for Intelligence Coordination, and U.S. Ambassador to the Ivory
Coast. A former Fellow of the Woodrow Wilson International Center
for Scholars, he is currently at work on a history of U.S.-Pakistani relations. Previously, he wrote *Estranged Democracies: India and the United
States.*

WOODROW WILSON CENTER SERIES

Continued on page following index

WOODROW WILSON INTERNATIONAL CENTER FOR SCHOLARS

The Center is the living memorial of the United States of America to the nation's twenty-eighth president, Woodrow Wilson. Congress established the Woodrow Wilson Center in 1968 as an international institute for advanced study, "symbolizing and strengthening the fruitful relationship between the world of learning and the world of public affairs." The Center opened in 1970 under its own board of trustees, which includes citizens appointed by the president of the United States, federal government officials who serve ex officio, and an additional representative named by the president from within the federal government.

In all its activities the Woodrow Wilson Center is a nonprofit, nonpartisan organization, supported financially by annual appropriations from Congress and by the contributions of foundations, corporations, and individuals.

WOODROW WILSON CENTER PRESS

The Woodrow Wilson Center Press publishes books written in substantial part at the Center or otherwise prepared under its sponsorship by fellows, guest scholars, staff members, and other program participants. Conclusions or opinions expressed in Center publications and programs are those of the authors and speakers and do not necessarily reflect the views of the Center staff, fellows, trustees, advisory groups, or any individuals or organizations that provide financial support to the Center.

Woodrow Wilson Center Press
Editorial Offices
One Woodrow Wilson Plaza
1300 Pennsylvania Avenue, N.W.
Washington, D.C. 20523
telephone: (202) 691-4010

India and Pakistan

The first fifty years

Edited by
SELIG S. HARRISON, PAUL H. KREISBERG, and
DENNIS KUX

WOODROW WILSON CENTER PRESS

AND

CAMBRIDGE
UNIVERSITY PRESS

PUBLISHED BY THE PRESS SYNDICATE OF THE UNIVERSITY OF CAMBRIDGE
The Pitt Building, Trumpington Street, Cambridge, United Kingdom

CAMBRIDGE UNIVERSITY PRESS
The Edinburgh Building, Cambridge CB2 2RU, UK   http: //www.cup.cam.ac.uk
40 West 20th Street, New York, NY 10011-4211, USA   http: //www.cup.org
10 Stamford Road, Oakleigh, Melbourne 3166, Australia

First published 1999

Printed in the United States of America

Typeface Sabon 10/13 pt.   *System* Penta [BV]

A catalog record for this book is available from the British Library.

Library of Congress Cataloging-in-Publication Data
India and Pakistan : the first fifty years / edited by Selig S.
Harrison, Paul H. Kreisberg, Dennis Kux.
p.   cm. — (Woodrow Wilson Center series)
Includes index.
ISBN 0 521 64185 3 (hc.). — ISBN 0 521 64585 9 (pbk.)
1. India—Politics and government—1947-   2. Pakistan—Politics
and government.   I. Harrison, Selig S.   II. Kreisberg, Paul H.
III. Kux, Dennis, 1931-   .   IV. Series.
DS480.84.I4854   1998
954.04—dc21   98-36434

ISBN 0 521 64185 3 hardback
ISBN 0 521 64585 9 paperback

Contents

vii

Figures and tables

Preface

In 1947, the independence of India and Pakistan signaled the beginning of the end of Western colonialism and the emergence of new nation-states in much of Asia and Africa. Fifty years after the achievement of their independence, India and Pakistan, with 20 percent of the world's population, have made significant economic, social, and political progress, but they continue to confront major challenges. The year 1997, the fiftieth anniversary of independence, offered an excellent milestone for assessing their progress, problems, and prospects. To accomplish this, the Woodrow Wilson International Center for Scholars organized a conference on June 3–4, 1997, in Washington, D.C. This volume represents the papers read at the conference.

Not only in the United States, but in South Asia as well, there is a wide range of opinion on every issue relating to the evolution of India and Pakistan. We found that to be true at the Wilson Center conference also. We believe, nonetheless, that the essays in this volume capture many, if not all, of the key issues and elements that should legitimately go into a fifty-year assessment. We did not attempt to organize an international conference; we relied primarily on American specialists on South Asia as authors and on Indians and Pakistanis who were residing in or visiting the United States as commentators.

We decided from the beginning to invite a diverse group of participants, each of whom brought a strong personal interest in, and professional knowledge of, the discipline and the region. The commentators offered their own views, participated actively in the discussions at the conference, and provided valuable ideas for the revised papers of the 10 authors. We would like to thank the commentators—Shahid Javed Burki, Inderjit Singh, and Anis Dani from the World Bank; Indian jour-

nalist Prem Shankar Jha; Vice-Admiral (ret.) K. K. Nayyar, chair of the
Delhi Study Group; Mustapha Kamal Pasha of American University;
Hasan-Askari Rizvi of Columbia University; and Stephen Coll of the
Washington Post—for their valuable contributions to this book, for
whose specific content and views, however, they bear no responsibility.
Pakistan's ambassador to the United States, Riaz Kokhar, and India's
chargé d'affaires, Shymala Cowsik, also offered their own views at the
start of the sessions. We sincerely welcome their involvement and encouragement.

We are deeply grateful to the Woodrow Wilson International Center
for Scholars for facilitating the conference and for its support to all three
organizers as Center scholars. We are also grateful to the director emer-
itus of the Woodrow Wilson Center, Charles Blitzer, for his backing and
help.

Without the financial assistance of the Kathwari Foundation, the En-
ron Corporation, the GE Fund, *India Abroad*, and the Infrastructure
Capital Group there would have been no conference and no book. We
warmly thank them for their interest and generous support.

Finally, and by no means least, we want to express our personal appreciation for the many hours and days of work by Beth Brimner, Li
Zhao, David Abruzzino, and Damon Daniels, members of the staff of
the Woodrow Wilson Center, for making sure that papers were received,
reproduced, and distributed; that invitations were sent out; and that
necessary administrative arrangements were undertaken in a timely manner; and for the innumerable contributions that only organizers of conferences can appreciate.

Introduction

SELIG S. HARRISON, PAUL H. KREISBERG,
AND DENNIS KUX

In 1826, fifty years after American independence, the new nation was still a work in very uncertain progress. It had not been long since the nation's capital had been sacked by foreign troops. Political campaigns were rife with slander and bribery. Parties and politicians were held in little repute. Outbreaks of violence and mob rule were common in major cities. Border tensions troubled relations with Canada and Mexico. Threats of rebellion and resistance to national policies in the southern states were beginning to confront the government in Washington. Intense debates raged between local interests over economic policies. No one in the country had any social safety net—except to move to the West.

The label of a potentially "failing state" might easily have been applied to the United States at the end of the 1820s as it entered the decades that would conclude with the Civil War. The American experience suggests the importance of caution in making prophecies about the prospects for India and Pakistan on the basis of their first half-century of independence, which ended on August 15, 1997. At the same time, a retrospective examination of these fifty years offers a valuable perspective.

Together, India and Pakistan constitute one-fifth of the human race. Pakistan is the second-largest Muslim state; and India, the second most populous country in the world. Although the British wisely left their Indian colony peacefully in 1947, the violence that accompanied partition sapped the development of the two states and set the stage for three wars between them. Both India and Pakistan have, nevertheless, made enormous strides in the last half-century, but the base from which each started and significant differences in political, economic, and social circumstances make direct comparisons difficult.

1

This volume has been intentionally structured so that India and Pakistan are evaluated on their own terms, although readers may see points at which comparisons occur. The editors offer some comparative assessments of their own in the introduction, but others may come to different conclusions.

The volume starts with chapters on domestic politics and governance. These are followed by chapters on economic development and on social change for the populations of India and Pakistan, which have trebled in the last half century. Two chapters address India's and Pakistan's foreign and security policies, and the final chapter considers U.S. policies toward the two states over the past five decades.

Short summaries of the key judgments in each of the chapters follow, along with comparisons of trends in the two countries by the editors at the end of each section.

POLITICAL DEVELOPMENT

Summary: Paul R. Brass's essay on Indian politics praises India for its success in building a solid constitutional structure where civil authorities have never been threatened by challenge from the military. India has passed the tests of assassinations of national leaders and of a declaration of a national emergency and the arrest of opposition political leaders. Regular transfers of power have taken place through free and generally fair elections in which participation has been strong. The judiciary has functioned for the most part with integrity. And new political forces have been able to emerge representing previously weak and underrepresented groups in society despite opposition from traditional power elites.

The heritage of colonial administrative rule, the dominance of the Nehru family and the Congress Party in politics, central control of the "commanding heights" of the economy, and socialist economic policies placed overwhelming power in the hands of the central government and its leaders through most of the first half-century of Indian independence.

Over the last two decades, however, as Brass notes, a shift has been taking place in the power balance between the central government and the states. Indian economic and social development as well as political power are increasingly likely to revolve around the tensions in this changing balance. The dominance of the Congress Party in Indian politics has ended. Upper castes are in the process of losing their dominance in Indian politics as regional elites and lower castes assume greater power both at the center and in the states. Brass does not predict what the consequences of these political trends will be for stability and democracy in India. He is, however, deeply concerned about the growth of corruption, criminalization, and violence in politics.

Tensions among ethnic, linguistic, and religious forces in India, Brass says, have been a key reason for India's obsession with maintaining political unity and territorial integrity at all costs, as well as for its emphasis on preserving a secular state. The strength of Hindu nationalism, which has grown in the last decade, will not go away, Brass says, particularly in northern India. But neither is it likely to prove successful in dominating India politically.

Brass concludes that India has been unsuccessful in providing its people with "the national self-respect they seek from the rest of the world" or the economic or social development that could have been achieved. Despite this, he sees the trends in India as potentially positive. Nothing would contribute more to this, he suggests, than a reduction of Indo-Pakistani tensions, which he argues have kept relations between Hindus and Muslims embittered, subject to manipulation, and prone to violence.

Robert LaPorte, Jr.'s assessment of Pakistan's political development since 1947 paints an uneasy and troubled picture. Pakistan is a state, LaPorte concludes, which after fifty years is "still in the making," still striving to find a stable and effective form of government. He sees the two and a half decades from 1947 to 1971 as a time in which ordinary citizens were denied a role in public policy making, regular military intervention in politics began, and efforts to reconcile the political and economic interests of Pakistan's two wings collapsed and led to civil war and division of the country.

Popular elections marked the beginning of the period from 1971 to 1988 but also heralded the consolidation and legitimization of "feudal" politics. Martial law and a return to military rule followed, along with the evolution of a new political power troika consisting of the chief of army staff, the president, and the prime minister.

The period 1988–97 was marked by repeated contests for power in an evolving two-party system. Judging from declining voting turnouts since the mid-1980s, however, the electorate has diminishing confidence in political processes that have not permitted any elected government to serve out its full term.

On the positive side, LaPorte sees an increasingly free and outspoken press in Pakistan, a decline in dominating political personalities, and some evolution away from rural feudal political power to more diverse forms of political influence. Although religion remains a key part of the country's political life, and despite concerns by many observers, Pakistan has not become a sectarian state. Religious political parties have failed to draw strong electoral support.

On the other hand, LaPorte expresses deep concern that institutions of governance at all levels—central, provincial, and local—remain weak. Corruption is widespread and deep. The independence of the judiciary from political influence has increased but is uncertain.

LaPorte hopes that a more open, participative, and responsible system will evolve and that government will develop the capacity to function impartially under the rule of law. It remains uncertain, however, whether democracy will become institutionalized in Pakistan or suffer a new set-back, probably ushering in another cycle of military governance.

Commentary: In contrasting the Brass and LaPorte views of political trends over the last half-century, it is clear that India has had a strong advantage in the continuity and viability of its basic political institutions. Its constitution, while much amended, has provided a stable and, by now, universally accepted legal and institutional structure. Pakistan has been less fortunate. The executive has been dominant in both countries, although in recent years the balance sheet of political power has become more complex. The pattern of strong leaders (or, in the case of Pakistan, military ones), with the personal authority to draw or command political support from a broad spectrum of the population, marked domestic politics in both India and Pakistan for long periods over the last fifty years. Barring major crises threatening the most fundamental institutions of government or national existence, this pattern seems unlikely to return in the national politics of either country.

Pakistan, since 1985, has seen a power struggle between the president and the prime minister, resulting in the dismissal of four governments. The most recent crisis, in late 1997, which also involved a raw confrontation between the constitutional powers of the chief justice, the president, and the prime minister, appears for the present to have settled the battle in favor of the prime minister. Nevertheless, it has cast a serious shadow on the working of Pakistan's constitutional structure and, once again, as so frequently in the past, raised the possibility of intervention by the army in resolving political tensions.

In India, while power remains nominally with the prime minister, the increasing fragmentation of political parties both regionally and by caste has reflected real shifts in power in Indian society. These changes have weakened the authority of prime ministers in successive governments, slowed consensus-building, forced more complex bargaining among centers of power, and complicated the formulation of national policies.

The Indian electorate has sustained greater confidence in electoral processes than that of Pakistan, at least as measured in terms of voter turnout. Nevertheless, cynicism about the honesty, integrity, and motives of politicians in both countries has grown steadily. Although the reform of politics and the elimination of corruption have emerged as central themes in both India and Pakistan, there has been virtually no effort in either country to alter the current state of affairs and it is unclear whether or how such reforms could be implemented. Neither Brass nor

LaPorte is optimistic that fundamental improvement in the quality of political life and governance will be forthcoming in the near future. The editors share this view.

The judiciaries of India and Pakistan have at times succumbed to pressures from the executive branch, or the military in Pakistan, or from more sordid inducements. Both legal systems suffer from a widespread perception that justice, usually long delayed—often for venal reasons—is, indeed, justice denied. Still, in recent years, the supreme courts in both countries have increasingly asserted greater powers of oversight and responsibility, and popular confidence in the courts, at least at the higher levels, has remained higher than in virtually any other institution of government.

From its birth, Pakistan has been pulled strongly by public sentiment and the views of political leaders toward greater conformity with Islamic principles and law. Long-standing disputes over who is a Muslim, the rights of minorities, and, in recent years, sectarian violence posed threats to political and social stability. India has faced parallel strains. Communal tensions between Muslims and Hindus, while uneven around the country, are deeply embedded in some areas. Both states have found that such tensions are partly open to remedy through education, economic development, legal recourse, and direct government action. They are, however, likely to persist in the future and offer opportunities for political exploitation that can seriously damage the democratic political system.

Pakistan has had a far more difficult time in sustaining its national integrity and unity than India. It lost part of this struggle in 1971 when the nation's eastern wing, East Pakistan, separated in a short but brutal civil war to become the independent state of Bangladesh. Sindhi, Baluch, and Pushtun grievances against the dominant Punjabi majority remain serious. Pakistan has also kept alive the bitter dispute with India over Jammu and Kashmir by diplomatic, military, and other political means. This issue has remained an important, if perhaps slowly declining, factor underpinning Pakistani politics and nationalism. Nevertheless successive Pakistani prime ministers have drawn back from any fundamental compromises on Kashmir that, while potentially opening the way to better Indo-Pakistani relations, might expose them to bitter recrimination and blame by domestic political rivals.

The sharply different roles the military has played in the two countries reflect in part this troubled history as well as the contrasting strengths of political institutions. The Indian military has been consistently apolitical and under full civilian control. The major role of the Pakistani army in the political life of the state has become a fact of life; civilian leaders regularly consult key military leaders on major political challenges facing the country.

While India has held the lead in developing and sustaining the political institutions of democracy, Pakistan has also made significant progress, particularly in recent years. At the same time, it is striking that both analysts see very similar political challenges: popular frustrations with politics, failings in legislative effectiveness, and threats to democracy from corruption and criminalization of politics and institutions.

The churning from new political forces generated by economic, social, and political change is stronger in India than in Pakistan, where traditional elites, particularly in rural and tribal areas, remain strong. Nevertheless, parallel changes have been occurring in Pakistan. The rise of ethnic-based politics in Karachi, shifting balances in tribal areas in the aftermath of the Afghan war, and the steady growth of urban politics and of the urban middle class are influencing the development of political institutions and the nation's stability.

Allthough democratic institutions in both India and Pakistan have weathered difficult challenges in recent years, Brass and LaPorte are uneasy about the future. Brass does not suggest fundamental changes in political institutions but worries about the ability of the existing institutions to respond to the demands of the years ahead. LaPorte's concerns are more fundamental. He wonders if Pakistan's present institutional and political structure will survive, although he does not question the survival of the state. The editors share these concerns and judgments.

ECONOMIC DEVELOPMENT

Summary: John Adams sees India's economic development over the last fifty years as reasonably steady and by no means unsatisfactory. The planned, socialist model of development adopted in the early 1950s was necessary, Adams believes, to lay the foundation for modernization and industrialization that the private sector was unable to undertake and for which only the state had the needed resources.

Nevertheless by the 1960s and 1970s, the burden of bureaucratic controls on the economy had begun to stifle growth. Mismanagement and inefficiency increased and the need for policy changes became increasingly urgent. At the same time, Adams argues, nationalization of banks in the early 1970s helped marshal resources from India's rural areas, and the benefits of the Green Revolution revived agricultural productivity. Adjustments in trade policy contributed to what became an increasingly rapid growth in Indian exports in the late 1970s, continuing in the 1980s, and increasing with further economic reforms in the 1990s.

Nevertheless at the beginning of the 1980s, it was clear that the overall economic growth of India was only modestly ahead of population growth and falling steadily behind that of other Asian economies. Adams believes the basic direction of Indian economic reform, which accelerated growth to 5 percent by the end of the 1980s, was set early that decade, gaining speed to reach first 6 percent and then 7 percent in the 1990s with the acceleration of reform after 1991. These two decades of unprecedented growth of the Indian economy are likely to continue, Adams argues. While he is fundamentally optimistic about the future, he warns that reform in democratic India will always be cautious, gradual, and marked by sensitivity to "making too many people uncomfortable at the same time."

Marvin G. Weinbaum's analysis of Pakistan's economic development is aptly summed up in his subtitle: "misplaced priorities, missed opportunities." Weinbaum shows that discontinuities of political policy and the abuse of power by entrenched elites have aggravated the impact of economic failures.

He argues that huge debts generated by domestic and international borrowing have not produced commensurate economic benefits but weigh heavily on the economy. A relatively high (6 percent) annual growth rate in the past enriched a few industrialists and large landowning families, but not the general population. Defense expenditures, generated by tensions around Pakistan's borders as well as by the political power gained by the Pakistani military over the last fifty years, siphoned off funds better spent on social welfare, health, and education programs. Inadequate investment in human infrastructure has impeded development of a workforce capable of enabling Pakistan to engage in economic global competition.

Although some of Pakistan's economic problems were consequences of international developments beyond its control, Weinbaum believes that many were the results of bad decisions by individuals and political groups within the country. Attempts at economic reform in the last fifteen years have been undercut by discontinuities in governance and difficulties in sustaining an economic policy vision. Low savings rates, poor work ethic, lags in infrastructure development, maldistribution of national income, and growing public cynicism about political and economic policies have led to a focus by those in both the public and private sectors on short-term advantage as opposed to long-term goals.

Even though Weinbaum believes prospects for the future may improve, like LaPorte, he argues that the most important need is to strengthen institutions, including reviving financial and banking systems, providing greater transparency in economic policy making, strengthening respect for legal norms including payment of taxes, and building an improved work ethic at all levels of society. Political normalization with India and peace in Afghanistan, in particular, would open new opportunities for subcontinental trade and for oil and gas links to Central Asia, which would be of great benefit to the Pakistani economy. Without fundamental systemic reform, however, Weinbaum is uncertain how successful the Pakistani economy will be in seizing such opportunities.

Commentary: Both India and Pakistan have tried different economic strategies of development since independence with varying degrees of success and at different times. Pakistan relied primarily on a market-based economic strategy in the 1950–70 period, shifted to a centralized economic approach in the 1970s and 1980s, and since has begun returning to a more market-based economy. Pakistan was able to sustain growth in its gross domestic product (GDP) of 4–6 percent throughout these years. But this growth was heavily dependent on foreign credits and remittances from overseas workers.

At the same time, Pakistan ignored or failed to follow through on agricultural reforms. It badly underspent on social and infrastructure needs, particularly health and education, and steadily sustained heavy military expenditures to deal with a perceived threat from India, the central focus of national strategy since 1947. Chronic and deep-seated corruption sapped economic vitality. As industrial productivity stagnated, economic growth began to decline in the 1990s. Major economic reform and restructuring have become imperative at the fiftieth anniversary of independence.

India pursued a very different economic course. Shortly after independence it initiated a planned economic development strategy that it essentially continued, and even strengthened, until the 1980s. All essential aspects of the economy, both domestic and foreign, were subject to close administrative control from New Delhi. Large subsidies were provided for agricultural inputs, high tariffs were sustained to protect domestic industry, and major investments were made in state-owned industry and infrastructure requirements. Greater attention was paid to social and human infrastructure, including rural land reform and education, than in Pakistan, but still not enough.

Much progress was achieved, as Adams notes, but less than was hoped for. Poverty levels have remained high. GDP rarely grew above 3 percent until the late 1980s, when it reached 5 percent. Industrial productivity stagnated. Foreign debt levels steadily grew. Major economic reform and restructuring became critical.

By the early 1990s, both countries had reached critical points in their economic development, but by very different routes. Both accepted the need to place greater reliance on the market and initiated reforms toward that end. There is no longer serious debate in either country over the importance of fiscal and budgetary reform in order to be able to control inflation, increase the tax base and make it more equitable, redistribute resources for the maximum economic and social return, and curtail the expansion of state enterprises and make them more efficient. But implementation of policies designed to achieve those goals, reduce government spending, and improve the efficiency of the market and the economy has been slow and shaky in both countries.

Finance and commerce and industry ministers in both countries understand and advocate the need for greater productivity in those sectors the state continues to control—and in principle agree on privatization of many of these—as well as in the economy as a whole so that manufactured and agricultural products and services are more competitive both internationally and domestically. They are intent on opening their markets to the outside world to encourage such competition and expanded exports. There is widespread realization of the importance of expanding regional South Asian trade, which has stagnated for most of the last half-century at minuscule levels, although political obstacles, especially in Pakistan, remain significant barriers.

India and Pakistan have already taken major steps to achieve some, but by no means all, of these goals. Both countries are encountering strong internal resistance—or, nearly as bad, apathy—as they try to move forward. Strong political groups agree in principle on the need for reform but continue to resist changes that affect their power bases adversely. And the political leadership in neither country has been strong enough to overcome this resistance.

Institutions and bureaucracies have a vested interest in slowing specific reforms and even in their failure. Large sectors of the publics in both countries have deeply embedded expectations of a continuation of the benefits—legal ones like fertilizer or food subsidies, illegal ones like pilfered electricity or water—they have received in the past. Fundamental infrastructual gaps in both countries constrain development, and not only shortages of capital but political resistance have made each step forward slow and difficult. Moreover, cultural and economic behavior, both malign and well intentioned—low savings rates, fear on the part of Indian companies of being overwhelmed by multinational corporations, a poor work ethic, and social indifference to the needs of the poor, as well as new concerns about the environment and ecology—hold back the pace at which economic reforms can proceed and continue to slow economic development in both India and Pakistan. The recent dramatic deflating of the East Asian economic "miracles" is likely to add to the caution with which India and Pakistan pursue economic reform.

SOCIAL DEVELOPMENT

Summary: Sonalde Desai and Katharine Sreedhar believe societal change in India has fallen short of aspirations at the time of independence. They see increasing disparities of wealth and living conditions. A growing Indian middle class benefits from the economic growth described by Adams. Hundreds of millions of Indians, however, remain deeply impoverished, with limited or no access to the better life offered by economic growth.

Desai and Sreedhar, nonetheless, see some areas of significant progress. Government programs over the last fifty years have doubled life expectancy and reduced infant mortality by two-thirds. Population growth has declined markedly. Male literacy has doubled and female literacy tripled, although levels in India still remain well below those in East and Southeast Asia.

But social programs are seriously underfunded and resources for these are diminishing, not growing. Malnutrition remains very high. General health services are of low quality and often totally unavailable to the poor. Regional inequities are enormous (with the Hindi-speaking heartland of northern India the worst off). Gender inequality continues to be rampant despite growing political pressure from organized women's groups.

Government programs focused on distributive justice and job creation, except for employment in state-owned enterprises or local and state offices, have not been successful. Although land reform has had impact in individual states, over half the rural population still farms economically marginal land or has no land at all.

Caste barriers, nominally illegal under the Indian Constitution, continue to be widespread. Despite the fact that these are yielding in some respects to political mobilization, Desai and Sreedhar emphasize that caste continues to limit the distribution of the economic benefits of growth throughout most of rural India and for many inhabitants of cities as well.

Redefinition of India's national security to include economic and social security for all is vital, Desai and Sreedhar argue, or there is likely to be little improvement in fundamental social services or in easing societal inequities.

Anita M. Weiss sees social development in Pakistan over the last fifty years, like that in India, marked by improvements in life expectancy and a decline in infant death rates, as well as greater access to information and transportation for ordinary Pakistanis. Nevertheless, again like Desai and Sreedhar, she sees broad neglect in many key areas. Pakistan is at a critical juncture, Weiss believes. The social contract envisaged at the time of independence—to improve the well-being of society as a whole—must be given new vitality and greater emphasis must be placed on social priorities.

Adult literacy, educational quality as well as access to schools for Pakistani children at every level, nutrition, sanitation and health, and women's rights in all respects have lagged badly. Inadequate financial resources, increasing rich-poor and urban-rural disparities, and the absence of consistent and viable national and provincial policy formation and implementation are all critical problems. Pakistan must also intensify efforts to reduce its rate of population growth. Politicians and government officials need to deal with the rapid growth of urban areas and the huge infrastructure and social changes these are causing. Weiss notes that when the next national census—seventeen years after the last census and seven years behind schedule—is held (in March 1998), this will underscore both the dramatic societal shifts that have occurred and the important policy changes that will be required.

Women's empowerment is a critical step in any fundamental effort to deal with Pakistan's social problems. Although there have been some advances in recent years, this continues to be a critical need. One area of hope is the recent growth of independent nongovernmental groups and organizations, which are working hard to strengthen civil society despite continued conservative resistance in rural and tribal areas.

Commentary: There are striking parallels in the achievements and the failings of India and Pakistan. Infant mortality has declined and life expectancy has risen along with *rising* rates of inoculation against disease. Adult literacy has improved, particularly in India, but growth is less impressive than in many other Asian countries, especially for women. Although birth rates have fallen in both countries, Pakistan's remain among the highest in the world. In both countries, there continue to be wide disparities in social indicators between different states (or provinces) and between urban and rural areas.

The goals of ending or even reducing poverty, providing adequate health care, offering educational opportunities for all, and reducing regional, urban/rural, and gender inequality remain targets for the future at the end of the first half-century of independence. The gaps between stated and legislated aspirations continue to be wide. Insufficient resources, scarcity of skilled professionals, lackluster administration, traditional cultural behavior patterns, and the very poverty of potential recipients all block or limit the effective implementation of governmental programs.

Desai, Sreedhar, and Weiss stress the complexity of reasons for the shortcomings in India's and Pakistan's social development programs but these are strikingly similar in both countries. Perhaps the most serious has been that other issues have persistently been given a higher priority by the top-level policy makers. Once funds were allocated, moreover, responsibility shifted to lower administrative levels, usually to state or provincial governments. There, except for provision of jobs and contracts, which has always enjoyed a high priority, local elites have influenced implementation in ways that have often minimized the benefits received by economically and culturally backward groups. Effective oversight of social programs has often been poor. There have been few penalties for those responsible for failing programmatic efforts and often few rewards for those with outstanding records of achievement.

Informal nongovernmental organizations (NGOs) and groups, which can act as a bridge for transferring technology and managerial skill to local groups and run interference against bureaucratic or political obstruction, are growing in both countries. Desai and Sreedhar see such efforts as useful at times but by no means a cure-all and are skeptical of many NGO efforts in India. Weiss sees them as of potentially greater importance in Pakistan and capable of making a real difference in both the formulation and implementation of policies in the future.

In India, traditional village and district local councils (*panchayats*) were given a new constitutional importance in the 1990s. They are now a formal third level of elected governance in the system (below the national and state governments and legislatures) through which the national and state governments will channel funding and administration for a wide range of social and economic programs. How this develops in practice is still being tested, and many of the obstacles to effective programs noted above may continue to operate at the *panchayat* level. Pakistan has no parallel structure and badly needs to pay more attention to building representative local institutions.

In both India and Pakistan, our authors believe—and the editors agree—effective change at lower levels of society is dependent on strong political leadership at every level. Major improvement in the quality of governance is critical, but particularly at the grassroots rural and urban levels where social policy and the people who are affected intersect. In both countries, changes in the values of those responsible for implementing policies, as well as those who are their beneficiaries, must gradually occur before the goals set out by India's and Pakistan's founders will be realized.

FOREIGN AND SECURITY POLICY

Summary: Indian foreign policy, Sumit Ganguly writes, focused initially on anticolonialism, global distributive justice, and nonalignment. These themes remained central over most of the first decades of independent India. Little emphasis was placed initially on defense and national security, but virtually unceasing tension with Pakistan and growing security concerns centered on China in the late 1950s and 1960s made national defense one of India's foreign policy priorities.

Relations with the major powers went through ups and downs. By the late 1960s, however, a chill in Indo-U.S. relations developed that persisted for much of the next two decades, while Indo-Soviet relations became warmer. Policy issues of importance to all three countries—the war in Vietnam, India's military involvement in the separation of Bangladesh from Pakistan, Sino-U.S. rapprochement, India's development of a nuclear capability in the 1970s, and renewal of U.S. military assistance to Pakistan in connection with the war in Afghanistan—were key factors. At the same time, the focus of Indian policy increasingly shifted from global issues to events relating to the subcontinent. While attention to nonalignment continued, India's global agenda took second place to its regional one. Moreover, internal security challenges—in the Punjab, northeastern India, Kashmir, and a number of other individual states—sometimes in part abetted from outside the country, have posed more difficult challenges than traditional external threats.

The end of the Cold War has presented new challenges to Indian policy makers, Ganguly suggests, and the need to evolve a new set of principles to cope with the altered international system. He sees three alternatives:

1. Renewing focus on "rich-poor" state issues and mobilizing international coalitions to resist economic pressures from the developed world. This strategy would conflict with India's own economic objectives and is unlikely to find common ground with the interests of many other developing states on a broad range of issues.

2. Developing India as a nuclear, great-power state that others would accept as such. Ganguly sees this as risking intensification of intra-Asian tensions and as inconsistent with India's rapid economic growth.

3. Centering Indian policy on strengthening economic and political cooperation in South Asia, including Pakistan, as well as with neighboring regions, and focusing on India's own economic growth and development. This would continue India's current policy direction and is more likely to enhance India's international status and reinforce its security than other options. This course, however, could compel either India (and Pakistan) or the other nuclear powers to find new ways of reconciling what at the fiftieth anniversary of independence had become strongly divergent views on nuclear weapons and their future role on the subcontinent.

Thomas Perry Thornton sees Pakistan's foreign policy since independence centered around a fifty-year effort to escape from insecurity. The central themes, which Thornton believes were pursued in generally sound, sometimes brilliant fashion with the help of outstanding diplomats, were links with other Muslim states and alliances or understandings with stronger states as a "balance" against India. A search for security against India, the stronger regional state whose dominance Pakistan has consistently feared, with which it has fought three wars and been in a state of almost unrelieved tension over Kashmir, has been the overriding focus of Pakistani security policy.

Hopes of support from the United States during the Cold War went through cycles, but the interests of both partners were only episodically synchronized. Beginning in the 1960s, Pakistan turned as well to China for support. This too, while rewarding, offered Pakistan no fundamental pillar of security. Efforts to gain political support among the nonaligned and Islamic states were rarely consistently successful in the face of a stronger Indian presence or other priorities that led to only lukewarm endorsement for Pakistan. The decision to pursue a nuclear deterrent in the 1970s was a response to uncertain efforts to find outside security balances and will not be abandoned barring a fundamental improvement in Indo-Pakistani relations.

Thornton suggests that after the Cold War Pakistan, in fact, faces no fundamental external threats, although events in Iran, Afghanistan, and elsewhere in Central Asia are clearly of concern. India has become a status quo power that does not threaten Pakistan and in terms of India's own international interests cannot afford to do so. Even though Pakistani military planners have not yet accepted this, there does seem to be a growing recognition that easing regional tensions is essential for Pakistan's national interests. Prospects may be better for achieving this now than at any time in the last twenty years.

Some Pakistanis, Thornton says, continue to look for new geopolitical scenarios that, like the Cold War, may heighten Pakistan's importance to other major powers. These are unlikely in the foreseeable future. The key factor affecting Pakistan's global role will be its ability to deal with its domestic challenges and become a more active player in the global economy.

Commentary: The assessments by Ganguly and Thornton accurately capture the congruence and divergence, as well as the continuities, in Indian and Pakistani foreign and security policies.

India began in the 1950s with a global view and a foreign policy focused on enhancing its international political stature as a leader of decolonized states. Between the 1960s and 1980s, wars with Pakistan and China, tensions with other South Asian neighbors, and emphasis on domestic economic and political priorities turned India inward. While never ignoring the rest of the world, particularly during the Cold War, Indian foreign policy under Jawaharlal Nehru's successors increasingly centered on the subcontinent itself.

International economic policy issues, except for international aid flows, were a distant priority for India throughout most of this period. Foreign trade and foreign investment were de-emphasized for over forty years. Indian economic policy makers focused their energies on promoting self-reliance and on protecting India's industries and agriculture from potential international competition.

India also pursued self-reliance in the military arena. Although it has achieved some successes, rapid technological change with which India has been unable to keep pace has steadily eroded the gains. India's long-term goal has been to ensure its military supremacy in the region. Even though it has clearly long achieved this on the subcontinent, policy makers have never resolved the question of how far beyond South Asia India needs to expand its security reach. India has, however, developed an independent capability to build nuclear weapons and missiles as deterrents against Pakistan, China, and any other potential adversary, and as a symbol of major power status. It is difficult to envisage India's relinquishing these capabilities in the absence of a global program toward the reduction and elimination of nuclear weapons by the existing nuclear powers.

It was only in the 1990s that India began to refocus its foreign policy, returning again to active global engagement but with a new emphasis on economics. The collapse of the former Soviet Union and the end of the Cold War were major factors for change in Indian foreign policy. But even more relevant was a growing awareness that India was being left behind in global economic and technological competitiveness. It is this set of priorities that Ganguly, correctly in the view of the editors, emphasizes as likely to set the primary direction of Indian policy in the future.

South Asia continued to be of major importance for India's policy makers. Even there, attention has increasingly turned to building economic linkages and resolving transborder economic and political issues. Although, in principle, this includes improved political and economic relations with Pakistan, progress is likely to come slowly.

Pakistan's foreign policy for the last half-century, on the other hand, has been and remains almost single-mindedly defined primarily in terms of the assumed threat from India and the unfinished business of partition, specifically the status of the former princely state of Jammu and Kashmir.

As Thornton observes, the search for reliable allies and security guarantors over the past fifty years has been largely unsuccessful. Pakistan sought military self-reliance, but its limited resource base has left it heavily dependent on imported weaponry, of which it can afford only modest supplies. Its nuclear capability has even more psychological importance for Pakistan's strategic planners as an "ultimate" deterrent than does India's capability. Pakistan's nuclear program, in contrast to India's, does not relate to aspirations for equitable global status and is focused only on the presumed security threat from India.

Continuing civil war in Afghanistan and U.S. tensions with Iran pose serious obstacles to Pakistan's taking advantage of its potential role in transshipment and development of petrochemical and refining industries drawing on Iranian and Central Asian oil and gas. Both offer major opportunities for Pakistan to broaden its foreign-policy focus to active cooperation with the Central Asian states and provide incentives for greater Indo-Pakistani energy cooperation. This would not only serve fundamental economic interests of both countries but also provide a stimulus for settlement of outstanding disputes.

The editors share Thornton's view that Pakistan suffers greatly from a foreign policy primarily based on zero-sum relations with India. The single-minded obsession with India has made it more difficult for Pakistan to cultivate relations with other countries and has limited its abilities to respond to the changing global environment. India has been trying to convince other states, particularly those in East and Southeast Asia as well as in the Middle East and Central Asia, that its tensions with Pakistan will not intrude into its relations with them. It has had some success, but ultimately there will have to be real progress toward resolving Indo-Pakistani tensions if this is to work.

Relations with the United States

Summary: American relations with India and Pakistan, argues Stephen Philip Cohen in the concluding chapter, have been marked by broad swings that have reflected U.S. global priorities at any given time as well as the fact that the United States does not have vital—as opposed to important—interests in South Asia. Concerns relating to the former Soviet Union, China, Vietnam, and the Middle East or to nuclear nonproliferation have generally guided U.S. policies. Support for democracy and economic development have been contributing elements, but often not determining ones in Washington's decision-making on issues relating to India and Pakistan.

Chronic tensions between the two countries have frustrated U.S. efforts to maintain good relations with both. The United States has never wanted to make an unequivocal choice and generally balanced moves toward one country by policy initiatives toward the other, often leaving both dissatisfied. The cumulative effect has been to breed resentment and suspicion about the United States in India and Pakistan, as well as a sense of frustration about the subcontinent in Washington.

Cohen argues that the primary U.S. foreign-policy challenge is to find a satisfactory formula for dealing with states like India and Pakistan, which are not threats to America's security, represent nonvital interests, and thus far are not major economic partners. Cohen suggests that U.S. policy should be "realistic, proportionate, and low-cost," aimed at encouraging economic liberalization and the development of trade and investment links, the strengthening of democratic institutions, and strategic normalization between India and Pakistan.

Washington should encourage India and Pakistan to address their differences without pressing for quick (and unrealistic) solutions. The United States should also encourage India and Pakistan to manage their nuclear capabilities without demanding that they abandon them, moderating U.S. legislative and national policies on this issue. Since the mid-1970s, nuclear proliferation issues, in particular, have dominated thinking in Washington, in Cohen's view, becoming an intellectual "bottleneck" in policy making toward South Asia. The United States, India, and Pakistan should finally, Cohen believes, develop bilateral and trilateral strategic dialogues about the rest of Asia, including China.

Commentary: The editors in general share Cohen's vision of the relationship and agree with much of what he believes needs to be done to strengthen U.S. ties with both countries. He fails, however, to acknowledge the depth of the enduring psychological and political damage to U.S. relations with both countries resulting from the U.S. Cold War alliance with Pakistan. In India, the U.S. tilt to Pakistan has left a legacy of distrust that continues to color the relations between New Delhi and Washington today. Moreover, since Pakistan wanted its U.S. military aid not for defense against communist aggression but to improve its balance of power with India, the American cutoff of military and economic aid in 1965 and 1990 has left a legacy of distrust in Islamabad as well. The editors share Cohen's assessment of nuclear policies in South Asia as a fundamental clash in national strategic policy objectives and interests on which compromise had become almost impossible as the two countries reached their fiftieth anniversary. American commercial interests in India and Pakistan and prospects for steady growth in economic interaction promise greater cooperation and increased U.S. attention to South Asia. Nuclear policy issues, however, remain a cloud through which it is uncertain that policy makers in New Delhi, Islamabad, and Washington will be able to navigate successfully in the coming years.

I

Political development

1

India: Democratic progress and problems

PAUL R. BRASS

DEMOCRACY IN INDIA

Democracy is one of the most overused and misused words in the vocabulary of politics, covering a wide variety of governmental forms, social systems, and political practices. It is a word that has become too imprecise to tell us much about any political order, including that of India, "the world's largest democracy." This chapter reviews a checklist of criteria that are commonly used to assess the strengths and weaknesses of contemporary developing democracies in relation to India's democratic evolution over the past fifty years. It will be necessary, however, to go beyond such a list to consider the more fundamental and persistent strains affecting the Indian political order in order to assess more fully its future prospects.

Let us begin with the features of India's political evolution that appear most positive to the view of India as a developing democracy. First among them is the entrenchment of parliamentary/electoral/competitive political practices. India, like Sri Lanka, but in contrast to Pakistan and Bangladesh and most other countries in the developing world, has never experienced military rule or even a serious attempt by the military to intervene in the political process. Indeed, again in contrast to both Pakistan and Bangladesh, senior military officers have never held ministerial office in New Delhi and have always accepted the authority of the civilian minister of defense. Thus, by one of the common yardsticks of a

I am grateful to Dennis Kux and Paul Kreisberg for their detailed criticisms of the first draft of this chapter, which led to several changes in it. I also want to thank Prem Shankar Jha for his role as a discussant when the draft was presented at the Woodrow Wilson Center conference on June 3, 1997, and for the exchange of views that followed afterward. The point of view expressed in this chapter, however, is entirely my own.

democracy—the maintenance of civilian control over the military—India's record stands unblemished.

The Indian Parliament is not exactly revered, nor does it have much power—neither does the British Parliament—but it has met regularly over the past fifty years and has also exercised the ultimate parliamentary authority of voting governments out of power. Although there have been occasions in the past—and not just during the Emergency—when some political parties have been banned and their leaders jailed for a while, on the whole Indian political parties have flourished, risen, and declined with few serious obstacles—except, in the case of most of them, their own organizational deficiencies, internal quarrels, and inability to mobilize popular support. Elections for Parliament and the state legislative assemblies have been held with great regularity, though at lower levels—in the cities, towns, and villages—they are held for the most part only when they can be won by the party in power at the state level. Some elections in some states have been marked by considerable electoral irregularities, and some violence, intimidation, "booth-capturing," and the like, always occurs, but most elections have been free and fair by international standards. Finally, elections at the state and national levels have become increasingly competitive and have occasioned numerous transfers of power in the states and several at the center. By that other great standard of a stable democracy, therefore, the ability to survive the transfer of power through competitive elections, India again stands as a rare case in the postcolonial world.

Separation of powers among the three great branches of government—executive, legislative, and judiciary—has also commonly been considered an aspect of democratic functioning insofar as it acts to prevent concentration of power and the possibility of its abuse by the executive. Insofar as the relationship between the executive and the legislative branches is concerned, it is the executive branch that has been dominant. Several struggles have also taken place since independence between the executive branch and the judiciary both at the central and the state levels. These have involved efforts by the judiciary to assert and by the executive to prevent judicial review of legislation, as well as efforts by the judiciary to protect fundamental rights from government infringements. They have also involved struggle over the power to appoint judges. Although the executive has often prevailed in limiting the Supreme Court's powers of judicial review and in limiting the application of fundamental rights through numerous laws providing for preventive detention or for the arbitrary arrest of individuals allegedly engaged in "terrorist" or other kinds of "disruptive" activities, the Supreme Court and some of the high courts in the states have managed to maintain a considerable degree of independence that has allowed them to reassert the authority of the courts from time to time on many matters. During the past few years, the Supreme Court and the high courts in some states have been especially assertive in overseeing the pursuit of civil and criminal cases involving corruption, forgery, and even complicity in promoting riots against dozens of former ministers in the union government and in the states, including former prime minister P. V. Narasimha Rao and the former chief minister of Bihar, Laloo Prasad Yadav.

There is, of course, one great blot in India's postindependence record on the above matters: the Emergency authoritarian regime established by Prime Minister Indira Gandhi between 1975 and 1977. During that period, most parliamentary conventions and practices were temporarily discarded or abused; the federal system was undermined; the judiciary failed to uphold even the right of *habeas corpus*; a cult of leadership was promoted; political hooliganism was fostered by Mrs. Gandhi's son Sanjay; tens of thousands of political figures were jailed, including many elected members of state legislatures and Parliament itself; and rigorous press censorship was enforced. Yet, for reasons that remain unclear, Mrs. Gandhi relaxed the Emergency after two years, held new, free and fair elections and lost them, thus inadvertently contributing to the achievement of that watershed in the heralding of an effectively functioning democracy, the first transfer of power from the ruling party, the Indian National Congress, to an alternative party, the Janata Party.

The Janata Party was formed toward the end of the Emergency by all the leading noncommunist leftist, centrist, and rightist parties, many of whose leaders had been jailed during the Emergency. The new party, formed for the sole purpose of providing an effective, united opposition to defeat Mrs. Gandhi and her dominant Congress (I) organization, won a bare majority in the Lok Sabha (House of the People) elections held in January 1977, and formed the first non-Congress central government in alliance with several other smaller and regional parties. Although it disintegrated as a consequence of internal conflict in July 1977, it passed legislation during its tenure restoring most of the important features of the previous parliamentary order, which remain in place today.

Two other features of India's competitive parliamentary system must be considered significant democratic achievements. The first concerns political participation. It is evident not only in high rates of electoral turnout, but in many other forms. With regard to turnout, the figures vary from election to election and from region to region, but they are generally higher than in the United States and, in some regions of India, as high as turnout rates in European countries. Turnout in Indian parliamentary elections has ranged from a low of 45.7 percent in the First General Elections, in 1952, to a high of 64.1 percent in 1984; it remained above 55 percent in every general election between 1962 and 1991. In contrast, participation rates in American presidential elections tend to range between 50 and 55 percent.

Furthermore, participation of Indians in other forms of political life is also extensive and involves rural as well as urban, poor as well as middle-class segments of society. Political marches, processions, and demonstrations of all sorts by innumerable groups are a regular feature of life in India that can be observed even by tourists during a short stay. Hundreds of thousands of peasants can be brought to Delhi to demonstrate before Parliament. They can also be mobilized in huge numbers to intimidate the civil administration in the districts and compel them to concede their demands on such issues as the timely provision of irrigation water or electricity. Hundreds of thousands can also be mobilized to march from many points in India to some central gathering place to participate in a grand political show of strength. All this, of course, goes back to the strategies of Mohandas K. Gandhi and a few of his predecessors, such as Bal Gangadhar Tilak, a leading nationalist figure from Maharashtra, prominent in the Indian National Congress in the late nineteenth and early twentieth centuries. These men developed a highly original array of mobilizational methods and tactics that represent one of the strongest supports for a participatory political life in India. Moreover, the proliferation of new tactics, devices, methods, and symbols used to mobilize large numbers of people for political causes in India is unending.

The second feature of Indian political evolution since independence that is especially favorable to the view of India as the world's largest democracy is the successive entry of new groups into the electoral/political process through caste succession and through the formation of new political parties mobilizing specific sections of society. The term "caste succession" refers to the fact that, in election after election, caste groups with large population concentrations in particular regions, districts, and constituencies, whose members previously either did not vote in large numbers or voted for persons from the dominant castes, have produced their own leaders who have given them a voice in the political process and access to political and economic patronage. This process of caste succession is one that filters upward from the localities rather than downward through mobilization from regional or national party head-quarters.

The latter process also has been at work, and massively so. Examples abound from virtually every state in the country. The most famous and best-documented case of the mobilization of non-Brahman castes oc-curred in Tamil Nadu in a process that began long before independence, in the late nineteenth century. In the postindependence period, the inher-itors of the non-Brahman movement of protest that displaced the Brah-mans from their overwhelming dominance in political and public life are two regional parties, the DMK (Dravida Munnetra Kazagham) and the AIADMK (All-India Anna DMK). These two parties have stood primar-ily for the advancement of the interests of the non-Brahman castes as well as for the regional cultural identity of the Tamil people and the protection of the Tamil language against any efforts to impose the use of Hindi in government administration, intergovernmental communica-tion, and the schools in their state. After the death of its founder in 1969, the DMK split into two separate organizations; the splinter organization added to the old designation the appellations "All-India" and "Anna" after the founder of the DMK, hence AIADMK. These two parties have alternated in power in the state government—completely displacing the Congress—since 1967.

In Kerala and West Bengal, it has been the Communist Party (Marx-ist) that has mobilized the lower castes, made it possible for them to participate effectively in electoral politics, and brought increased wages to agricultural laborers and increased security to tenant farmers and small landholders. Other regional parties and movements that have mo-bilized the lower and backward castes have formed in Maharashtra, Gujarat, and Karnataka. The effectiveness of such movements in increas-ing the political awareness and participation of the lower castes can be seen in the electoral turnout rates in these states for state legislative assembly elections. In Kerala, for example, between 1957 and 1987, turnout ranged between 72.3 percent in 1980 and 84.4 percent in 1960. In Tamil Nadu, turnout between 1952 and 1989 ranged from 64.3 per-cent in 1957 to 76.6 percent in 1967.

In north India, the mobilization of the backward and lower castes has occurred more recently and has been more divisive than in most other parts of the country. The first party to mobilize successfully a considerable range of new groups into the political process in north India was the radical socialist party under the leadership of Ram Manohar Lohia, whose party at its height was known as the SSP (Samyukta [United] Socialist Party). Lohia, who died in 1969, founded the movement to mobilize the backward castes into an effective force in north Indian politics, something done much earlier in the south and west of India. He tried also to speak for all other disadvantaged and minority groups as well as women, but his greatest success and that of the SSP was to further the process of political incorporation of the backward castes and to mobilize them as part of a broader attack on Congress and upper caste dominance in the Indian political order.

A second party arose in north India in the late 1960s to extend the process of incorporation of nonelite groups as effective political participants in the Indian political order. That party, initially called the Bharatiya Kranti Dal (BKD), later the Lok Dal, was created by Chaudhuri Charan Singh, who defected from the Congress in the state of Uttar Pradesh (U.P.), the largest and politically most important state in India, with a small group of followers in 1967. His defection brought down the Congress government in that state, which was replaced by the first non-Congress government in its history, with Charan Singh as chief minister. Although this government remained in power for less than a year, it transformed party politics in the state and made it much more competitive. Moreover, within a few years, Charan Singh established the BKD as the preeminent representative of the middle peasantry of north India. The BKD manifesto, written by Charan Singh personally, was an extremely sophisticated statement concerning the economic and political advantages of sustaining a system of peasant proprietorship in India—as opposed to either landlordism or collective farming. Intended to appeal to all the middle peasants irrespective of caste, the manifesto appealed especially to the broad band of so-called backward castes who resented the political and economic dominance of the elite castes in the rural districts of north India.

In 1974, the two principal parties representing the middle-peasant backward castes merged into the Bharatiya Lok Dal (BLD), which, in 1977, became the principal force in the Janata Party that defeated the Congress in the post-Emergency elections. Several party splits and changes in leadership and party nomenclature have occurred in the intervening years, but some party or other representing the middle-peasant backward castes has been a major force in every election from 1969 to the present in the Hindi-speaking states, particularly U.P., Bihar, and Haryana. The political descendants of Ram Manohar Lohia and Charan Singh today in north India are the two leaders from the backward caste known as Yadavs: Mulayam Singh Yadav, from U.P., whose party is the SP (Samajwadi [Socialist] Party); and Laloo Prasad Yadav of Bihar, who leads the Rashtriya Janata Dal.

A further spurt in political mobilization has taken place with quite dramatic consequences in the last few elections in north India since the formation of the BSP (Bahujan Samaj Party) under the leadership of Kanshi Ram and Mayawati. The BSP stands for the unity of all nonelite castes and backward Muslims against the dominance of upper-caste Hindus in Indian political life, but its primary base is among the lowest or "Scheduled" Castes (also called Dalits, meaning "oppressed"). Although Kanshi Ram, the BSP's head, comes from the Punjab, the party has less support and influence there than in U.P. The party won 6 seats out of 85 in the 1996 parliamentary elections from U.P. and only 4 in the 1998 elections, but it has become a powerful force in recent state legislative assembly elections and a critical alliance partner in the unstable coalition politics of government formation. The party also has some electoral support in Madhya Pradesh, where it won 2 parliamentary seats out of 45 in the 1996 elections, although it won none in 1998. Mayawati, Kanshi Ram's protégée and close companion, is an educated woman of Dalit origin with a law degree from the University of Delhi.

I have argued in my earlier work on party and electoral politics that, during the first four decades of parliamentary politics in north India, the Scheduled Castes had been merely pawns in a political process in which the principal lines of conflict were between parties representing mostly the upper castes and parties representing the backward castes. In north India, the Congress, representing primarily upper-caste Brahmans, Rajputs, and Bhumihars, nevertheless retained the support of the lower castes who had no important, respected leaders from among their own ranks, excepting Jagjivan Ram from Bihar. The Scheduled Castes remained pawns in the sense that they were used to sustain the Congress against challenges to its dominance, in return for which they received some benefits from various poverty alleviation programs, but little substantial political power or influence beyond that exercised by Jagjivan Ram. Jagjivan Ram remained a member of the Congress for most of his political life until he broke with the party at the end of the Emergency in 1977 and joined hands with the opposition. During his long political career, he was a member of every Cabinet in New Delhi from August 15, 1947, until July 28, 1979, when he served as deputy prime minister in the Janata government headed by Morarji Desai. He commanded influence in the Congress and the Janata Party because of his prestige among Scheduled Caste members of Parliament (MPs), but he never sought to mobilize the Scheduled Castes into a separate political party.

This has now changed very dramatically in U.P. The party of the Scheduled Castes in that state now commands the votes of the great majority of the Scheduled Castes. Mayawati has twice become chief minister of the state. In Bihar, Scheduled Castes have been critical in keeping the Janata Dal of Laloo Prasad in power, though they lack powerful leaders of their own there. Nevertheless, it is of great importance that the Scheduled Castes in both states now form a critical and independent voting bloc in the electorate and in the legislatures, whose support or withdrawal of support may determine the fate of governments. Even more important in my view is that Scheduled Castes, as well as backward castes, are now being recruited in large numbers into the higher levels of the civil administration and the police.

In sum, the principal achievements in postindependence Indian politics that justify India's designation as the world's largest democracy are the entrenchment of parliamentary institutions and practices, including repeated transfers of power through free elections; the extensive participation in the political process, reflected both in voting and in collective movements of all types; and the successive incorporation and mobilization of new groups as effective agents in politics. It should also be noted that—again, with the exception of the Emergency period—India's press has not been subjected to state censorship.

PROBLEMS

Satisfaction with these developments of half a century must, however, be tempered by a consideration of the problems and trends that run counter to democratic consolidation. First, centralizing tendencies have been present in Indian politics from the beginning. These tendencies have been reflected in ideology, government practices, and political leadership in New Delhi. They have recently been given a major jolt as a consequence of elections since 1993 that have brought to the forefront their opposite—

namely, regional and decentralizing tendencies and forces. Nevertheless, the tension between centralizing and regionalizing forces remains of decisive importance for the future of Indian politics.

Centralism as a faith and an ideology has been the creed or the unspoken assumption of nearly all national leaders of India since independence, including Jawaharlal Nehru, India's prime minister from 1947 until his death in 1964; Sardar Vallabhbhai Patel, deputy prime minister under Nehru and his political rival in the Congress until Patel's death in 1950; Indira Gandhi, Nehru's daughter and prime minister from 1966 to 1977 and again from 1980 until her assassination in 1984; her son, Rajiv Gandhi, prime minister from 1984 to 1989; and most other leaders from north India as well. The justification for centralism has been India's desire to become a modern, industrialized society and a strong state, the equal of the Western powers—and entitled to their respect. All the main policies, institutions, and practices that have weakened Indian democracy and frustrated most of its proclaimed goals of equality and social justice derive from the underlying ideology of centralism and the strong state. They include the maintenance of the principal institutions inherited from the British colonial authoritarian-bureaucratic empire, including the elitist civil service, the multifarious preventive detention laws, and the recurrent practice of imposing central rule over individual states according to the whim of the central leadership rather than the guidelines of Article 356 of the Constitution, which allow central rule only under certain restricted circumstances. They include also the system of centralized economic development planning that retarded Indian economic growth for thirty years or more and prevented any serious efforts to provide for the basic minimum needs of the country's population. They include further the brutalization of the police, paramilitary, and even to some extent the military forces through their unrestrained use in the suppression of any real or imagined threats to the unity of India.

Insofar as the practice of parliamentarism is concerned, India has also experienced specific deviations from those associated with the Western model. Most legislation passed both by the central government and the states does not emerge from parliamentary debate and open discussion in the press, but through ordinances issued by the government and later ratified by the legislature.

Dynasticism has been one of the principal routes to power not only in New Delhi, but in states, districts, and localities throughout the country. While dynasticism has confronted other forces in the states and districts, such as the processes of caste succession and political mobilization discussed above, it has been an especially corrosive force at the national level. The degeneration of the Nehru-Gandhi family as the mantle of power passed from father to daughter to sons has had serious consequences for Indian political institutions and practices. The daughter set out to dismantle the parliamentary system and the federal union. One son introduced hooliganism as a political practice of the ruling party. A second son brought massive corruption to the very center of the Indian political order.

Although, as noted above, India has more than once passed the test of peaceful transfer of power from one set of leaders to another in New Delhi, on two occasions the transfers have been preceded by assassinations. Moreover, on the first occasion, after the murder of Mrs. Gandhi, the transfer of power to her son emphasized dynasticism—and that through irregular procedures. Furthermore, highly placed members of the Congress and the government proceeded in the midst of the funeral ceremony for Mrs. Gandhi and the transfer of power to Rajiv Gandhi to launch a pogrom against the Sikh community in Delhi and in other urban areas of north India as "revenge" for the killing of Mrs. Gandhi by her two Sikh bodyguards. The second assassination was that of Rajiv Gandhi in May 1991 in the midst of the parliamentary election campaign. His killing precipitated a sympathy vote that tilted the balance in favor of the Congress. The new prime minister, P. V. Narasimha Rao, was then elected and appointed according to the accepted conventions of parliamentarism.

Although these assassinations and their aftermath, especially the first, must qualify one's satisfaction over the process of transfer of power in India, they have been no more frequent than in the United States. Nor have assassination and execution of elected heads of government become as critical in transfers of power in India as they have in other countries in South Asia, including especially Sri Lanka, Bangladesh, and Pakistan.

India, like the United States, is a federal union. In such systems, the maintenance of a balance between central and state powers is an important protection against the potential abuse of central power. For two decades after Nehru's death, the years dominated by Mrs. Gandhi and her sons, the centralizing tendencies to which I referred above were accompanied by a corrosion of the federal system manifested in the frequent use of President's Rule to remove governments led by opposition parties or even by Congress leaders who showed signs of independence from the central leadership or who had any significant political bases of their own. A further consequence of this corrosion of the federal system and the centralization of power in New Delhi was the growth of political sycophancy in the states as well as at the center.

Representative institutions in the states have themselves not met the highest standards of democratic functioning. While elections in most of the states have been regular, highly competitive, mostly free and fair, and accompanied sometimes by very high rates of turnout, governance in all but a few of the states has not been consistent with democratic norms. There has been little real legislative participation in state-level government in most states, where rule by ordinance is routine. Legislatures meet primarily to ratify the selection of a chief minister—sometimes actually to select one—but then the game is to prevent the legislature from ever meeting again or to have it meet only rarely and briefly. The fear, indeed often the expectation, is that the chief minister and the government will be voted out of power should the legislature meet—not on any policy grounds, but because of the discontent of those in the majority party or coalition who have not received what they consider to be their due in the form of political patronage and the distribution of sources of corrupt income, such as a ministerial portfolio or chairmanship of a public-sector corporation.

In such a context, it should not be surprising that there is an absence of policy making at the state level. The principal actions of ministers and of the government are directed toward amassing wealth through corrupt means, recognizing particular groups in society for special benefits such as caste reservations, destroying one's enemies by various measures, and preventing elections at the local level that might allow one's rivals to establish local bases of power.

Politics have been very considerably criminalized at the local and state levels in India in a way that goes far beyond ordinary patronage politics and corruption. Urban mafias and rural *dacoits* (gangs of armed robbers), often in collusion with the police, have proliferated in many parts of the country, particularly in the north and in the west. Criminals, including drug barons and murderers, are elected in large numbers to many state legislatures and to Parliament as well. The police themselves have become a scourge in some parts of the country, colluding with criminals, carrying out routine acts of beating, torture, and rape in police stations, and attacking and looting villages on one pretext or another. In Punjab and Kashmir, of course, police actions have gone far beyond even

these forms of behavior to include extreme atrocities, collusion with terrorists, drug smuggling, and more. The consequence of this criminalization of politics and the police is that personal safety for ordinary citizens
is not among the values guaranteed by the state, as in Hobbes's prescription, but is merely one among several values for which one must strive
and that require political protection.

Politicians have felt the consequences of criminalization as well, some
dangerous, some prestige-enhancing. Political and other forms of violence have increased at all levels in Indian society, making it increasingly
imperative for the politicians to carry arms and to be accompanied by
bodyguards. It has also become common for a political leader in power
to be accompanied by a retinue of cars and jeeps wherever he or she
goes, including a platoon of trim and smart-stepping "Black Cats,"
armed and dressed in black uniforms, who jump out at each destination
before the leader to provide protection that may or may not be needed,
but certainly the prestige he or she desires. Many of these politicians,
however, do in fact need constant protection; their stately bungalows
have become virtual armed encampments.

The world of persons abroad interested in India has been kept informed of the abhorrent violations of human rights and dignities in the
Punjab that persisted throughout the 1980s and into the early 1990s and
that have been in progress without cease in Kashmir since 1989. It is less
commonly known that such practices occur from time to time in police
stations everywhere in north India and that some of them constitute
routine political practice.

To return to the matter of corruption, it needs to be noted that the
practices that have become standard are not the quaint custom of giving
bakshish (literally meaning a gift, but in practice suggesting a bribe) nor
the occasional scandals that come to the surface in every democratic
country. What exists in India is pervasive, systematic, structured, and
graded corruption running from the bottom to the top of the political
order. Few are exempt from it, untouched by it, immune from it—from
ordinary villagers to prime ministers of the country. The bureaucracy
also, from top to bottom, including the once pure elite cadre of Indian
Administrative Service (IAS) officers, has become thoroughly corrupted.
Postings and transfers to lucrative districts—where district magistrates,
civil engineers, irrigation engineers and inspectors, health officers, and
many others occupying high-income-producing posts can make a lot of
money—are sold by the ministers of government to the bureaucrats in

their departments. So are police postings. The judiciary too, especially at the lower levels, has not been free from the taint of corruption.

Finally, behind the stable facade of Indian parliamentarism, an incessant and tumultuous struggle for power persists without end. Struggle and competition for power are of the essence of any democratic political order. In a federal and parliamentary system such as India's, functioning in such a heterogeneous and factionalized society, it is hardly surprising that there is not even a temporary respite. Nevertheless, the consequences of such incessant struggle undermine and reinforce some of the antidemocratic tendencies noted above, as well as others. They include the abdication of policy-making responsibilities by most ministers to the bureaucrats, concentration of the ministers on political maneuvering, amassing wealth for themselves and their family members, and the longing for an authoritative personality to provide a source of final authority in the system.

THE POLITICAL CONSEQUENCES OF CENTRALIZED PLANNING AND THE NEW ECONOMIC POLICY

Most modern conceptions of political democracy include an assumption of relative economic equality, if not in fact, at least in either opportunity or as a policy goal. On the face of it, the achievement of economic equality was included among the long-term goals of economic development policies in India after independence, based on socialist ideology and the mechanism of centralized planning. In practice, in reality, and even in the admission of those who developed these early economic plans, the actual goals were different.

Socialism was a borrowed concept of the upper castes and classes of India that served several purposes. It fed into the desire for a strong centralized state; indeed, centralized economic development planning became its *raison d'être*. It made it unnecessary for the upper-class, upper-caste elites to face in the present most of the inequalities, oppressions, and discriminations in their society, which would all be taken care of in the future when the grand new industrialized state of India would come into being. It also made it unnecessary for them to exercise their minds, to examine realistically the structure of their society, its resources, and its actual potential, providing instead a ready-made formula derived from a universal model of political economy and world history. It helped to keep them in power—for only they knew the world formula and how to implement it—while providing a *chapati*-in-the sky long-term goal of reconstructing India's economy and society.

There is one important exception to this argument, namely, the abolition after independence of the exploitative tax farming system dominated by big landlords and princes. In this case, some serious analyses of conditions in the countryside were undertaken and policies implemented to eliminate the control of the ex-landlords and princes over the land and its tenantry and to establish in their place a countrywide system of peasant proprietorship, in which title to the land—or effective control— was transferred to the former cultivating tenants. This was done for a number of reasons. First, the landlords and princes had been the principal collaborators with the British in ruling India and could therefore be attacked fairly and revengefully as enemies of both the nation and the people. Second, it made good political sense in an electoral system based on adult suffrage because the landlords and princes were the strongest potential rivals to the Indian National Congress and the socialist parties that developed out of it; their elimination would provide tens of millions of hopefully grateful new landowning voters. Third, it also fit into some long-term socialist schemes for ultimately reorganizing Indian agriculture through land reforms, land redistribution, and even cooperative farming, none of which were ever carried through very far or at all. Finally, it obviously would not promote the image of India as a country striving to achieve the goal of creating a modern, socialist, industrialized state to have all these big landlords and princes around acting as intermediaries and buffers between the state and the people and strutting about, even riding about on elephants, like feudal potentates.

The system of centralized economic development planning began to fall apart in the mid-1960s and its death blows have been administered by all governments since 1991, with the help and upon the insistence of the World Bank and the International Monetary Fund. The death blows, however, are being administered rather slowly. It is not the pace of the reforms that concerns me here, but the havoc wreaked upon the country and its political order by the system that functioned for four decades and the fact that the economic reforms may not be sufficient by themselves to undo all the damage done to politics and society.

Clearly, the system of centralized planning stifled the entrepreneurship of the Indian business classes. Releasing the energies of these classes into productive channels is one of the most likely consequences of the liberalization of the Indian economy. However, there were other consequences of the old policies that are less easily rectified. The pseudoso-cialist economic order that prevailed for forty years created instead of a vibrant entrepreneurial class, a stultifying, enormously corrupt bureau-cratic system. Furthermore, the imperatives of centralized economic de-velopment planning provided Indian elites with a justification for fob-bing off the needs and demands of the majority of the ordinary people of India with "symbols and shadows" rather than the substance of eco-nomic well-being or even a life lived in dignity with at least their basic minimum needs provided. In addition, among the most dramatic and pervasive consequences of the economic policies of those years were their contribution to the creation of the vast armies of unemployed college graduates and students who see their life chances as so bleak that they are easy recruiting fodder for every movement of protest—particularly linguistic, religious, and cultural—that comes along claiming to provide them all with the high-status jobs they crave.

THE OBSESSION WITH NATIONAL UNITY AND INTEGRITY

This brings me finally to the political consequences of ethnic, linguistic, religious, and regional conflicts in India and their connection with the growth of the centralized state and the political economy that went along with it. Partition affected the thinking of the leadership on virtually all issues of language and religion that came up in the years thereafter. Under Nehru, however, a balance was struck and compromises were reached that allowed for the recognition of a multiplicity of claims made by distinct language—but not religious—groups and for the creation of a national consensus on some very divisive matters such as linguistic reorganization of states and official language policy. That balance too was undermined by the policies of Mrs. Gandhi and her son Rajiv, which exacerbated regional ethnic animosities and contributed to the rise of Hindu-Muslim tensions. These results were brought about, on the one hand, by the desperateness of Mrs. Gandhi to hold on to power by whatever means, impelling her to intervene in local conflicts in all the states of India and to align even with persons and groups who would later be condemned as extremist, militant, and secessionist. On the other hand, her and then her son's desperate clinging to power led them both to shift Congress policies away from protecting minorities to pandering to Hindu politico-religious sentiments. The political consequences in the form of actual secessionist movements and increased Hindu-Muslim tensions in turn magnified the obsession with maintaining the national unity and territorial integrity of India at all costs.

At the same time, it needs to be recognized that the preoccupation with national unity and territorial integrity does not arise only from the scars of partition, genuine anxieties over the possibility of disintegration of the country, or the manipulative and self-defeating policies of particular leaders sacrificing the interests of the country in favor of their own. A set of values associated with the idea of a strong centralized state underlay and preceded all these events, concerns, and practices. Even before independence, India's national leaders—with the exception of Mahatma Gandhi and his followers and disciples—considered such a state an absolute necessity to make of independent India a great and respected country in the world. Associated with this doctrine was also the belief that a consolidated nation was essential to provide the foundation for such a state. The idea of turning such a diverse and heterogeneous country as India into a nation-state was tempered during Nehru's lifetime by pluralist policies and the acceptance in practice of India as, in effect, a multinational state—though the word itself could not be used in a society whose nationally oriented elites would be offended by its implications. For the latter, the unity and territorial integrity of India is the ultimate value, for whose preservation any and all means will be used, as the world has so clearly seen in Punjab and Kashmir.

It is also necessary in considering the consequences of this obsession with national unity to note its contribution to the failure to resolve the most divisive of all matters pertaining to India's national unity, namely, the status of India's Muslims and Hindu-Muslim relations. The national ideology of India cannot provide a framework for the settlement of these matters despite the insistence of India's leadership that Indian secularism, in contrast to Pakistan's "medieval" religious nationalism, provides a common home for Hindus and Muslims. The emphasis on secularism—and the absolute necessity of a strong centralized state to preserve it—itself stands in the way, for this is a secularism that calls attention to divisions, rather than setting them aside, by proclaiming that secularism requires a strong centralized state to protect minorities—read "Muslims"—whose very status as perpetual and endangered minorities is required to justify the existence of the state. For, without the dangers produced by Hindu-Muslim conflicts—most especially the unending conflict with Pakistan—the ideological justification for such a state would be reduced and demands for decentralization of the Indian polity would acquire greater force. But how can one grant, for example, regional autonomy when the very term conjures up a special status for Indian states such as that which Kashmir was supposed to have? This leads to another burning issue in contemporary Indian politics, namely, the rise of militant Hindu nationalism.

Those who have faith in the persistence, and ultimately the complete triumph, of democratic practices in India discount the more extreme aspects of militant Hinduism: its communal prejudices, jingoistic rhetoric, and destructive manifestations. At the north Indian town of Ayodhya, on December 6, 1992, a huge crowd of militant Hindus massed in the culmination of a movement that had been in progress for several years under the leadership of a "family" of militant Hindu organizations, including the BJP (Bharatiya Janata Party), and destroyed the mosque there known as the Babri Masjid, said to have been built on the ruins of a Hindu temple in the sixteenth century. The destruction of the mosque was followed by countless riots throughout the country in which mostly Muslims were killed.

There are several affiliated organizations in the militant Hindu family. The parent organization, the RSS (Rashtriya Swayamsevak Sangh), founded in 1925, stands for the consolidation of all Hindus into a united community. The BJP is its political arm, whose goal is to unite Hindus politically to achieve power at the center and to transform India into a Hindu nation-state. The VHP (Vishwa Hindu Parishad), the spearhead of the Ayodhya movement, has been largely responsible for the mass mobilizations of Hindus that converged on Ayodhya on several occasions, including December 6, 1992. Also important has been the Bajrang Dal, an organization of armed gangs that use violence during mass Hindu mobilizations allegedly to protect Hindus against Muslims, but probably more often to attack Muslims.

It is said that Hindu militancy may ultimately fade and that the BJP in power will conform to the prevailing parliamentary practices and traditions. The BJP came to power after the 1998 general elections as the largest party in a multi-party coalition government with numerous other small regional parties and independents. The new government under Prime Minister Atal Bihari Vajpayee won a vote of confidence in Parliament on March 28 with a narrow majority, garnering 274 votes against 261 in opposition. In order to form its fragile coalition, the BJP was compelled to put aside for the time being several of its principal policy goals, including the building of a new temple to Ram at Ayodhya, the establishment of a uniform civil code for Hindus and Muslims alike, and the abrogation of the special constitutional status of Jammu and Kashmir. However, the BJP has not given up its adherence to these policies in the event that it comes to power in a future government on the basis of its own strength.

The electoral evidence, however, suggests that the strength of the BJP, the political manifestation of militant Hindu nationalism, has crested where it matters most, in the north, and that it remains overwhelmingly a regional party of the Hindu-speaking states, Gujarat, and Maharashtra. At the same time, I do not believe that Hindu nationalism itself will go away, for several reasons. First, it has always been a powerful, though a somewhat subterranean, force in modern Indian history and politics. Moreover, it has now become entrenched as the predominant ideology of upper-class, upper-caste Hindu society in north India. Third, educated Indians in general are an intensely and self-consciously nationalistic people. Fourth, there is no all-embracing ideology that has the potential for bringing about a genuine national consolidation in India other than Hindu nationalism. I say "potential" both because it does not yet exist and because I continue to believe it is not possible, for many reasons that cannot be taken up here.

Finally, a matter that requires more elaboration because of its significance for Indian national sentiment and because it is never made explicit, the Indian state has failed to provide Indians with the national self-respect they seek from the rest of the world. India is not recognized as an equal by the great powers. Postindependence economic development policies have not succeeded in turning India into an economically powerful country and have failed to improve the lives of its people in a manner that the industrial and postindustrial societies of the world would recognize as sufficient, though the general well-being of some segments of the poor has increased somewhat over the years. The failure of Indian leaders and their economic policies to transform the Indian economy and to bring about dramatic changes in the lives of ordinary people and, in addition, the fact that millions upon millions of people are living in the most degraded conditions continue to tarnish India's image and greatly embarrass its leaders and educated classes.

Failures of national development have often produced scapegoats; in India, the scapegoats for these failures are the Muslims and any other so-called minorities whose actions are deemed to threaten the Indian state, its national unity and integrity. These failures and the existence of convenient scapegoats provide an essential basis for the recent rise of militant Hindu nationalism, which was not really about a mosque in Ayodhya, but about India's place in the world. Heedless of the fact that their actions in Ayodhya made of Hindu nationalists and of India itself an object of derision in the rest of the world, they insisted rather that they had struck a blow for Hindu freedom from Muslim slavery, from an insufficiently Hindu state, and from any acceptance of ideas derived from the West while the whole basis of their ideology and their political religion comes from the West and is directed at mimicking the rise of the West.

FUTURE PROSPECTS

Over the years in presenting the negative side of Indian democracy, I have noticed that academic audiences, like the general public that attend Hollywood movies, like a happy ending. There are two important recent developments that suggest such a possibility. The first is the decline of the Congress, the party mostly responsible for most of the ills that India has suffered since independence. It is unlikely that the Congress—even with the decision of Sonia Gandhi, wife of the assassinated former prime minister Rajiv Gandhi, to take over its leadership and thereby bring dynasticism back to the center of Indian politics—will recover from its illness, which is probably terminal. The demise of the Congress will sharpen one of the oldest tensions that has existed in all states and empires in Indian history: that between centralizers and decentralizers, empire-builders and regional kingdoms. In contemporary India, that tension is manifested in the contest between proponents of militant Hindu nationalism in the BJP and the other organizations in the RSS family, on the one side, and the parties representing the lower and backward castes in north India and regional sentiments in other parts of the country. In today's India, the latter two sets of forces—not the Congress—constitute the main political and ideological bases for both secularism and decentralization.

The United Front governments that came to power after the defeat of the Congress in the 1996 parliamentary elections, staving off as well the establishment of a BJP government, represented the latter forces. Moreover, this was something new in postindependence Indian political history. The previous non-Congress governments at the center were not so clearly dominated by backward-caste and regional parties and leaders as those that came to power in the late 1990s. The coming to power of the United Front government in 1996 constituted a reversal of previous history in several respects. It marked not only the defeat and probable demise of the Congress as the centering force in Indian politics but the end of upper-caste dominance in the Indian political order. It also partly reversed the political practices of most previous governments. The central government and its ruling parties in the past all engaged more or less deeply in interventionist practices designed to favor their subordinate units and party allies in the states and to undermine their opponents. Although these practices continue, the major significance of the United Front governments of Prime Ministers H. D. Deve Gowda and Inder K. Gujral was the opposite: the penetration of the central government itself by regional elites and parties.

The important question for the future, however, is whether a watershed has been reached in the evolution of the Indian polity in favor of both regionalism and decentralization as well as the rise of the lower half of Indian society to political predominance. I believe these governments did mark a watershed. As noted above, the BJP itself had to compromise with mostly regional political parties in order to form a government in March 1998. Compromises with leaders from the backward and lower castes in several states have also posed problems for the internal cohesion of the BJP, which continues to be dominated by upper-caste elites. Compromises on issues of regional autonomy for the states are not likely to be made explicit, but the more any central government has to depend upon regional parties for its existence—whether dominated by a heterogeneous coalition or a BJP-led government—the more likely it is that, gradually and without much fanfare, the states of India will become increasingly autonomous.

The second recent promising development, highlighted by the meeting between Inder Gujral and Pakistani Prime Minister Nawaz Sharif at the 1997 SAARC (South Asian Association for Regional Cooperation) conference and subsequent meetings, is the desire of both India and Pakistan for better relations, including some kind of tacit settlement of the Kashmir dispute that would make it possible for both sides to put the issue aside and establish normal relations between these two inheritors of the British Raj. Nothing has since come of these meetings. On the contrary, violent clashes continue to occur between the Pakistan and Indian armed forces across the line of control in Kashmir. Furthermore, BJP pronouncements in March 1998 regarding its desire to incorporate nuclear weapons into the military equipment of the Indian armed forces received a strong negative counterresponse from Pakistan. Yet nothing could be more conducive to the triumph of secularism and democracy in India than the ending of the conflict between India and Pakistan that has kept the relations between the two predominant religious communities of South Asia embittered, subject to malevolent and malicious political manipulation, and prone to violence.

SUGGESTED READINGS

Anderson, Walter K., and Shridhar D. Damle. *The Brotherhood in Saffron: The Rashtriya Swayamsevak Sangh and Hindu Revivalism.* Boulder, Colo.: Westview Press, 1987.

Brass, Paul R. *Ethnicity and Nationalism: Theory and Comparison.* New Delhi: Sage, 1991.

  The Politics of India since Independence, 2nd ed. Cambridge: Cambridge University Press, 1994.

  Theft of an Idol: Text and Context in the Representation of Collective Violence. Princeton, N.J.: Princeton University Press, 1997.

Butler, David, et al. *India Decides: Elections 1952–1991*, 2nd rev. ed. New Delhi: LM Books, 1991.

Frankel, Francine, and M. S. A. Rao, eds. *Dominance and State Power in Modern India: Decline of a Social Order*, vol. 2. Delhi: Oxford University Press, 1990.

Gould, Harold A., and Sumit Ganguly, eds. *India Votes: Alliance Politics and Minority Governments in the Ninth and Tenth General Elections.* Boulder, Colo.: Westview Press, 1993.

Jaffrelot, Christophe. *The Hindu Nationalist Movement and Indian Politics: 1925 to the 1990s.* London: Hurst, 1997.

Kochanek, Stanley. "Briefcase Politics in India: The Congress Party and the Business Elite," *Asian Survey* 27, no. 12 (December 1987): 1278–301.

Kohli, Atul. *Democracy and Discontent: India's Growing Crisis of Governability.* Cambridge: Cambridge University Press, 1990.

  The State and Poverty in India. Cambridge: Cambridge University Press, 1987.

Rudolph, Lloyd I., and Susanne H. Rudolph. *In Pursuit of Lakshmi: The Political Economy of the Indian State.* Chicago: University of Chicago Press, 1987.

Sisson, Richard, and Ramashray Roy, eds. *Diversity and Dominance in Indian Politics*, vol. 1: *Changing Bases of Congress Support.* New Delhi: Sage, 1990.

Varshney, Ashutosh. *Democracy, Development and the Countryside: Urban-Rural Struggles in India.* Cambridge: Cambridge University Press, 1995.

Wade, Robert. "The Market for Public Office: Why the Indian State Is Not Better at Development," *World Development* 13, no. 4 (April 1985): 467–97.

——— "The System of Administrative and Political Corruption: Canal Irrigation in South India," *Journal of Development Studies* 18, no. 3 (April 1982): 287–328.

Weiner, Myron. *The Child and the State in India: Child Labor and Education Policy in Comparative Perspective.* Princeton, N.J.: Princeton University Press, 1991.

2

Pakistan: A nation still in the making

ROBERT LAPORTE, JR.

As late as 1986, thirty-nine years after independence, a scholar of Pakistan could entitle his book *Pakistan: A Nation in the Making*.[1] A decade later, the title remains valid. As Pakistan reaches the half-century mark, it remains a nation in the making.

The Islamic Republic of Pakistan began its political life with what is formally described as a federal parliamentary government. But it was a federal parliamentary government under siege, so to speak. Within the thousand miles separating Pakistan's west wing from its east wing was a hostile India. The demands of developing a unified government dictated little margin for error and a great concern for control. The new leadership of Pakistan used the viceregal system inherited from the British. Civil servants were given vast powers to administer. As the first governor general, Mohammad Ali Jinnah dealt directly with civil officers, often bypassing the ministers who were theoretically in charge of ministries. This arrangement lasted for about one year, until Jinnah's death. Following his death, and that of his successor, Liaquat Ali Khan, in 1951, a significant leadership void emerged that was not filled until the first martial-law period in 1958. But elements of the viceregal system continue even until today.

Pakistan's quest for a constitution over a period of twenty-six years (1947–73) produced three documents. The first two (the 1956 Constitution and the 1962 Constitution) limited terms of the participation of ordinary citizens in public decision-making. The 1956 Constitution was promulgated by Governor General (later to be president) Iskander Mirza

---

[1] Shahid Javed Burki, *Pakistan: A Nation in the Making* (Boulder, Colo.: Westview Press, 1986).

on March 23, 1956, and abrogated by President Iskander Mirza on October 7, 1958. The concept of representation was limited in this constitution as a result of the One Unit Plan (the merger of the four western provinces into one province). Since no elections took place during the short period of time when this constitution was the basic document of Pakistan, the extent to which the franchise was limited is a "what if" question.

The 1962 Constitution was promulgated by General Mohammed Ayub Khan on June 8, 1962, and abrogated by General Agha Mohammed Yahya on March 29, 1969. This document intentionally limited participation by restricting the franchise to the several thousand "Basic Democrats" (elected local officials). In addition, an indirect procedure was introduced to elect the president. Even with this procedure and government-based patronage, Ayub won an unimpressive victory in the 1965 presidential election over Fatima Jinnah, the sister of the *Quaid-i-Azam*, or Mohammed Ali Jinnah.

Although not a constitution, the Legal Framework Order of 1969 issued by General Mohammed Yahya Khan, who had succeeded President Ayub, was an interesting document. The Legal Framework Order abolished the One Unit Plan, provided the framework for the development of a new constitution that included direct elections for the Constituent Assembly (to draft the constitution), and stipulated a time limit of 120 days to complete the constitution-making process. It also reserved the right of the president (in this case, Yahya) to authenticate the constitution produced by the Constituent Assembly. The Legal Framework Order set the stage for the 1970 elections, the first direct elections based on universal suffrage in Pakistan's history.

FOUR GOVERNMENTAL CONSTRUCTS

Pakistan's search for a suitable form of government resulted in four constructs during the period from 1947 until 1988. Three of these ended in martial law (1958, 1969, and 1977) and these three periods of martial law lasted a combined total of about fifteen years.

The first construct can be described as nonrepresentative parliamentary government (1947–58). Although there were provincial assembly elections, no national elections were held. Two constituent assemblies functioned as the legislative bodies during this time period with power in the system alternating between the governor general (later president) and the prime minister. This form of government was abolished with the installation of the first martial law period in October 1958.

Nonrepresentative parliamentary government failed because it ran out of stakeholders. The 1956 Constitution was written by the civil service under the supervision of a nonelected governor general, Ghulam Mohammed (1951–55), who had been a civil servant himself and had dismissed the original Constituent Assembly, whose task it was to draft the constitution. By 1955, he had been retired. His successor, Iskander Mirza, was a military bureaucrat famous for his contempt for politicians, his preference for the viceregal system, and his declaration of martial law on October 7, 1958. Mirza had no stake in the 1956 Constitution and his support base, the military, disliked what Mirza called the "prostitution of Islam for political ends," that is, the Islamic trappings of this constitutional order.[2]

The second form of government tried was the "tutelary democracy" of Mohammed Ayub Khan (1962–69). His government was a strong, centralized presidential system with the legislature acting as a rubber stamp. This construct ceased when the second martial law period began in March 1969 and lasted until December 1971, when General Agha Mohammed Yahya Khan transferred power to Zulfikar Ali Bhutto.

Ayub's tutelary democratic scheme was well liked by the 80,000 Basic Democrats (the number of which was increased to 120,000) who profited from government largesse, but those on the outside developed into sources of discontent. Ayub disliked politicians and did not believe Pakistan was ready for democracy. Most politicians, lawyers, and intellectuals, in turn, disliked Ayub. In 1959, the government announced the Elective Bodies (Disqualification) Order (EBDO) and used this device to prohibit more than one hundred former ministers and other leading politicians from holding public office for several years.

Some scholars also maintain that Ayub's system collapsed because it tried to modernize Islam in Pakistan. The Muslim Family Laws Ordinance of 1961, coupled with efforts to promote family planning, did not sit well with many of the *ulema* (Muslim clerics). When Ayub was forced out of office in 1969, few advocated a continuation of his form of government. The martial-law regime installed under Yahya Khan turned out

---

[2] See Richard S. Wheeler, *The Politics of Pakistan: A Constitutional Quest* (Ithaca, N.Y.: Cornell University Press, 1970), 106.

to be a transitional regime designed to lead Pakistan to democratic elections as a prelude to a new constitution.

THE BHUTTO-ZIA PERIOD, 1971–88

The 1970 elections were free, but the results—an overwhelming victory in the east for Mujibur Rahman and a strong majority in the west for Zulfikar Bhutto—helped split the country apart. After failure to agree on a governmental formula, President Yahya Khan declared martial law in the east and banned Mujib's party, the Awami League. Many died in the brutal military crackdown that culminated in the 1971 Indo-Pakistani War and the independence of Bangladesh. Yahya handed over power after the war to Bhutto, whose People's Party of Pakistan (PPP) had captured a majority of the Constituent Assembly seats in the western provinces in the 1970 elections. One of the major items on the political agenda was the development of a third constitution. Basically, Bhutto had a "clean slate" with which to work. The nation that was left was demoralized, the military weakened, the civil service uncertain as to its future, and the traditional major power holders, the landed "feudals,"[3] outside the constituency that elected Bhutto.

Except for the period from 1977 to 1985, when it was shelved, the 1973 Constitution has proved to be Pakistan's most durable constitution. It provides for the direct election of members of the National Assembly and the four provincial assemblies. Participation through voting is a fundamental component of this constitution and five elections have been held under it (1977, 1988, 1990, 1993, and 1997). The 1973 Constitution was originally designed to promote a strong parliamentary form of government. The principal government leader was to be the prime minister, with the president playing a titular role. Curbs on the roles of non-elected officials (i.e., the military and the civil bureaucrats) were initiated. No longer would there be a commander-in-chief of the Pakistani army in uniform; instead, there was to be a chief of the army staff (COAS). Civil servants no longer had constitutional guarantees of tenure as provided in Pakistan's two previous constitutions.

---

[3] The term "feudal" as I am using it includes *zamindars* (principally Punjab-based land-owners), *waderas* (Sindh-based landowners), *maliks* (North-West Frontier Province and tribal-area leaders who may or may not hold substantial amounts of land), and *sardars* (the term used to describe tribal leadership in Balochistan and parts of Sindh). As in the case of *maliks*, *sardars* may or may not possess large tracts of land.

Initially, the third construct marked an attempt to return to the parliamentary form of the first decade of independence, with some changes. It established a ceremonial presidency (instead of an activist presidential role) and legislative bodies—the National Assembly and the four provincial assemblies—that were truly representative (i.e., based on direct elections). Critics of this period, however, maintain that the promised parliamentary democracy degenerated into a Bhutto dictatorship and his broad misuse of state institutions.

The governmental form introduced by the 1973 Constitution had not been functioning long enough to be judged a failure when the military removed Bhutto in 1977. The populist nature of the regime, however, changed when Bhutto himself had decided to drop leftist elements in the PPP and instead to cultivate more conservative feudals. In the elections of 1977, more feudals were given PPP tickets for seats in the National Assembly and the four provincial assemblies. Bhutto moved to the political right and his populist experiment, the so-called Islamic Socialism, ended. After the opposition charged widespread rigging of the elections, disorder shook the country and Bhutto was ousted by a military coup led by General Mohammad Zia ul-Haq in July 1977.

With the coup, the 1973 Constitution was placed in limbo. Zia ruled the country under martial law until December 30, 1985. The constitution was suspended, however, not abrogated. On March 18, 1985, President Zia promulgated the Revival of the Constitution Order of 1985, adding new amendments to the 1973 Constitution. One of these specified that "the president's orders made since the 5th of July 1977, shall not be altered, repealed or amended without the previous sanction of the president." Another, the Eighth Amendment, substantially increased the powers of the president.

From the time of the 1977 coup until December 30, 1985, Pakistan experimented with a policy approach that promised Islamization. The Zia government was politically dominated by the military and run by civilian bureaucrats. Zia ruled with military officers and civil servants occupying positions that elected officials would normally have held. Incrementally and over time, Zia made important changes. In late 1979, he abolished the local government/rural development scheme that had been put into place by Bhutto. Zia's replacement, called the "local bodies" scheme, included direct elections on a nonparty basis in 1979, 1983, and 1987, for local councils designed to focus on rural development. In December 1981, Zia appointed a 350-member national assembly. On

February 25, 1985, nonpartisan elections on the basis of universal suffrage were held for the National Assembly. From members of this assembly, Zia selected Muhammad Khan Junejo to become Pakistan's first prime minister in almost eight years.

The last years of the Zia period (1985–88) were a fourth construct that might be labeled semidemocracy. This was not a drastic government reform but, rather, an evolution from what had already begun to develop immediately after the lifting of martial law on December 30, 1985. Power in this period was shared between Zia and Junejo in a sort of halfway house toward genuine parliamentary democracy. Ultimate power, however, remained with Zia, who used his prerogatives to dismiss Junejo and his government on May 29, 1988. Within this time frame, Pakistan witnessed the development of a press that was virtually uncensored compared to the early years of the Zia period. Both the Urdu and English presses openly criticized the government and began to become part of the transparency and accountability processes for government.

Zia's approach to governance seemed at times to be two steps backward, one step forward. Over time, however, political participation gradually increased. From July 5, 1977, until February 25, 1985, only appointed officials, both military and civilian, held government positions. The three nonpartisan elections for local bodies and the referendum on President Zia held on December 19, 1984, were the only elections held during this time period. The nonpartisan elections to the National Assembly held on February 25, 1985, introduced civilian politicians into government office. The Revival of the Constitution Order on March 18, 1985, and the lifting of martial law on December 30, 1985, helped to "civilianize" government even further.

POLITICAL DEVELOPMENTS IN THE POST-ZIA PERIOD

The post-Zia period (1988 to the present) has been marked by further significant changes as Pakistan has moved toward becoming a full democracy, the fifth construct. As noted above, the political system that took root first during the Bhutto period was suspended, modified, and then reinstalled in somewhat altered form by Zia, but was not scrapped. In fact, the order of succession established by this system (the chairman of the Senate serves as acting president until new elections can be held) was followed in 1988 when Zia died in an as yet unexplained plane crash. Perhaps because of the human desire to personalize history, the "great person" approach to governance has an attraction for laypersons as well as scholars. In the political history of Pakistan, four dominant personalities (Jinnah, Ayub, Bhutto, and Zia) have emerged. In the post-Zia period of Pakistan's history, no single political personality has emerged; it has been a time of constant struggle for power between two individuals—Benazir Bhutto, Zulfikar Ali Bhutto's daughter, and Nawaz Sharif, the political protégé of the Zia regime.

Concentrations of power

Prior to April 1, 1997, when the National Assembly and the Senate approved unanimously legislation to change the Eighth Amendment to the Constitution, three institutions shared power: the presidency, the prime ministership, and the military. Known as the troika, this arrangement was rather like an unsteady three-legged stool. During the troika years (1988–97), the struggle for power involved principally the president and the prime minister, with the military observing and occasionally siding with one or the other or mediating between the two. The army corps commanders, acting like a board of directors, have contributed to both the staying power of governments as well as their downfall. It was the corps commanders who told Ghulam Ishaq Khan to retire in 1993 by refusing to support him in his battle with Nawaz Sharif and the Supreme Court. The constitutional provisions revised in April 1997 eliminate the power of the president to dismiss elected governments and to appoint armed-forces chiefs. As in the heyday of Zulfikar Ali Bhutto, the locus of power now rests with the prime minister and Parliament.

Distribution of power

Although Pakistan is a federal system on paper, the powers of the provinces in reality are minimal and the powers of local government are even less. There is virtually no decision-making autonomy outside of the central government. Provincial secretariats are officered by centrally appointed civil servants and local government powers are exercised by the centrally appointed civil officers. With the exception of Punjab, the four provinces are financially dependent upon federal funds and have no significant source of revenue apart from the funds that flow from the center. Local governments are even worse off financially than the provincial governments. After fifty years of independence, decentralization of power is still very elusive.

The executive

From 1988 until 1997, the central executive saw a power-sharing arrangement between presidents and prime ministers. The former president, Sardar Farooq Ahmed Khan Leghari, started in the civil service before joining the PPP. The previous president, Ghulam Ishaq Khan, spent a career in the civil service, rising from the North-West Frontier Province provincial service to hold every major federal secretaryship before becoming federal finance minister, chairman of the Senate, and finally president of Pakistan. The two post-1988 prime ministers, on the other hand, have come from a major landowning political family (Benazir) and from a middle-class business family (Sharif). The recent past reveals that neither has been above using the institutions of the state to harass the opposition. Parliamentary government in Pakistan has not been government by a first among equals but rather a collection of equals led by a more-than-equal person.

One new institution in recent years is that of the caretaker government. After the dismissal of Junejo in 1988, a caretaker government was formed but accomplished very little. Again, in 1990, another caretaker government was formed after the dismissal of the first Benazir government and, again, little occurred. A third caretaker government was formed in 1993 after Ghulam Ishaq Khan dismissed the Sharif government, but the Supreme Court declared the president's action null and void on May 26, 1993. On July 18, 1993, after the joint resignations of Ghulam Ishaq Khan and Nawaz Sharif, a fourth caretaker government was appointed. This time, the caretaker prime minister was Moeen Qureshi, retired senior vice president of the World Bank. The extensive agenda that this caretaker government tried to follow was, perhaps, not as successful as planned, but nonetheless was ambitious.

After the dismissal of the second Benazir government on November 5, 1996, by President Leghari, a fifth caretaker government was appointed. The major problems facing this caretaker government were public finance and the state of the economy. It is perhaps too early to judge its success, but it should be obvious that trying to correct fifty years of trial and error with ninety days of concerted effort may well be pursuing an impossible dream.

Over the past nine years, then, Pakistan has had caretaker governments holding office for a total of slightly more than one year. The caretaker governments are the closest that Pakistan has come to national unity governments. But the knowledge that decisions taken by a caretaker government during its brief tenure may then be reversed by the incoming regime has worked against efforts to use the caretaker governments as instruments for major reform.

The legislature

Since 1988, the National Assembly has been elected on a partisan basis. Four general elections have been held for members of the National Assembly. That is the good news. The bad news is that no elected government has ever served its allotted tenure. On the whole, these elections have been fair, with few complaints of important rigging.

In the national legislature, party discipline should be an important power that the prime minister and the leader of the opposition have at their disposal. In practice, however, party discipline has been weak and has not prevented members of the assemblies from crossing the aisle and joining the opposition. The 1973 Constitution tried to prohibit party changing, or "floor-crossing," as it is termed in Pakistan, but to no avail. One of the 1997 campaign promises of Nawaz Sharif was the passage of constitutional amendments ". . . to ban floor-crossing in the assemblies and eliminate horse-trading."[4]

Although floor-crossing is an issue that generates heartburn for the political party leadership, a more fundamental question is how much real power legislative bodies exert. In fact, the National Assembly formally possesses power but does not use it. The assemblies may raise questions and debate issues, but all major decisions, including those relating to budgeting and financial matters, have been made for them by the executive (i.e., the prime minister). The provincial assemblies exercise even less power than the national legislature. However, the background of members of the National Assembly (MNAs) and the provincial assemblies (MPAs) reflects the country's power structure, which continues to be dominated by rural landowning elites, the so-called feudals. Outside of urban areas, traditional tribal and clan ties remain the strongest social and political glue in Pakistan. The fact that fifty years after Pakistan's

[4] Zaffar Abbas, "Can the Tiger Roar?" *Herald*, March 1997, 29.

birth the imposition of an agricultural income tax remains a sensitive political issue is testimony to the staying power of the rural elites.

The judiciary

Since the death of Zia, the judiciary—the Supreme Court and the four high courts (at Karachi, Lahore, Peshawar, and Quetta)—has asserted itself on important political issues confronting the nation more often than in any previous period. The starting point was the Supreme Court's October 2, 1988, decision that elections for the National Assembly and the provincial assemblies would be held on a party basis. A second dramatic decision was rendered by the Supreme Court on May 26, 1993, voiding President Ghulam Ishaq Khan's dismissal of the Sharif government on the grounds that the president had overstepped his powers. More recently, Benazir's refusal to adhere to court recommendations to depoliticize judicial appointments was one of the factors that led to her dismissal in late 1996.

Only time will tell whether the judiciary will continue to play a more independent role in checking the abuses of governmental power and holding government officials more accountable for their actions. In the past, the executive's attempts to control the judiciary usually worked. The Supreme Court upheld the Lahore High Court's execution order in Zulfikar Ali Bhutto's case by a margin of only one vote, but that one vote was enough.

The higher civil service

There does not appear to be any marked change in the behavior of the higher civil service with the current resurrection of parliamentary government. Civil servants may exercise influence more subtly in dealing with elected officials but there have been no large-scale purges of the centrally recruited services reminiscent of the Zulfikar Ali Bhutto period. The viceregal system, with some alterations, is still in place. The higher civil service is still able to recruit some of the best talent in the country. In fact, approximately 15,000 persons take the examination each year for about 150 entry-level officer positions, and more applicants have been coming from the sciences in recent years (including medical doctors). In addition, more applicants than ever in the past have been women, so the male gender bias of the services may have been somewhat modified. One area in which women as civil officers may be having positive effects is in taxation. According to one senior civil servant, women officers in revenue and taxation have developed the reputation of being utterly honest, incorruptible, and efficient, much to the chagrin of some citizens.

Political parties

Despite the PPP's poor showing in the 1997 elections, a two-party system has developed over the last decade. Although the PPP traces its origins to the late 1960s, the present PPP is different from its founding organization and appears to have no discernible left wing (as it did in the 1960s and 1970s). PPP politics for all intents and purposes are centrist and focused on the personality of its leader, Benazir Bhutto, a two-time prime minister with the dubious distinction of having twice been dismissed from office. In the 1997 elections, the PPP suffered heavy losses in the Punjab and now finds its principal support base in Sindh province, Benazir's home base.

The Pakistan Muslim League/Nawaz (PML/N) currently enjoys a large majority in the National Assembly and the prime minister, Nawaz Sharif, is its leader. Its principal support base lies in Punjab Province. The PML/N traces its roots back to the Muslim League that was formed in 1907 and campaigned successfully for the creation of Pakistan. The PML/N, which emerged in the late 1980s when Zia allowed political parties, is largely the creation of two individuals, the late prime minister Muhammad Khan Junejo and Nawaz Sharif. Its politics are centrist-right. Policy differences are minimal and personalities are the major distinction between the PPP and PML/N. Benazir, like her father (the PPP's founder), is an articulate Western-educated scion of a wealthy feudal family. Nawaz, in contrast, is a Pakistani-educated, less articulate product of a middle-class family that made a considerable fortune in industry in the Lahore area.

A major concern about the viability of a two-party system is the state of the PPP. During the last election, Benazir's party lost substantially, winning only eighteen seats in the National Assembly. Earlier signs that the PPP was losing its urban support base in the Punjab Province[5] appear

---

[5] See Andrew R. Wilder, "Changing Patterns of Punjab Politics in Pakistan: National Assembly Election Results, 1988 and 1993," *Asian Survey* 35, no. 4 (April 1995): 377–93.

to be supported by the results of the 1997 election. The PPP still retains
the characteristics of a mass movement rather than a disciplined political
party. Benazir continues to dominate the organization with the assistance of a few close advisers. The PPP has to alter its modus operandi
and become a more open and better-organized party. If not, it is likely
to decline further and end up as a regional party speaking largely for
Sindhis.

The media

The flourishing of the media in Pakistan is one of the most significant
developments of the last decade and a half. The Zia government dropped
censorship and permitted the print media to blossom. The first Benazir
Bhutto government implemented changes in Pakistan Television and
opened up the television airwaves to foreign broadcasters. Hence, Pakistanis were exposed to live CNN telecasts of the U.S. Senate debating
the Gulf War resolution and the reporting of other important events
around the globe. Dozens of news publications now report on what
government does or does not do. Questions are openly raised about the
behavior of government officials as well as politicians. To a degree, government accountability has been introduced through the pages of both
the Urdu and English-language presses.

One area where the print media has done an exceptionally fine job
has been in covering election campaigns and reporting and analyzing the
voting. An example is the pre- and post-election coverage by the *Herald*,
the monthly news magazine published by the *Dawn* group. *Dawn* itself,
long the leading English-language newspaper in Pakistan, has in recent
years emerged as an excellent daily providing serious coverage of domestic, regional, and international events. Together with the *Nation* and the
News, the Pakistani English-language press has made rapid progress pro-
fessionally and now provides the public with a far less biased and fuller
picture of developments than in Pakistan's first four decades, when the
government largely ran or guided the press. What impact has the mass
media had on politics in Pakistan? No systematic study has been com-
pleted, but it appears that government officials are more cautious in their
actions and politicians are trying to learn how to deal more effectively
with the press.

Major problems

The governments of the post-1988 era inherited political, social, and economic problems of great magnitude. Until recently, even seemingly simple issues such as Pakistan's failure to conduct a census since the early 1980s have long-range implications for a political system that desperately needs to make decisions based on reliable population information. The list of institutions that have deteriorated and are in need of massive reform, in many cases rebuilding and restructuring, is long and includes most of the basic public institutions that are critical to productive endeavors in any society. In this category are public education, public health, social welfare, and institutions related to the care of the elderly. Some of these institutions have decayed, while others have simply been overwhelmed by the pressure of a population that is approaching 140 million.

Legitimacy

At one time, when the population of Pakistan was about 90 million, I was told by an observer of Pakistan that the country had "90 thousand citizens among ninety million subjects." Participation in elections is one crude way of measuring legitimacy. The estimates of the turnouts for the past five elections for National Assembly seats show a depressingly downward trend: the non-party February 1985 election, 53.7 percent; the November 1988 election, 43.1 percent; the October 1990 election, 45.5 percent; the October 1993 election, 40.3 percent; and the February 1997 election, 35.1 percent. The trend raises the question of whether the decline in participation measures a drop in support for the political system, a growing lack of public confidence in the National Assembly as an effective government institution, or voter weariness over having so many elections in a relatively short time period. Whatever the explanation, it is not a good sign for Pakistan's fledgling democracy.

Corruption

Rampant corruption has also had erosive effects on the quest for legitimacy. Among intellectuals, good governance is the same in Pakistan as in the United States or Europe. The lament is over the "slip from cup to lip." Positive terms and practices such as "accountability," "responsibility," and "openness" in government operations are contrasted with negative terms and practices such as "corruption," "favoritism," and "nepotism." Three governments in the course of eight years have been dismissed in part on charges of corruption. Recently, the government dismissed more than eighty high-ranking civil servants on charges either of corruption or of other abuses of office. It is impossible to attach a figure to the leakage of public funds into private coffers, but it must be substantial and has earned Pakistan the unenviable prize of being considered among the most corrupt nations in the world.

In addition to corruption, widespread favoritism has eroded public confidence in government. According to one source, ". . . corruption, nepotism and patronage are all part of privatization. When the government sold 4 or 5 cement plants, the price of cement rose 20–30 percent in one month!"[6] However, few Pakistanis having personal connections with those who make decisions (about who gets what, when, and how) would in reality wish to risk replacing this system with one that provides broader, impartial, equal treatment for all under the law.

The role of Islam

Despite the centrality of religion in the formation of Pakistan and its continuing importance, none of the religiously based political parties has been able to seriously challenge either the Pakistan Muslim League or the People's Party of Pakistan in any election. The success of the Jamaat-e-Islami, the best-known religious party, in mobilizing its members to demonstrate in the streets has not been matched at the ballot box. The inability of religion to play a major role in politics is due, to a large degree, to the diversity found within Islam in Pakistan. Jinnah and Ayub may not have been able to eliminate religion as a factor in politics, but the leadership of the religious parties has not been able to make Pakistan a sectarian state.

The feudals

In an interview conducted in July 1994 with officials connected with a nongovernmental organization attempting to promote the development

---

[6] Interview with retired government official, April 6, 1995.

of democracy in Pakistan, the following observation was made regarding Pakistani politics:

The dominant class from which Senators and MNAs [members of the National Assembly] come is feudal (about 70 percent of the membership of both bodies comes from the feudal class). And the feudal class operates on the thesis that "once an enemy, always an enemy" and that revenge is the only course of action when a wrong has been committed. The culture of feudalism continues today.[7]

Landownership is still an important form of wealth. In portions of Punjab and Sindh landlords still extract services from their peasants much in the same fashion as hundreds of years ago. Feuds between landowning families occasionally spill over into urban areas and account for some of the crime statistics. Landownership and family ties explained a good portion of political behavior in Pakistan in the past and may still today. However, the face of feudalism may be changing, although slowly. The sons (if not the daughters) of feudal landlords have been entering the civil service and nonagricultural business. At the same time, feudalism is being challenged by middle-class businesspeople and professionals.

The military

For roughly half of its first fifty years, Pakistan has been ruled by the military, either under martial law or by a government led by the army commander and supported by the military establishment. A decade after the death of the last military ruler, Zia, and despite four democratic elections, the military—essentially the army, which remains the dominant service—continues to play a considerable, if behind-the-scenes, role in the governance of the country. Although the last military takeover was twenty years ago, in 1977, the military remains a potent political factor. During the most recent caretaker cabinet, there was a move to entrench the military into the governmental structure in a more formal manner by establishing a mixed national security council including both military and civilian leadership. Created by President Leghari in January 1996, the Council for Defense and National Security (CDNS) membership included the president (as chairperson), chairman of the joint chiefs of staff committee, the three armed services chiefs, the prime minister,

---

[7] Interview with three officials of a nongovernmental organization, July 28, 1994. Interestingly, these pessimistic observations did not prevent all three officials from voting in the 1993 elections.

and the ministers of defense, foreign affairs, and finance. After Nawaz Sharif took office, the CDNS was shelved, but the institution may reappear at some time in the future, perhaps in modified form, as a way of formally involving the military in the governmental process.

CONCLUSIONS: WHITHER PAKISTAN?

This is Nawaz's second opportunity to serve as prime minister. Given his majority in the National Assembly (134 out of a total of 204 seats—close to a two-thirds majority) and the repeal of the Eighth Amendment, he has a free hand to design and implement public programs to address the needs of the nation. Some maintain that Pakistan has opened a new chapter in parliamentary democracy under a moderate leader who does not represent the interests of the feudal class. So far, he has (1) repealed the Eighth Amendment, (2) called for a nationwide census that began on March 2, 1998, (3) supported a tax on agricultural incomes, and (4) supported a reduction in Indo-Pakistani tensions. But will he succeed in further institutionalizing democracy? Can he successfully deal with the dire economic situation that has put Pakistan on the edge of bankruptcy? Can he deal with the underlying social ills that afflict the country? Can he improve the appallingly poor performance of government? Can he deal effectively with serious law-and-order problems that have created a deep sense of insecurity throughout much of Pakistan in recent years?

During the last caretaker government (November 1996–February 1997) and into the February campaign for the National Assembly and the provincial assemblies, there was public discussion of Pakistan's "last chance" to provide a workable, effective, and efficient governmental system. The question arises as to what happens if leadership once again fails. What does failure mean?

It does not mean that Pakistan as a state will collapse. However, it probably does mean the end, for the time being at least, of Pakistan's recent experiment with democratic government. Despite the clamor, the *ulema* are unlikely to gain power and turn Pakistan into a sectarian state à la Iran. The religious fundamentalists remained badly fractured into numerous groups despite the pervasive influence of Islam in Pakistani life. The most likely consequence of another failure of parliamentary government will be yet another period of military rule. Although at present the generals are content to remain in the background, were Nawaz

Sharif or a successor to fail and were the domestic situation in Pakistan to continue to deteriorate badly, their attitude could well change.

In sum, fifty years after its birth, Pakistan remains "a nation in the making."

SUGGESTED READINGS

Ali, Chaudhri Muhammad. *The Emergence of Pakistan.* New York: Columbia University Press, 1967.

Baxter, Craig, ed. *Zia's Pakistan: Politics and Stability in a Frontline State.* Boulder, Colo.: Westview Press, 1985.

Baxter, Craig, and Charles H. Kennedy, eds. *Pakistan in 1997.* Boulder, Colo.: Westview Press, 1998.

Burki, Shahid Javed. *Historical Dictionary of Pakistan.* Metuchen, N.J.: Scarecrow Press, 1991.

Pakistan under Bhutto, 1971–1977. London: Macmillan, 1980.

Burki, Shahid Javed, and Craig Baxter, eds. *Pakistan under the Military: Eleven Years of Zia ul-Haq.* Boulder, Colo.: Westview Press, 1991.

Callard, Keith. *Pakistan: A Political Study.* London: George Allen and Unwin, 1957.

Feldman, Herbert. *The End and the Beginning: Pakistan, 1969–1971.* Karachi: Oxford University Press, 1976.

From Crisis to Crisis: Pakistan, 1962–1969. Karachi: Oxford University Press, 1972.

Revolution in Pakistan: A Study of Martial Law Administration. London: Oxford University Press, 1967.

Hardy, P. *The Muslims of British India.* London: Cambridge University Press, 1972.

Korson, J. Henry, ed. *Contemporary Problems of Pakistan.* Boulder, Colo.: Westview Press, 1993.

LaPorte, Robert. *Power and Privilege: Influence and Decision Making in Pakistan.* Berkeley: University of California Press, 1975.

Sayeed, Khalid B. *Pakistan: The Formative Phase.* 2nd ed. London: Oxford University Press, 1968.

Weiss, Anita M. *Islamic Reassertion in Pakistan: The Application of Islamic Laws in a Modern State.* Syracuse, N.Y.: Syracuse University Press, 1986.

Wheeler, Richard S. *The Politics of Pakistan: A Constitutional Quest.* Ithaca, N.Y.: Cornell University Press, 1970.

Wilcox, Wayne A. *Pakistan: The Consolidation of a Nation.* New York: Columbia University Press, 1963.

Woodruff, Philip. *The Men Who Ruled India.* 2 vols., "The Founders" and "The Guardians." London: Jonathan Cape, 1953 and 1954.

Ziring, Lawrence. *The Ayub Khan Era: Politics in Pakistan, 1958–1969.* Syracuse, N.Y.: Syracuse University Press, 1971.

Pakistan in the Twentieth Century: A Political History. Karachi: Oxford University Press, 1997.

II

Economic development

3

India: Much achieved, much to achieve

JOHN ADAMS

India became an independent nation in 1947. After the adoption of the country's constitution in 1950, the new democratic government embraced economic planning as the cardinal means of instigating and sustaining economic development. With full awareness of the breadth and depth of India's needs, and an impatience stemming from long-denied freedom, Prime Minister Jawaharlal Nehru and the Congress Party leadership voiced complex and ambitious intentions. Their goals entailed altering the structure of the economy from predominantly agricultural to conspicuously industrial, attacking poverty and inequality, and achieving an acceptable rate of economic growth. Commitments were made to provide the country's 550,000 villages with basic amenities such as primary schools, clinics, potable water, sanitary facilities, and electricity. The decision to press toward what became known as the Socialist Pattern of Society incorporated the doctrine that India would rely on pervasive government ownership and strong-handed public direction of the industrial, financial, communications, and transport sectors.

The origins of India's fervent preference for aggressive planning and the lively political economy of the early plans have been extensively rendered in excellent studies by A. H. Hanson, George Rosen, Sukhamoy Chakravarty, and Francine R. Frankel.[1] There is no need to recapitulate the heady early days of one of the great national economic-policy exper-

---

[1] A. H. Hanson, *The Process of Planning: A Study of India's Five-Year Plans, 1950–1964* (London: Oxford University Press, 1966); George Rosen, *Democracy and Economic Change in India* (Berkeley: University of California Press, 1966); Sukhamoy Chakravarty, *Development Planning: The Indian Experience* (Oxford: Clarendon, 1987); Francine R. Frankel, *India's Political Economy, 1947–1977: The Gradual Revolution* (Princeton: Princeton University Press, 1978).

iments of the twentieth century. India has traversed an eventful fifty years of economic development and social progress; a fresh millennium is about to dawn. The global imperatives of economic integration are changing the rules of the game for every national economy, including formerly diffident giants such as the United States, Russia, China, and India, leaving reduced scope for sovereign policies. During the last five decades, an enormous amount has been learned from the comparative analysis of growth experiences in the rich and poor countries. Prevailing economic principles have swung 180 degrees in favor of free enterprise and narrowly focused state responsibilities.

This historic juncture in modern economic history affords a unique opportunity to assess India's record and to speculate where the future will lead. This chapter will outline patterns of long-run change with an accent on continuities rather than on erratic perturbations in the economy or on those trivial tilts in planning priorities or ostensible policy adjustments that have so often attracted the transient attention of cocksure pundits. For convenience, the past half-century of economic progress will be divided into three phases, each roughly fifteen years in length: Nehruvian Planning, 1950–64; Contrary Currents, 1965–80; and The Golden Growth Path, 1981–98. Broadly speaking, the planning era sought and attained the desired industrially biased structural change. The second phase witnessed the rise of redistributive politics and an explicit confrontation with food needs, poverty, and inequality. Planning during this period was less focused and industrialization and growth lost pace. The third period has brought to the fore policy expediency and the pursuit of rapid growth. Interestingly, the achievement of brisk economic expansion preceded rather than followed India's initiation of deep-cutting economic reforms in the early 1990s.

Another way of characterizing the three postindependence phases is to look at the substance of relations between the government and India's citizenry. In the Nehruvian period, governance was paternalistic, in some ways even patronizing. Parliament was overweighted with English-speaking urbanites. Although voter turnout was heavy, the large Congress majorities elevated the party's elite to power and dampened direct links between local popular politics and New Delhi. After 1966, central politics became more competitive and more pluralistic. Those holding power used redistributive means such as subsidies and food programs to woo voting blocs. Parliamentary representatives were increasingly non–

English-speaking, poorly educated ruralites. In the first fifteen years after independence, government pushed the people; in the second fifteen, the people began pushing government. After 1980 and into Rajiv Gandhi's time on the stage in the third era, many Indians began moving toward a more materialistic, achievement-oriented outlook. Demands arose for continued growth, ideology declined, and parliamentary politics became even more complicated, culminating in the post-1996 coalition governments of the United Front. As of 1997, popular sentiment was swinging toward expecting more accountability, less corruption, and better performance from government at all levels.

One caveat must be offered: the ensuing analysis is predicated on one strong belief and one mixed sentiment. The belief is that the economic and political context in which economic policy decisions have been taken, from 1950 to the present, has always been tightly binding, certainly more so than cavalier commentators usually concede. There is scant space to second-guess. The ambivalent sentiment is at once laudatory, about how much India has achieved, and tinged with sadness, over hopes unfulfilled.

NEHRUVIAN PLANNING, 1950–64

Typically, as a people's average income rises, secular change in the productive structure of their nation's economy follows a well-worn path. Hollis Chenery used comparative economic data covering large sets of countries to demarcate universal patterns of evolution in the structure of employment, the demographic transition, and the profile of the foreign sector. These transformations had taken place in the first wave of countries that underwent economic modernization, mostly through haphazard reliance upon private enterprise and the market system.[2] The dominant intention of Nehru and India's economic planners after 1950 was to rely purposively on governmental initiative to create an integrated industrial sector. At independence, India's private sector operated important capacity in cotton and jute textiles, manufactured selected consumer products, and owned iron and steel mills. The national railway system, although worn down by the war effort, was an important asset. Irriga-

---

[2] Hollis Chenery and Moises Syrquin, *Patterns of Development, 1950–1970* (New York: Oxford University Press and the World Bank, 1975).

tion canals in the northwest and parts of the south created tracts of considerable agricultural potential. Nonetheless, India's economic backwardness was patent.

The reasons for adopting an industry-first development program were manifold and irresistible. Industrialization was associated in almost everyone's mind with urbanization and modernization. Postwar economics emphasized the strong linkage effects of establishing, through a big push or critical minimum effort, an interlaced set of basic and consumer firms, which could depend upon each other for inputs and as markets. A strong infrastructure would generate externalities—cost advantages—in production, because of plentiful power, cheap transport, and accessible telecommunications. Only the state, with its full overview of the economy, could mobilize the amounts of capital needed to jump-start development across many fronts and allocate investment funds across projects so as to maximize social returns. India's strategic interests were folded into the industrial scheme: indigenous capacity to produce military supplies and equipment was paramount for India to assert a position as a self-reliant regional power in the postwar arena.

The Industrial Policy Resolution of 1956 divided India's industrial sector into three spheres. The state assumed exclusive future responsibility for heavy industrial enterprises; power, including atomic energy; coal, oil, and most minerals; air and rail transport; telecommunications; and defense goods. Existing private firms in these areas would be allowed to continue, for the most part. In the second sphere, mixed participation of public and private businesses would occur in machine tools; drugs, dyes, and plastics; fertilizers; pharmaceuticals; and road and sea transport. All other activities were left to the third sphere, which would be primarily private. State firms could enter even here, however, and private firms would be subject to extensive oversight and direction. To appease the Gandhian strand of thought, cottage, village, and small-scale industries were promised support and preferences.

The Second Plan (1956/57–1960/61) and Third Plan (1961/62–1965/66) were predicated on these principles, which set the contours of India's formative industrial development. The broadening and deepening of India's manufacturing sphere took precedence over achieving rapid growth. Thirty years later the imprint of this planning structure is plainly evident in the architecture of the economy. India's present slowness in privatizing segments of the public sector stems from continuing adhesion to the 1956 paradigm. Although the initial commitment to public initiative was well grounded in economic analysis, by the mid-1960s public corporations were overstaffed and weakly managed. Subsidies kept many afloat. Incentives to innovate, secure profits, and improve worker productivity were paltry or nonexistent. Today, efforts to revamp or privatize state enterprises confront a resistant nexus of interlocking worker and manager interests threatened by competition and change.

In retrospect, the first fifteen years of India's experiment with state planning are as remarkable for what the nation's leaders downplayed as for their aggressive pursuit of industrialization. Because of their emphasis on inward-looking self-reliance, they sought import substitution rather than an export orientation. Economic planners expected that aid flows rather than trade earnings would cover any shortfalls in domestic resource mobilization. The physical targets set in the planning exercises were not coordinated with realistic estimates of fiscal revenue; it was brazenly assumed that funding gaps would be covered by domestic windfalls or foreign largesse. Lip service was paid to employment generation, but the plans never incorporated forecasts of labor needs either in total or by skill categories, nor did they establish a network of educational and training institutions designed to ensure the availability of appropriate workers. A disproportionate share of resources was devoted to higher education, and no dedicated effort was made toward attaining universal primary schooling. The legacy of these deficiencies is that India's labor force at the end of the century has noticeably low levels of literacy and skills compared to workers in East Asia, Southeast Asia, and much of Latin America, although its cadres of engineers and technicians are the largest in the developing world.

The initial inattention to agriculture and its related industries is salient. Although a primary goal was to grow enough food for the nation to feed itself, the rural sector was treated as a cheap handmaiden in terms of its claims on resources; it was expected to do much with little. Just as there was export pessimism there was peasant pessimism. India's elite leadership believed that the rural masses could not be enlisted in the development effort until centuries-old habits and institutions were transformed. Hence land reform, community development, and village self-rule, or *panchayati raj*, were needed to break down inequality, passivism, and casteism. Cooperatives would bring villagers together and release them from their dependence upon putatively exploitative middlemen for marketing access and upon moneylenders for credit. Presumably, as irrigation spread, these coordinated institutional changes would enable an increase in agricultural product. As luck would have it, mostly good monsoons in the 1950s and early 1960s confirmed this illusion, although expressions of alarm were becoming more common by the time severe droughts struck in the mid-1960s. As with industry, the pursuit of growth was sublimated to a broad strategy of changing the rural sector's fundamental fabric.

Table 3.1 compares the changing structure of India's economy over the past fifty years with patterns of change in six Asian peer countries. Broadly speaking, the push to shift India's economy toward industry has been successful. Agriculture accounted for 49 percent of gross domestic product (GDP) in 1960. This share was reduced to 31 percent in 1990 and fell below 25 percent by 1997. Over the 1960–90 period, the proportion of GDP originating in industry rose from 21 to 29 percent. These changes are in line with those in Pakistan, more defined than those of Nepal and Bangladesh, but less sharp than the transitions in Indonesia and Thailand, countries that enjoyed more rapid industrial expansion. India began with a relatively high fraction of industrial output because of its cotton and jute textile factories.

The residual tertiary or service sector shares are not shown in Table 3.1, but India's climbed from 33 to 40 percent between 1960 and 1990. Despite the commitment to the Socialist Pattern of Society, the stake of central government–owned enterprises in India's GDP rose from 9 to only 12 percent from 1971 to 1991. In the group of six peers, the range for the government sectoral share in GDP in 1991 is 9 (Indonesia, Philippines) to 13 (Pakistan). India's public enterprises encompassed about two-thirds of the capital invested in large-scale manufacturing by 1975, but the economy remained a hybrid, mixing social control of the commanding heights with multifarious private enterprise in farming, rural industry, commerce, small business, and many industries.

Economic historians like to pose counterfactual mind experiments to imagine how alternative policies or lines of development might have worked out. So what if India had turned its back on the most persuasive postwar economic ideas, overcome the nation's popular mindset, and eluded the constraints of domestic political realities that made the adoption of planning effectively inevitable? It is implausible that domestic enterprise could have moved as forcefully as state initiative did to develop heavy industries, defense capabilities, and capital-demanding infrastructure. The reasons are exactly those provided by the early development economists. Private firms could not have reasonably expected to

Table 3.1. *Agricultural and industrial sector*
contributions to GDP, India and peers,
1960–90 (percent of GDP)

Country	Year			
	1960	1970	1980	1990
Agriculture				
Nepal	72	67	62	52
Bangladesh	57	55	50	37
India	49	45	38	31
Pakistan	46	37	30	26
Indonesia	52	45	24	22
Philippines	26	30	25	22
Thailand	36	26	23	13
Industry				
Nepal	9	12	12	16
Bangladesh	7	9	16	16
India	21	22	26	29
Pakistan	16	22	25	25
Indonesia	15	19	42	39
Philippines	28	32	39	36
Thailand	19	25	29	37

Source: World Bank, *World Development Report,* various years.

earn rates of return on most of these investments, at least in the early stages, that would have enticed them to commit their limited capital. India's financial markets were so underdeveloped, and the national savings rate so low, that private-sector mobilization of the resources needed was impossible. Nothing in the history of the early postwar international economy can lead one to believe that a legion of foreign-aid donors and corporate investors was lined up on India's borders, waiting to provide needed funds, technologies, and management talents.

During the period of Nehruvian planning, India successfully used the powerful push of the public sector to achieve structural change and an industrial dynamism that is continuing through the 1990s, albeit with variations in pace. Figure 3.1 provides a long-run overview of the annual growth rates of India's industrial production from 1952/53 to 1994/95. Industrial output more than doubled from 1951/52, the initial year of the First Plan, through 1965/66, the final year of the Third Plan. The average rate of industrial growth rose from about 6 percent in the First Plan to 8 percent in the early 1960s. Then a great deal began to go

Figure 3.1 Annual change in industrial production in India, 1952/53–1994/95

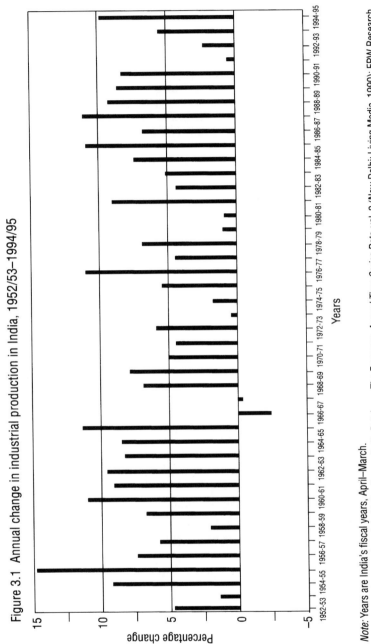

Note: Years are India's fiscal years, April–March.
Source: H. L. Chandhok and the Policy Group, *India Database: The Economy, Annual Time Series Data*, vol. 2 (New Delhi: Living Media, 1990); EPW Research Foundation, *National Accounts Statistics of India, 1950–51 to 1994–95* (Mumbai, 1996); *Economic and Political Weekly* (Mumbai), various issues.

wrong. After the war with China in 1962 India's fiscal and foreign-reserve position came under stress. Nehru died in 1964 and his successor, Lal Bahadur Shastri, had a fatal heart attack in January 1966. In 1965/66 and 1966/67 brutal droughts reduced food-grain availability and put upward pressure on prices. Planned levels of government investment were scaled back and industrial output actually fell for the first time. The regime of controls became more obstructive than facilitative of private-sector expansion, while the public-sector enterprises, operating under social and political compulsions, were as a group mismanaged and inefficient. For three years, through 1968/69, annual plans were adopted before the fourth five-year exercise could be started.

In spite of all these criticisms, India entered the 1970s with a significantly enhanced range of industrial capacities. The authors of the Fourth Plan (1969/70–1973/74) said, "In spite of this rather uneven performance, significant achievements contributing towards the realization of diversified industrial structure were made. . . . A fairly solid base for future growth has been laid."[3] They go on to mention engineering products; machine-building industries; heavy electricals; iron and steel; indigenous capacity in rail and road transport equipment, communications gear, sugar, and cement mills; fertilizers; rayon; and petrochemicals. Industrial growth perked up in the late 1970s, then slumped in conjunction with a 15.2 percent decline in agricultural production in 1979/80 and the second oil shock, both of which restricted supplies of inputs to industry and, consequently, raised prices. Cumulating bottlenecks in power and transportation worsened supply and shipping problems, the trade balance deteriorated, and monetary policy was tightened. Industrial expansion resumed a rapid tempo only when India moved onto the Golden Growth Path of the 1980s and 1990s.

CONTRARY CURRENTS, 1965–80

India's political processes and the progression of economic development entered a period of severe turbulence in the mid-1960s. When viewed from a long-term perspective, the effects on the economy of such disconcerting events as the wars with Pakistan in 1965 and 1971, Indira Gandhi's Emergency of 1975 to 1977, the ouster of Congress from power in

[3] Planning Commission, Government of India, *Fourth Five-Year Plan, 1969–1974* (New Delhi, 1970), 297.

the election of 1977, and the oil shocks of 1974 and 1980 are to a degree smoothed out. In addition, one risks overlooking points of transition in the long-run movement of important components of the economy if one's microscope is too finely focused. The period of Nehruvian planning had ignored or made overly conjectural estimates about three key processes, each central to attaining a particular long-run national objective: growing enough food by dissolving existing agrarian relations, raising the national savings rate in order to attain a high rate of capital formation, and generating sufficient exports to ease the foreign-exchange constraint on imports and domestic economic activity.

Growth is a dynamic process characterized by the emergence of leading sectors and the interactive behavior of constituent components. Policy decisions can have substantial effects on the rate and sources of growth. These principles are well illuminated by sea changes in the behavior of the food, savings, and export constituents of India's development course, all of which occurred amid the contrary currents of the stormy years 1965–80.

The bad monsoons of the 1960s added urgency to mounting concerns inside and outside India that not enough was being done to raise food output. It was evident that with its ample water supplies and fertile soils, India's low yields could be doubled or trebled by the application of scientific agriculture, and yet still would not become comparable to the world's best. Land reforms had not been effective in changing India's agrarian relations, although ceilings on the amount of land a farmer could hold had some impact on the maximum size of holdings. The cooperative movement had never caught fire because the hierarchies of caste and power in India's villages made it difficult to get all cultivators to work together to channel credit and inputs, or jointly to market their crops. Somehow, a more directly active formula had to be found.

In 1959, a Ford Foundation report on the stasis in India's food supplies recommended much keener focus on research, extension, intensive modern input use, and incentives. By 1965, a consensus emerged in India, radiating from Prime Minister Shastri and C. Subramaniam, the agriculture minister, that new high-yielding varieties of wheat should become the centerpiece in an input-intensive strategy designed to raise the rate of agricultural growth. Especially in the states of Punjab and Haryana, the quickly orchestrated nationwide extension program met with a sympathetic response from wily, independent farmers. A key innovation was the creation of regional agricultural universities, modeled on the public land-grant schools of the United States. The use of fertilizers, power tillers, pumps, and credit soared as the new varieties of wheat were adopted, first by larger farmers but soon by almost all. The input- and incentive-oriented strategy of this Green Revolution was at odds with the plans' stress on institutional change and community development; it favored what was already India's richest region and, at least at first, the bigger farmers, rather than the marginal cultivators and landless laborers. An urgent pragmatism had overcome New Delhi's idiom of peasant pessimism.

Figure 3.2 shows the upward movement of India's food-grain production after 1950. Allowing for the vicissitudes of the monsoon, the post-1968 period is one of expansion at a rate sufficient to exceed by a small margin the pace of population expansion. Usually, India has held some 20 million tons of grain in reserve, has not had to depend upon foreign supplies of food, and has become a net exporter of agricultural products. The spread of the Green Revolution into the eastern rice areas of West Bengal in the 1980s began to bring overdue income and employment gains to India's poorest region. Despite a sequence of good monsoons, growth in food-grain output in the 1990s has been disappointing, only a bit above population increase. Agriculture will require continued investment and innovation in an environment of fixed land supply, rising marginal costs of increasing output, and a mounting burden of environmental damage associated with fertilizer runoff and pesticide application.

From the beginnings of the plans, it was intended that a large portion of the gains of growth would be soaked up as taxes by the government or as deposits by the banking system, forms of savings that the government could recycle into new capital formation. This was intrinsic to Nehru's stratagem and wholly consistent with contemporaneous development philosophy. Yet, from an average rate of savings of 10.3 percent of national income in the First Plan, India's propensity to save climbed only to 13.2 percent during the Third Plan. Arguably, a rate over 20 percent was needed. The failure to elevate the nation's savings effort was substantive in itself, but was also symbolic of the weakened planning system, the recurring food crises, and indolent overall growth. The consensus that Nehru had been able to sustain while alive was fragmenting. After 1964, India experienced swings in policy orientation as numerous ideas, interests, and individuals jousted for influence.

Through the economic exigencies of the mid-1960s, strategy swung from a mild relaxation in controls on prices and investments under Shas-

Figure 3.2 Production of foodgrains in India, 1952/53–1994/95 (Index: 1969–70=100)

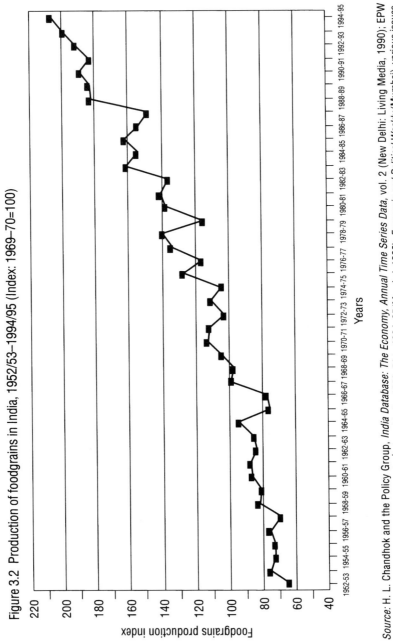

Source: H. L. Chandhok and the Policy Group, *India Database: The Economy, Annual Time Series Data,* vol. 2 (New Delhi: Living Media, 1990); EPW Research Foundation, *National Accounts Statistics of India, 1950–51 to 1994–95* (Mumbai, 1996); *Economic and Political Weekly* (Mumbai), various issues.

tri, toward more radical politics as Indira Gandhi took control of a wing of the Congress Party and sought to marshal popular support before and after the election of 1971. At her initiative and despite judicial opposition, questionable parliamentary measures were adopted to make it easier to acquire large landholdings or industrial assets without full compensation, threatening private property rights and dampening entrepreneurial ardor. An antimonopolies act was passed, the biggest industrial houses were to have less access to licenses for new manufacturing capacity, and the insurance and coal industries were nationalized. In 1969, the largest private banks were taken over and put in the public sector, with the intent of directing them to provide more credit to prioritized rural and small-business clients. Although Indira Gandhi's impatient and radical economic policies can be faulted on a number of grounds, the nationalization of banks was followed quickly by a huge increase in the number of rural and suburban branches. India's nationalized banks had about 8,000 branches in June 1969 and over 62,000 branches in 1995, with much of the expansion coming in the 1970s. The earmarking of certain proportions of credit to farmers and other groups traditionally neglected by private bankers shunted voluminous flows of loans to entirely new clients.

The chief consequential effect of the opening of branch banks, including savings windows offering a mix of account options, was to draw a large inflow of deposits from India's households. The numbers of accounts rose sharply, as did the amount of savings. As Figure 3.3 indicates, after 1968/69, India's savings rate climbed sharply to the levels thought necessary to sustain investment deployments that would in turn put India's economy on a higher growth track. With savings and investment rates stabilizing in the 20–25 percent range, there was an expectation that yearly output growth would move toward 7 percent or more, on average. This relationship, of about 3 units of savings to 1 unit of growth, which was thought to be routinely mechanical, broke down when India began using its capital stock with less efficiency than expected, so that added savings had a smaller impact on output increments than earlier. Notwithstanding, Indira Gandhi's gut instinct, rather than cool economic judgment, led to bank nationalization, the diffusion of branches, and, assuredly, to the attainment of the target rate of savings hoped for in the 1950s. This is not to say that liberalizing financial reforms such as those that began in the early 1990s should not proceed rapidly in the very different circumstances that now prevail.

Figure 3.3 Gross domestic savings as a percentage of GDP, 1952/53–1994/95

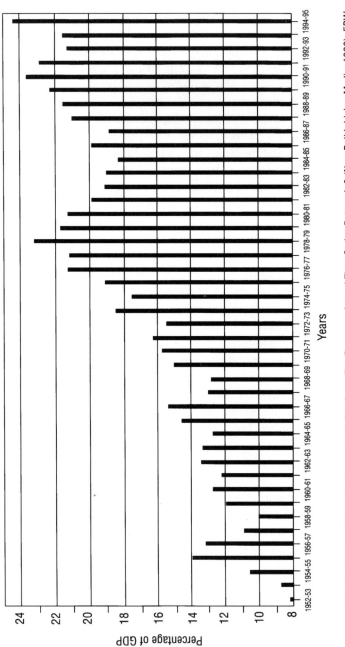

Source: H. L. Chandhok and the Policy Group, *India Database: The Economy, Annual Time Series Data*, vol. 2 (New Delhi: Living Media, 1990); EPW Research Foundation, *National Accounts Statistics of India, 1950–51 to 1994–95* (Mumbai, 1996); *Economic and Political Weekly* (Mumbai), various issues.

The Nehruvian plan frame was predicated on the assumption that exports did not matter or were not necessary. Such export neglect was consistent with most thinking about economic development, particularly as applied to a large country such as India that had diverse resources and a potentially large domestic market. The economic problems of the mid-1960s and considerable reassessment of policies led to modest reforms in trade procedures that were favorable to exporters. The centerpiece of the policy changes was the controversial devaluation of the rupee in 1966, which eventually brought India's overvalued currency more closely into line with its likely market value and made India's exports more attractive. India began to experience ascending export growth in the early 1970s, setting in train a process that has continued into the 1990s. Figure 3.4 shows the weakness of India's exports in the First and Second Plans, and the moderate growth in the Third Plan and annual plans. After 1971, in the Fourth and Fifth Plans, India's exports take off rapidly, pause, and then again resume more rapid gains in the late 1980s and 1990s. The impact on the national economy as a whole was initially not great because exports comprised only 3.6 percent of GDP in 1970/71, but this breakthrough does mark the point at which exports began to play an increasingly positive role in India's economy.

Many factors have been involved in determining India's export performance after 1970. The import-substitution policy, coupled with the broadening of the industrial structure, did generate product lines in which India was globally competitive. Agricultural and fisheries goods have acquired salience. Growth has come almost entirely from new exports such as iron and steel, metal manufactures, chemicals, engineering goods, prawns and other seafood products, transport equipment, and gems and jewelry, mostly polished diamonds. India's private firms were slow to develop export divisions capable of discovering market opportunities. Quality and reliability problems have long stigmatized Indian exporters in world commerce. Nonetheless, over the past three decades, India has developed an extremely diversified set of trading partners in East Asia, the Middle East, Europe, and North America. The extensive array of goods represented in the export mix, and the wide gamut of exterior markets, ensure that India is well insulated from vicissitudes that may affect a particular commodity or buyer. The fall of the Soviet Union disarranged a large portion of India's trade, but overall exports were not much affected, and ties are being restored.

The lessons of the records of wheat, savings, and exports are that

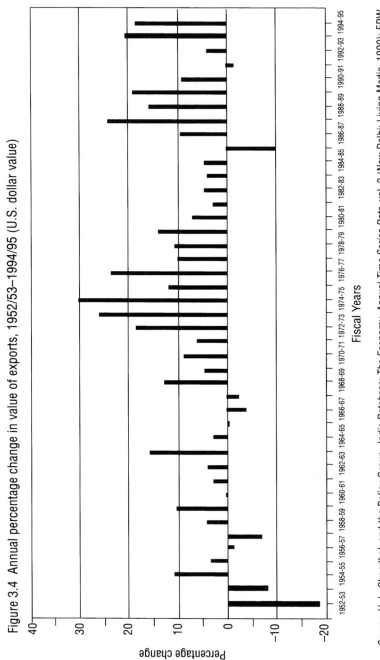

Figure 3.4 Annual percentage change in value of exports, 1952/53–1994/95 (U.S. dollar value)

Fiscal Years

Percentage change

1952-53 1954-55 1956-57 1958-59 1960-61 1962-63 1964-65 1966-67 1968-69 1970-71 1972-73 1974-75 1976-77 1978-79 1980-81 1982-83 1984-85 1986-87 1988-89 1990-91 1992-93 1994-95

Source: H. L. Chandhok and the Policy Group, India Database: The Economy, Annual Time Series Data, vol. 2 (New Delhi: Living Media, 1990); EPW Research Foundation, National Accounts Statistics of India, 1950–51 to 1994–95 (Mumbai, 1996); Economic and Political Weekly (Mumbai), various issues.

policy matters and that problem-solving reform has been a significant constituent of India's development strategy. This pragmatism is wholly consistent with a democratic mode of governance, which often involves trial and error. What is involved is not simply a choice between state and market mechanisms, but of the relations and coordination between them, and with the broader legal, political, and cultural environment.

THE GOLDEN GROWTH PATH, 1981–98

During the 1980s India became one of the world's most rapidly expanding economies. The reasons for what amounted to a sustained doubling of the nation's rate of per capita income expansion are imperfectly understood. The period has not been subjected to anything like the range of analysis that probed the slowdown of the late 1960s and 1970s. It is unlikely that economic policy changes played much of a role, if any, although it is common to point to Indira Gandhi's post-1980 government, and Rajiv Gandhi's after 1985, as having set in motion sequences of liberal reforms in industrial licensing, imports, and foreign investment. Plausible reasons for the upswing to a higher growth path include enhanced efficiency in the power and transport sectors, the coming on line of long-gestation infrastructure projects, increased absorption of foreign technologies, the spread of middle-class consumerism, and certainly most importantly, the effects of a Keynesian-style expansion of government deficit spending, alongside monetary and import laxness.

A notion of the change in India's growth trajectory after 1980 can be obtained by looking at the country's performance in the 1970s. Table 3.2 contrasts the rates of growth of per capita gross domestic product, industrial output, and agricultural production in the 1970s and 1980s, and provides comparable data on the same six peer countries included in Table 3.1. India's per capita growth rates slightly more than doubled in the 1980s. Agricultural output switched from lagging just behind population growth of about 2 percent per year in the 1970s, to 3.1 percent in the 1980s. Similarly, industry swung from a disappointing average rhythm of expansion of 4.5 percent in the earlier decade to a robust 7.1 percent rate of annual growth in the 1980s. During the 1970s, India's per capita, agricultural, and industrial performance was decidedly inferior to those of its higher-income peers, Pakistan and the suite of Southeast Asian states. Then, in the 1980s, India's aggregate growth rates

Table 3.2. *Economic growth, India and peers (average annual rate, percent)*

Country	(1) Per capita GDP (in dollars) 1991	(2) Growth in per capita GDP 1970–80	(3) Growth in per capita GDP 1980–90	(4) Growth in agriculture 1970–80	(5) Growth in agriculture 1980–90	(6) Growth in industry 1970–80	(7) Growth in industry 1980–90
Nepal	180	−1.0	1.5	0.5	4.0	4.0	6.0
Bangladesh	220	0.5	1.9	0.6	2.7	5.2	4.9
India	330	1.5	3.1	1.8	3.1	4.5	7.1
Pakistan	400	1.9	3.2	2.3	4.3	6.1	7.3
Indonesia	600	4.7	4.3	4.1	3.4	9.6	6.9
Philippines	730	3.2	−1.4	4.0	1.0	8.2	−0.9
Thailand	1,570	5.1	5.8	4.4	4.0	9.5	10.9

Source: World Bank, *World Development Report*, various years.

move into the bracket occupied by these counterparts and generally out-paced those of its poorer neighbors Nepal and Bangladesh.

A long-run overview of India's growth performance is presented in Figure 3.5, which reports annual percentage variations in GDP. The four years of subzero growth, in 1957/58, 1965/66, 1972/73, and 1979/80, are each associated with severe declines in agricultural production that resulted from very poor monsoons. In the era of Nehruvian planning, GDP expanded at an average rate of 4.1 percent per year. From 1965/66 through 1979/80, the period of Contrary Currents experienced average annual growth at 2.9 percent, less than 1.0 percent over population accretion. Then, in the post-1980/81 epoch of the Golden Growth Path, India's total output has enjoyed a mean yearly rise of 5.4 percentage points. Per capita gains in this period have equaled those of the prior three decades combined.

Table 3.3 gives the average growth rate by decade. The average growth in each of India's first three decades falls in the range of 3.0 to 4.0 percentage points per year. As Figure 3.5 conveys, the amplitude of year-to-year variations was high. Rainfall shortages, oil shocks, wars, or moments of careless fiscal, monetary, and foreign-reserve management created short-run problems. The ambit of a five-year planning horizon was far too brief to allow the contrivance of cogent judgments about how well the economy was doing, with the result that the nation's leadership, foreign observers, and India's politically alert citizens often subjected themselves to excessive and unnecessary swings of mood. Yet it is clear with hindsight that the long-run trend was reasonably steady and by no means unsatisfactory; one could describe it as a stately tempo, consistent with India's large size and deliberate progressions. Of course, a 3.0–4.0 percent growth rate ran only a bit ahead of population's average annual expansion of about 2.1 percent through the 1970s. Joined with continuing poor performance in the state enterprises, overcontrol of private initiative, and the realization that other Asian economies were moving ahead much more rapidly, this regal sluggishness created the widespread appreciation by 1980 that it was time to hope for, and to seek to engineer, an acceleration.

Then, without a radical change in policy mode and for no obvious reason, 1980/81 became exactly such a wished-for turning point. The simple numbers show that India has thereafter avoided years of negative or very poor positive growth. A consistently more favorable monsoon

Figure 3.5 Annual change in GDP, 1953/54–1994/95

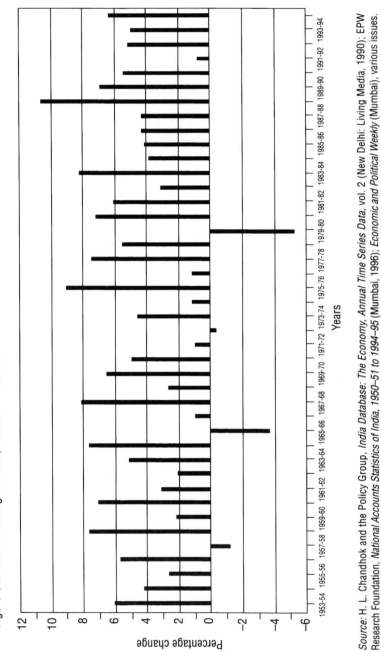

Source: H. L. Chandhok and the Policy Group, *India Database: The Economy, Annual Time Series Data*, vol. 2 (New Delhi: Living Media, 1990); EPW Research Foundation, *National Accounts Statistics of India, 1950–51 to 1994–95* (Mumbai, 1996); *Economic and Political Weekly* (Mumbai), various issues.

Table 3.3. *GDP growth rates by decade (average annual percent)*

Decade	Growth rate (%)
1951/52–1959/60	3.6
1960/61–1969/70	4.0
1970/71–1979/80	3.0
1980/81–1989/90	5.7
1990/91–1994/95	4.5
1995/96–1999/00 (est.)	6.0

Source: Same as Figure 3.5; author's estimate.

has been happily fortuitous. The only obvious downward blip took place in 1991/92 when the reform transition occurred. A cynic could point to this episode as the only interruption that has punctuated the post-1980 Golden Growth Path. It is too widely unnoticed that India's reforms followed a decade of unprecedented growth. Policy adjustments in the early 1990s were catalyzed by fiscal and balance-of-payments imbalances. The reforms were implemented on the watches of Prime Minister P. V. Narasimha Rao and Finance Minister Manmohan Singh, lineal heirs of the Congress Party mantle, with the approbation of other party stalwarts and, seemingly, rested on a vast Indian concordance that was as unexpected as it was broad. One conjecture is that through the 1980s Indians developed on a mass basis, for the first time, progrowth expectations. Poverty rates fell, even as the middle and business classes flourished and then flaunted their new wealth, in most unsocialist fashion. The collapse of the Soviet Union in economic disgrace took any remaining air out of planning's sails. The appropriate responses to crises of external and internal financial balance of the rather modest magnitude India experienced by 1990 are rather easily sorted out by domestic professionals and outside prompters. They do not require a full recasting of economic ideology or policy motifs.

Entering the 1990s, Indians of many economic strata, political parties, and regional loyalties had experienced robust growth for a full decade, liked it, and were willing to have the government make sufficient policy accommodation to return to the Golden Growth Path. At the same time, past attitudes and policies were not jettisoned. Nothing of importance was privatized, foreign corporate entries were still closely modulated, and the leash on the private sector was let out only a couple of notches, not taken off the neck. Workers were sedated by retention of rules that prohibited their discharge and that stopped even sick firms from going out of business. The number of workdays lost to strikes declined by over half. There was appreciable change, but India exhibited a democracy's sensitivity to making too many people uncomfortable at the same time. After all, the administration of shock therapy is incompatible with a culture known for pursuing cures through the patience of yogic meditation and the application of subtle ayurvedic balms.

THE FUTURE

India's future economic progress will be built on the foundations of the past fifty years. Continuing economic reforms ensure that industrial growth will remain rapid. Opening and deepening the financial sector will encourage expansive flows of foreign and domestic investment. Enhanced regulatory oversight will reassure investors in India's stock market. It is now widely understood that power, transport, communications, and urban services must be rapidly upgraded if private-sector expansion is not to be strangled by infrastructure bottlenecks. International firms are being encouraged to participate aggressively in power generation and distribution. The emergence of a national consensus in favor of pragmatic economic reform makes it unlikely that any political party or coalition government will pursue other than a centrist and progressive strategy. If—and it is not a particularly big if—policy management continues to be constructively handled by India's extremely able strategy technocrats, then GNP should remain on the Golden Growth Path of 6 to 8 percent a year. Industrial expansion will be two to three points higher as India's managers and workforce respond to competitive challenges. Agricultural growth of 4 to 5 percent a year is feasible, with renewed levels of investments and technical diffusion, as a second wave of the Green Revolution is extended into high-value fruits, vegetables, meats, and dairy products.

From 1950 through 1990, the international economy played little role in India's economic development. By 1995, exports still comprised only 12 percent of GDP. Foreign technical assistance in agriculture was the most dramatic instance of the impact of foreign-aid programs, but technological borrowing was also key to developing steel mills, chemicals, transport equipment, and defense goods. On a per capita basis, net foreign-aid transfers were never large enough to make a decisive difference in a country the size of India. The policy of self-reliance precluded significant inflows of foreign investment, and the pressured exit of companies such as IBM and Coca-Cola sent a strong negative signal to Western corporations. Only after 1991 have foreign collaborations and fully owned direct investments been welcomed, following changes in India's foreign-investment codes. No single country, not even the United States or Japan, will predominate in India's trade or capital flows; rather, a spectrum of foreign markets and corporate investors will prevail. This diversity will help lay to rest once and for all the specter of domination or loss of autonomy that has haunted Indian policy makers since the end of colonial rule.

India's location in South Asia does not place it astride the world's most dynamic commercial pathways. India needs to be aggressive in securing links to the economies of the Pacific Rim on the one side, and those of the Middle East and the European Union on the other. The United States will in all likelihood remain the primary source of foreign investment as American multinationals stake out large positions in agribusiness, industry, and infrastructure. Steps by the post-1991 governments of Prime Ministers Rao, H. D. Deve Gowda, and Inder K. Gujral to work toward economic cooperation with India's South Asian neighbors in the fields of water, trade, and power should pay rich dividends. If economic accords are accompanied by a winding down of political tensions, most apparent between India and Pakistan, this comparatively poor part of the world will begin to close the gap between itself and the richer lands to the west and east. A supportive and vibrant international economy should smooth the path of accelerating growth that India has moved along since 1950. The decisive factors will remain the decisions taken or not taken in Delhi and the state capitals, and the everyday economic choices made by India's one billion consumers, workers, and managers. Indians are in full control of India's economic future.

SUGGESTED READINGS

Adams, John. "Breaking Away: India's Economy Vaults into the 1990s," in *India Briefing, 1990*, ed. Marshall M. Bouton and Philip Oldenburg. Boulder, Colo.: Westview Press in conjunction with the Asia Society, 1990, 77–100.

"History and Context: 1947–1975," in *Regional Handbooks of Economic Development*, vol. 2: *India*, ed. C. S. LaRue. Chicago: Fitzroy Dearborn, forthcoming. The section "Contrasting Currents" in this chapter draws upon a portion of this essay and includes some overlapping language.

"Reforming India's Economy in an Era of Global Change," *Current History* (April 1996): 151–57.

Ahluwalia, Isher J. *Industrial Growth in India: Stagnation since the Mid-Sixties*. Delhi: Oxford University Press, 1985.

Chakravarty, Sukhamoy. *Development Planning: The Indian Experience*. Oxford: Clarendon Press, 1987.

Chenery, Hollis, and Moises Syrquin. *Patterns of Development, 1950–1970*. New York: Oxford University Press and the World Bank, 1975.

Ford Foundation. *India's Food Crisis and Steps to Meet It*. New Delhi, 1959.

Frankel, Francine R. *India's Political Economy, 1947–1977: The Gradual Revolution*. Princeton, N.J.: Princeton University Press, 1978.

Government of India, Planning Commission. *Fourth Five-Year Plan, 1969–1974*. Delhi, 1969.

Hanson, A. H. *The Process of Planning: A Study of India's Five-Year Plans, 1950–64*. London: Oxford University Press, 1966.

Joshi, Vijay, and I. M. D. Little. *India: Macroeconomics and Political Economy, 1964–1991*. Washington, D.C.: The World Bank, 1994.

India's Economic Reforms, 1991–2001. Oxford: Clarendon, 1996.

Lewis, John P. *India's Political Economy: Governance and Reform*. Delhi: Oxford University Press, 1995.

Nayar, Deepak, ed. *Industrial Growth and Stagnation*. Delhi: Oxford University Press, 1996.

Rosen, George. *Democracy and Economic Change in India*. Berkeley: University of California Press, 1966.

Useful data sources are H. L. Chandhok and the Policy Group, *India Database: The Economy, Annual Time Series Data in Two Volumes*, vols. 1 and 2 (New Delhi: Living Media India, Ltd., 1990); Economic and Political Weekly Research Foundation, *National Accounts Statistics of India* (Mumbai, 1996); Reserve Bank of India, *Report on Currency and Finance* (Bombay, annually). All charts and tables were constructed from data in these sources.

4

●━●

Pakistan: Misplaced priorities, missed opportunities

MARVIN G. WEINBAUM

Retrospectives on Pakistan at fifty are likely to give prominence to the country's failure to realize its aspirations as a democratic and Islamic state. Pakistan's economic performance to date similarly evokes disappointment—despite advances in absolute terms since 1947. At independence, the country began with a resource disadvantage in comparison with the physical and human capital available to India. But not-inconsiderable assets, including an inherited irrigation system and the entrepreneurial skills of recent refugees, offered Pakistan potential for economic development. From the vantage point of the early 1960s, Pakistan, in fact, seemed a better bet to succeed economically than Korea, Indonesia, or Malaysia. Over the years, various indicators have at times suggested that Pakistan stood poised to cross over into the ranks of "middle-income" countries. But an accounting today finds Pakistan struggling to cover its deficits, hurting for investment and savings, and mired in debt.

In some respects, Pakistan's economic problems seem straightforward and, with dedicated leadership and rational policies, largely correctable. The country can reverse its economic imbalances and support growth by living within its means, investing its wealth more wisely, creating new incentives, and obliging its better-off citizens to pay their fair share of taxes. Diagnosed differently, the country's troubles are more complex and deeply structural. The intimately linked economic and political systems pose formidable obstacles to reform. Both are dominated by elites whose self-interest dictates a firm defense of a nonrepresentative, unaccountable decision-making process. Chronic political instability and an obstructionist bureaucratic culture mar prospects for good government and sound economic growth. A population increase of more than 3 per-

cent per annum and a deteriorating economic infrastructure further undermine future prospects. Gains registered to date for industry and agriculture have also done little to reduce the sharp income and social
inequalities among citizens. Burdensome debt servicing is unavoidable,
and the country's huge spending for national defense is politically un-
touchable.

Factors largely beyond the control of the country's decision makers—
including international prices, access to global markets, and unreliable
aid benefactors—are in part to blame. Plainly, a country heavily in-
debted and lacking self-sufficiency in energy, food, and technology is
vulnerable to international circumstances and pressures. Still, the discre-
tionary behavior of those making and implementing domestic policy is
mostly responsible for Pakistan's economic plight. Over the years, the
mismanagement of Pakistan's economy can be attributed to bad politics
and, no less, bad administration. As we shall see, Pakistan's economic
history has been marked by misplaced priorities and missed opportunities, expressed by often inconsistent and ill-conceived economic policies.

THE VARIEGATED PAST

In the first ten years after partition, Pakistan's fledgling economy was in
the hands of an urban-oriented elite that had migrated from India. This
small group of *muhajirs* emphasized industry over agriculture. Private
entrepreneurs were encouraged with easy credit, tax breaks, and other
government incentives. The boom in Pakistan's embryonic industrial development seemed to have launched the country toward a predominantly
private-sector economy. Initially at least, Pakistan followed a liberal import policy. By the mid-1950s, however, the economy was in shambles.
Pakistan was unable to feed itself and was heavily dependent on U.S.
aid. It also lacked the foreign exchange needed to stimulate its new industries.

The ousting of the squabbling civilian politicians by a martial law
regime headed by General Mohammed Ayub Khan (1958–69) saw a
shift. The Western-oriented Ayub government's approach for the most
part favored a free market economy, a strategy that focused the country's energies on modernization and economic development. Pakistan
was expected to diversify its economy through the fostering of industry
that would, among other things, contribute to its military defenses. General Ayub encouraged new industrial entrepreneurs from the army and

the bureaucracy, as well as some transfers of wealth from the landed aristocracy. He also sought domestic private investment in industry and undertook privatization of state-owned firms. Many exports were freed of administrative controls. Private banks made money available, and a capital market developed. But the economy also took on planned features with the creation of a Planning Commission given wide discretion. Import-substitution policies erected high protective barriers for the industrial sector. The manufacturing sector grew at a very rapid pace during this period, between 8 and 16 percent per year, and agriculture also began to prosper. Overall, the economy experienced solid expansion, averaging 5.5 percent per year.

Ayub, as Pakistan's president, succeeded in winning for his bureaucratic-military government the backing of an expanded business class. His indirect electoral system, called Basic Democracies, mostly served to ensure no serious challenge to government policies. Nor was there much that was redistributive in Ayub's government-assisted economy. Industrial wealth accrued mainly to a few families. Some twenty-two families were said to control the bulk of the financial and industrial resources in the country. Meanwhile, Ayub's Green Revolution policies, which raised agricultural production impressively, contributed to the increasing affluence and power of the larger landlords.

Under Prime Minister Zulfikar Ali Bhutto after 1971, Pakistan's economy underwent far-reaching structural changes. Bhutto, campaigning on a highly populist platform, had been the top vote-getter in West Pakistan during the 1970 elections. With the army's defeat and the loss of East Pakistan in December 1971, his government replaced a humiliated military regime. Despite accusations of economic exploitation of West Pakistan by East Pakistan's Bengali leaders, the grievances that galvanized people involved political underrepresentation and military repression. The creation of Bangladesh proved to be more psychologically devastating than economically damaging. On balance, Pakistan was probably advantaged by the divorce of its heavily populated, noncontiguous, economically depressed eastern half.

In office, Bhutto implemented his campaign pledge to alter the previous industrial policy and address the inequities that had occurred under Ayub. His program was designed to replace a largely open economic system with a more state-centric one. From 1972 to 1974, banks and insurance companies were nationalized, as were industrial enterprises in ten basic industries. Within a few years, more than 20 percent of the

total output in the nonagricultural part of the economy was from the
public sector. In Bhutto's hands, the economy moved sharply toward
centralized administrative control, and the state exercised considerable
influence over domestic markets. Stronger import and export controls
were introduced, as well as price controls over agricultural commodities
by public-sector departments.

The government's nationalization policies and market controls proved
to be detrimental to the economy. State-owned industries were inefficient, budgetary deficits were created, and investment fell off sharply. In
an effort to cover deficits and restart economic growth, the government
became heavily dependent on foreign loans. It also came to rely on workers' remittances. As a by-product of a foreign policy intended to attract
economic assistance and political backing from oil-rich Arab states, hundreds of thousands of Pakistanis found employment in the Middle East.
Many highly skilled people were drawn off, but work abroad provided
critical foreign exchange and a political safety valve by absorbing much
of Pakistan's surplus labor.

Bhutto's policies alienated important social groups, namely the country's large and mid-sized farmers, merchants, industrialists, and, eventually, urban professionals. A poorly performing economy left little opportunity to satisfy his key constituencies—the lower classes, rural and
urban. Bhutto did succeed in introducing labor reforms, carrying the
promise of a stronger political role for workers, but in time he grew
suspicious of an energized civil society. Land redistribution was a much-
awaited reform. On paper, it was progressive, limiting holdings to one
hundred acres. However, as with earlier legislation under Ayub it contained major loopholes that enabled large landowners to hold on to most
of their property, particularly the best-quality land. By the end of his
time in office, Bhutto had done very little to improve the income maldistribution among urban and rural populations. The main beneficiaries of
his policies were his party leaders and their families, bureaucrats, and
others employed by the industrial empire acquired by the state.

The military's reascendance in July 1977, following discredited national elections in March, restored little of the laissez faire of the Ayub
era. Despite revived attention to agriculture and smaller industries, especially the producers of agricultural inputs, the new strongman, General Muhammad Zia ul-Haq (1977–88), preferred an economy that tam-
pered little with the status quo. Aside from undoing some of his
predecessor's most disastrous schemes, including the government take-

over of cotton milling, he declined to reverse Bhutto's nationalizations. The state bureaucracy and managers were not keen on giving up the power they wielded in government enterprises, nor were workers anxious to lose the job security that public employment provided. The financial sector remained tightly in government hands, despite promises of deregulation. The somewhat greater freedom to participate in economic development activities provided opportunities for corruption and misuse of public funds that were not overlooked by well-positioned members of the military.

At least for a time, Zia and his advisers, exhorted by the international lending agencies, kept deficits and inflation under control. Overall, the Zia years saw an impressive growth rate of 6.3 percent, nearly two points higher than under Bhutto, and growth in the manufacturing sector almost six points higher. The successes registered in Pakistan's balance of payments over much of the 1980s, mostly from externally generated inflows, enabled the government to avoid addressing more fundamental structural problems in the economy. Remittances from workers abroad, totaling over $25 billion in the 1980s, helped greatly. Foreign assistance was also a vital component. Largely in connection with the Afghan war, Pakistan received generous military and economic assistance from the United States and Saudi Arabia, among others. Humanitarian aid to Afghan refugees and weapons for the resistance, funneled through (and in part siphoned off by) Pakistani hands, proved to be a strong stimulus to the domestic economy. Although it enriched the North-West Frontier Province in particular, the aid also left a legacy of crime and drugs throughout the country.

With the election of Prime Minister Benazir Bhutto following Zia's sudden death in August 1988, there was some further opening of the economy—largely at the insistence of the International Monetary Fund (IMF). Benazir's first government made a clear break with her father's public sector–oriented policies. The prime minister tried to overcome suspicions about her intentions by encouraging nongovernmental investment in industry. Reforms focused on the exchange-rate policy and the removal of agricultural input subsidies. Also contained in a three-year reform program of stabilization and adjustment measures were a sales tax and lowered tariffs.

Hamstrung as she was in governing by Pakistan's president, Ghulam Ishaq Khan, and by the army, Benazir Bhutto was unable to give sufficient focus to the economy and made no sustained efforts to denationalize the state's assets or liberalize regulations. Development expenditures were lowered to accommodate budget cuts, but military spending continued to grow. Pakistan's social and physical infrastructure suffered; its economic growth was sluggish and uneven. In August 1990, President Khan, supported by Army Chief of Staff Aslam Beg and the chief minister of Punjab, Nawaz Sharif, ousted Benazir on charges of corruption, nepotism, and misrule. There was sufficient popular dissatisfaction with her performance that later in the year, in a reasonably honest election—when the rapacious style of her administration stood as a major issue—she was easily defeated by the opposition, headed by Sharif.

As prime minister, Sharif, scion of an industrialist family, seemed determined to accelerate the liberalization process. Early in 1991, his government announced a package of economic reforms. Included were measures to stimulate growth through attracting greater private-sector investment and increasing productivity. The reform policies were supposed to liberalize the economy by reducing the state's role with further denationalizations and deregulation. The government seemed prepared to create a better climate for private enterprise by intervening less in industrial and agricultural pricing and deregulating entry into the markets. It announced that it was ready to embrace liberal international trade and investment, and would offer tax and tariff incentives to new industries as well as liberalize foreign exchange.

Significantly, this period marked the maturing as a political force in Pakistan of a new breed of industrialists, traders, and smaller entrepreneurs, and many others in the urban middle class distrustful of the landed aristocracy and the grassroots populist appeals championed by Benazir Bhutto. Had Sharif been able to complete his term in office, he might have reduced the influence of the rural elites. In any event, the government's fiscal policies laid to rest any early prospects of realizing economic stabilization. In hopes of stimulating the economy, Sharif ran up heavy external debts. The opposition had no trouble unearthing evidence of corruption involving kickbacks and misappropriated funds. In July 1993, the military intervened to force both the prime minister and President Khan to resign. A former World Bank vice president, Moeen Qureshi, became the transitional prime minister pending new elections.

Qureshi put in place policies clearly dedicated to furthering economic liberalization. His three-month tenure saw a number of changes in Pakistan's financial and revenue structures, and an austerity program. He introduced a tax on agricultural income, reduced the budget deficits, devalued the rupee, cut government subsidies, and prepared Pakistan to qualify for IMF loans. These and other changes became possible because as a political outsider and interim leader not beholden to special-interest groups, he was freer to act. However, Qureshi did not have the benefit of democratic legitimacy—necessary if he were to undertake efforts to expose government corruption. Rather than attack his policies directly, Qureshi's critics tried to discredit him for the coincidence of his views with those of the World Bank and the IMF.

After Benazir Bhutto's return to office in October 1993, she again insisted on her commitment to liberal reforms. The legitimate purpose of government, she announced, was to do for the people only what they cannot do for themselves. Indeed, her macroeconomic plan proposed deregulation and decontrol that included trade liberalization and fiscal and financial reforms. The list of privatizations included industry, telecommunications, power generation, electricity-distribution companies, commercial banks, and other financial institutions. The government also introduced a broad-based value-added tax (VAT) on manufacturing, made domestic currency fully convertible, and lifted restrictions on current account transactions. Tariffs were reduced to lower the costs of important inputs. Development plans centered most on infrastructure, primarily targeting the energy sector. The pace of economic reforms was expected to increase with the approval by the IMF of a $1.55 billion, three-year credit that would assist in the implementation of structural adjustment policies.

For a time the Benazir government succeeded in restoring macroeconomic stability. However, by 1995–96, after she had been in office two years, the fiscal discipline and reform had disappeared. The government had fallen far short of IMF-set targets, and Pakistan could no longer qualify for the promised financial assistance. Pressured to find additional revenues to reduce a widening budget deficit, Bhutto resorted by mid-1996 to heavy, highly unpopular new taxes that painfully squeezed the urban middle class but seemed to leave the higher bureaucracy and economic elites largely untouched.

In the fall of 1996, President Farooq Leghari leveled at Benazir a now-familiar litany of charges: mismanaging the country's economy, abetting corruption, and misusing government powers. Using constitutional powers created by General Zia in 1985, the president ousted the prime minister from office in November 1996 and installed a caretaker government led by Meraj Khalid. The interim government undertook a number of administrative initiatives and managed to restore some confidence in the tottering banking system. It steered mostly clear, however, of the politically sensitive task of trying to broaden the tax base. The Khalid government was under continual political sniping, largely inspired by its close affinities with Pakistan's international creditors and their liberal economic orthodoxies. When power was relinquished in February 1997, it went to Nawaz Sharif, victor in an election that awarded his party an overwhelming parliamentary majority.

AN ACCOUNTING

Nawaz Sharif assumed power for the second time with the economy in a severe crisis. By late 1996, Pakistan's foreign exchange reserves were virtually depleted, and the country faced being unable to cover its import bills. A serious international trade imbalance prevailed. Exports had been in the doldrums for some time. Annual export growth that averaged 7 percent for thirty years slumped to less than 2 percent over 1994–96. The trade deficit hovered around $3 billion, 5 percent of gross domestic product (GDP). The balance of payments was in the negative to the order of $4.4 billion. Overseas remittances from more than 3.5 million Pakistanis working abroad had been declining since the early 1980s.

GDP growth dropped to an estimated 3 percent. It had expanded at a respectable 6 percent overall during the 1980s and ran a three-year average of 5 percent until the 1996/97 fiscal year. Overall industrial growth, having reached only an average 2.6 percent in recent years, recorded no growth in the large-scale manufacturing sector during 1996. Meanwhile, the country was laboring under a huge budget deficit, the result, most observers would agree, of flagrant overspending. The deficit that had reached 6.3 percent in 1995–96 stood at 8 percent of GDP. The IMF target was 4 percent. Driven by its obsessive fear of India's intentions, Pakistan has continued to spend heavily on defense, a severe drain on its economy. Along with loan servicing, defense accounts for roughly 70 percent of appropriated funds. The military takes between 6 and 7 percent of GDP and upward of 30 percent of the budget allocations. Moreover, these expenditures are largely free from scrutiny or audit.

Pakistan began 1997 with debts of more than $51 billion, $30 billion of it owed to foreigners. Debt servicing alone has recently consumed more than 50 percent of the total taxes collected and about 35 percent of budget spending. With payments of $3 billion due to foreign lenders through the latter half of 1997, only about $900 million remained in the national treasury. Pakistan has become a net exporter of capital and is increasingly dependent on its bilateral creditors. Concessional aid was more difficult to obtain. Pakistan had misapplied its short-term external aid by using it to finance budget and current-accounts deficits rather than to sustain development. To further liberalization, the IMF demanded that tariffs be cut from a maximum of 70 to 45 percent. The Bhutto government, however, succeeded in lowering tariffs only to about 65 percent. Because of missed fiscal and budgetary targets, the IMF had in 1995 suspended the structural adjustment agreement and in February 1997 ended an $810 million standby loan arrangement.

Pakistan's physical infrastructural sector compares poorly with other countries in the developing world. Roads and public utilities are crumbling. Public enterprises and federal bureaucratic departments still command power generation, railways, roads, and telecommunications. Provincial and local governments are responsible for water supply, sanitation, and management of irrigation facilities that were developed by the federal institutions. Aside from projects funded by foreign sources, infrastructure development is at a standstill, as the heavy debt burden has soaked up available financial resources. The continuing change of governments has upset long-term planning, as leaders are preoccupied by short-term issues.

A high priority in Pakistan's development planning has been placed on the attraction of private investment as a means to finance industrial expansion and create employment. Foreign direct investment totaling $800 million was officially recorded in 1996. As much as $5 billion in power-sector private investment has been committed in recent years. But Pakistan still has a long way to go if it is to provide an attractive investment climate. Even with improvements in the country's regulatory environment, investors have had to contend with the anomalies in the tax system, the poor state of public services, and bureaucratic bottlenecks. The plan in 1996 had been to privatize twenty-seven public-sector companies. Privatization was supposed to draw down the country's debt, but the lack of transparency in transferring some enterprises during the second Benazir Bhutto term, along with fears of unemployment and limited investor interest, had stalled denationalization.

Pakistan's investment potential is also affected by its embarrassingly low savings rate. It finds itself behind ten other Asian countries, including India and the Philippines, in its gross domestic saving as a percentage of GDP. The country is also stuck with Rs 135 billion in defaulted bank loans—mainly the result of unsecured borrowing by privileged members of the economic elite over more than a decade. By mid-1995, the nationalized banking system had virtually collapsed under the weight of bad loans. Heavy government borrowing from the banks has left little credit available for the private sector.

Smuggling takes a heavy toll on the economy. Lost customs duties played a major role in the shortfall in government revenues. It is estimated that the Afghan smuggling trade costs $3 billion a year in uncollected revenues, and the estimate for the whole of Pakistan is three times that amount. The smuggling of wheat out of Pakistan to Afghanistan in 1997 created severe shortages and raised domestic prices. Smuggling of goods from India into Pakistan has fueled the latter's inflation rate. Third countries, often involved in this indirect trade, collect fees for their role, which unnecessarily boosts the price of traded goods. As much as $650 million worth of goods is traded with India, but only $150 million is through legal channels. Just what happens to the black money that is generated is not clear. Some of it undoubtedly leaves Pakistan; much of it goes into luxury items, including cars and houses.

A broadened tax base has appeared high on the agendas of several governments. Tax collection, most of it indirect, accounts for less than 15 percent of GDP, a very poor take compared to all lower- and middle-income developing countries. Because of its failure to collect tax revenues, the country has one of the highest tax rates, an average of 65 percent. There exists widespread resistance to taxes, which are considered neither fair nor equitable. Blatant discrimination exists in the provision of exemptions. Under Benazir Bhutto's tax scheme, for example, individuals in private-sector employment were taxed at a higher rate than those in government service. Evasion is rampant and the collection process scandalous. Owing to evasion, it is believed that no more than 50 to 60 percent of what is supposed to be taxed is actually collected. Somewhere between 0.8 and 1 percent of the population actually pays income tax. Corruption and favoritism have become even more blatant in recent years. Allegedly, no important transaction involving a government contract can occur without a kickback or commission. According to an international business survey, Pakistan is considered the most corrupt country in Asia.

Pakistan's record of land reform and the survival of a traditional rural society stand as barriers to both a more progressive agriculture and a greater social and economic equality. Despite IMF and World Bank prodding, its governments have failed to raise water rates or exact taxes from farm incomes (or, for that matter, business profits). Agricultural commodities are dominated by monopolies or government parastatals, and officials continue to set prices below world market levels. Were prices set right in agriculture, output would probably increase. Pakistan has the potential to achieve self-sufficiency in food and even become a net exporter.

Deficiencies in human capital also retard productivity growth and lower profits from investments. Pakistan's low literacy rate (around 35 percent), high fertility rate (5.7, compared with 3.8 for all low-income countries), and the absence of women from much of the workforce have implications for its goal of building an export-oriented economy. Meager spending on education has most seriously depreciated the country's human capital. Although there is statistical evidence that absolute poverty in the country has declined, income inequality has increased. Inflation in 1996, officially 13 percent, was believed by many to be as high as 20 percent. With consumer subsidies reduced, the inflationary impact has naturally fallen most heavily on the least well-off sectors in the society. In the absence of formal systems of unemployment insurance, public welfare, and health care, the country is poorly positioned to absorb an economic transition. When the hardships of reform inevitably fall unevenly, many people may be unable to adjust to the changes.

Pakistan's continuing economic distress has been dealt with repeatedly through ad hoc solutions. Reform policies are often described as "stop-go." Recent governments have mostly focused on coping with narrow budgetary and debt-payment issues. Not since the days of Ayub and Zulfikar Bhutto have there been serious attempts at a long-term policy based on a coherent and internally consistent vision. Policy making has remained elitist, largely in the hands of a patronage-oriented civil service wedded to the status quo. It has neither been instructed by the best economic expertise nor been able to mobilize support for its policies from active and informed publics.

THE CHALLENGES AND HOPES AHEAD

Early in Pakistan's golden jubilee year, there were renewed hopes that the country would finally face up to its formidable array of economic and political problems. If Nawaz Sharif had made mistakes his first time as prime minister, there were high expectations that he would not repeat them, especially given the way Benazir Bhutto had forfeited public support. Sharif exhibited an early determination on the political front. In April 1997, the constitutional provision that had since 1985 given the president the discretion to dismiss a popularly elected government was removed by amendment, along with important presidential appointment powers. Backed by a large parliamentary majority, Sharif seemed emboldened as well to take risks in order to remove structural impediments in the economy.

The government moved quickly to try to bolster foreign currency reserves, stimulate investment, and attempt to realize additional revenues with stepped-up production. Legislation lowered personal and corporate taxation and cut tariffs. Sharif promised to pursue the privatization of state-owned enterprises at an accelerated pace, and to move ahead with government downsizing and deregulation. Plans were laid for undertaking a long-delayed national census—without which rational planning had been impeded and just representation of citizens denied. Making the weekly holiday Sunday instead of Friday, mainly to please the country's internationally minded business community, offered an early sign of political courage. Overall, a new policy dialogue seemed to be taking place, one prepared to entertain ideas about structural reform that left some talking about a possible "paradigm shift" in the country's economic policy framework.

Pleased with the direction that Sharif and Finance Minister Sartaz Aziz were taking, the IMF, the World Bank, and bilateral creditors gave the government extended time to bring down the budget deficit and implement other reform programs. After lengthy negotiations, the IMF agreed to a $1.6 billion three-year loan; and other international and regional financial institutions promised an additional $750 million in assistance. For the time being, Pakistan's creditors were willing to discount the prime minister's firm refusal to cut the defense budget as well as his failure to use his influence on provincial governments to enact an effective tax on agricultural income. Sharif's about-face on legislation to create a fairer and more yielding General Sales Tax, instead settling for a low flat rate as a concession to angry merchants and traders, also went unchecked.

At the core of Sharif's plans for economic recovery was an investment-driven policy. It relied on a more confident business community willing and able to take the lead in growing the economy. Supply-side strategies called for the middle and lower classes to bear most of the pain of economic discipline and belt-tightening, at least in the near term. However, if the package of mainly probusiness incentives was supposed to stimulate industrial growth and narrow the country's budget deficit, it was a clear failure. By early 1998, currency reserves remained low; tax collection had declined; and serious trade imbalances had failed to improve.

To deflect public criticism, Sharif had through 1997 reverted to the kind of populist policies for which he had gained a reputation during his first term as prime minister. Decisions were made to raise the pay of civil servants, postpone electric and gas price increases, introduce a novel expatriate saving scheme to help manage debt repayments, and further Islamicize the constitution with a pledge of interest-free banking. The completion of a motorway from Lahore to Islamabad—begun during Sharif's first government—was also supposed to win wide acclaim. Instead, it politically backfired as critics called attention to the road's weak economic rationale and the high, unrecoverable costs that siphoned funds off from other more justifiable infrastructural projects.

The initially high popular expectations about economic improvement have worked strongly against Sharif. Mass apathy and cynicism about politics and the economy are again visible. Much of this is occasioned by a major constitutional crisis in the second half of 1997, largely of the prime minister's own making. Drawing on his presumed electoral mandate, Sharif sought to further amass political power by instigating confrontations with the country's judiciary and presidency. By the end of 1997, Sharif had prevailed over his chief adversaries, who were forced from office. But over many months, he and his government had virtually ignored the country's sagging economy. Partly in consequence, and despite the optimism of government ministers, the economic program in 1998 has been struggling to regain momentum and find direction. Much depends on whether the prime minister will use his consolidated power to reach the necessary hard decisions on economic reform—overcoming vested group and class interests—or whether he will be inclined to use his enhanced authority to trample on the country's political liberties.

A checklist of objectives for correcting Pakistan's economy will have to include dealing with its budget imbalances and high inflation. Production must be revived; only by developing its export-oriented industries can Pakistan overcome its chronic balance-of-payments problems and expand employment opportunities. The outstanding external debt and its servicing need to be lowered, and exchange reserves should be built up to cut the cost of high-interest loans. An improvement in the legal and political climate for more foreign direct investment is essential. Accelerated privatization and deregulation are additional goals, as is a revamped tax administration. For Pakistan to come into conformity with the new global trade regime, further trade liberalization measures are unavoidable. Ultimately, the sacred cow of defense spending will have to be addressed.

For a sustainable, more self-reliant economy, Pakistan also requires strengthened economic and political institutions, including a reinvigorated civil society. Institutional reforms, including a fully independent judiciary, a sound financial and banking system, and an attractive securities market can be enhanced with proper legislation. Other changes, such as more transparent decision-making processes, a strengthened work ethic, and greater respect for the rule of law, will take longer to evolve. Rational economic planning will be furthered by elected governments serving out their mandate, and wider democratic participation should allow the cultivation of popular constituencies in favor of reform. The freedom of organized interests to engage in regular dialogue with the state may also help to legitimate those policies that require further public sacrifice. Additionally, without investment in the social agenda for primary and secondary education, family planning, and health, most of the other objectives are likely to be undermined.

Regional developments could help to determine Pakistan's chances of a short-term economic turnaround and its longer-term opportunities for growth. Hopes for opening new markets for the export of goods to Central Asia run high in policy circles but are unlikely to be realized without peace in Afghanistan—the land bridge to the now-independent Muslim republics of the former Soviet Union. A reasonably stable central government in Kabul is needed to ensure unimpeded road traffic and to negotiate the oil and gas pipelines that will allow Pakistan to profit from transshipments and help meet its own future energy requirements. Tensions between Pakistan and Iran, largely brought on by their opposing political alignments in the Afghan conflict, can be expected to disappear with a peaceful settlement, probably enhancing the prospects of economic cooperation through the regional associations to which they both belong. Increased official trade is also certain to result from any progress from talks on political normalization with India. Although Pakistan may be at an initial disadvantage with its weaker export industries, the competitiveness of the country's goods and services can be expected in time to strengthen and the comparative advantages of its economy to be better identified.

Even if Pakistan falls far short of its development goals, it will, in all probability, avoid bankruptcy. In the past it has muddled through, staving off financial collapse through remitted incomes from abroad, illicit dollar flows, and the timely arrival of donor aid—features of a rentier economy that have enabled governments in many developing countries to put off policy discipline and reform. The international economic community will be reluctant to allow so large an economy and so politically sensitive a country, one now nuclear armed, to fall to its knees. Pakistan will in all likelihood be rescued through debt restructuring before it defaults on its loans and becomes a drag on the international economy.

But merely getting by will leave Pakistan noncompetitive, relatively impoverished, and prone to political instability. Should its economic development stagnate further, rapid population growth will cut back living standards, and endemic sectarian and interprovincial tensions will surely worsen. By contrast, an expanding economy, able to distribute its proceeds more equitably, stands a far better chance of dealing with the underlying causes of domestic discontent and disorder. Such a Pakistan, having better prioritized its development needs and exploited its economic opportunities, will be prepared to join an integrated and vigorous regional trade system that could improve prospects for political conciliation across South Asia.

SUGGESTED READINGS

Blood, Peter R., ed. *Pakistan: A Country Study.* Washington, D.C.: Library of Congress, 1995.

Burki, Shahid Javed. *Pakistan: The Continuing Search for Nationhood.* Boulder, Colo.: Westview Press, 1991.

Chaudhry, M. Ghaffar. "Economic Liberalization of Pakistan's Economy: Trends and Repercussions," *Contemporary South Asia* 4, no. 2 (1995): 187–92.

Kennedy, Charles H., ed. *Pakistan: 1992.* Boulder, Colo.: Westview Press, 1993.

Kennedy, Charles H., and Rasul Bakhash Rais, eds. *Pakistan: 1995.* Boulder, Colo.: Westview Press, 1995.

Korson, J. Henry, ed. *Contemporary Problems of Pakistan.* Boulder, Colo.: Westview Press, 1993.

Malik, Sohail Jehangir, Safiya Aftab, and Nargis Sultana, eds. *Pakistan's Eco-*

nomic Performance, 1947 to 1993: A Descriptive Analysis. Lahore: Sure Publishers, 1994.

Monshipouri, Mahmood, and Amjad Samuel. "Development and Democracy in Pakistan: Tenuous or Plausible Nexus?" *Asian Survey* 35, no. 100 (November 1995): 973–89.

Noman, Omar. *Pakistan: A Political and Economic History since 1947.* London: Kegan Paul, 1990.

Samad, Abdus. *Governance, Economic Policy and Reform in Pakistan: Essays in Political Economy.* Lahore: Vanguard Books, 1993.

III

Social development

5

India: Growth and inequity

SONALDE DESAI AND KATHARINE F. SREEDHAR

> The present and the future inevitably grow out of the past and
> bear its stamp.
>
> Nehru, *The Discovery of India*, p. 515

THE WAY WE WERE

It is impossible to understand the changes in Indian society without recognizing the state of the country on the eve of independence, in 1947.
For the first time, the independence movements of 1931 and 1942 had
created a sense of purpose and unity among the diverse and divided
peoples of India. But they had barely papered over the country's deep
divisions.

In spite of leaders like B. R. Ambedkar and Mohandas K. Gandhi,
India was still ruled by locally entrenched economic and political hierarchies based on caste, gender, class, region, and religion. In many areas,
the *jamindari* system of feudal relations dominated a primarily rural
society and included three broad classes: landlords, tenant farmers, and
landless laborers. India lacked financial and technical resources, basic
and modern industries, social services, and enough food to feed itself.
Most people worked in the informal sector, with little access either to
productive resources, land, water, forest, and capital or to education and
employment, and were not represented in decision-making bodies.
Women, children, and bonded laborers, as well as the Scheduled Castes
and tribes, were ignored and therefore suffered disproportionately.

The founding fathers (women's roles were primarily unrecognized)
expected the central government to play the main role in solving these
problems. Their goals were, first, to unify the nation; next, to build a

modern industrial state and promote economic growth; and in the course of those achievements, to reduce poverty and inequalities. Gandhi laid this out clearly: "Recall the face of the poorest and the weakest man whom you may have seen and ask yourself if the step you contemplate is going to be of any use to him. . . . Will it restore to him a control over his own life and destiny? In other words, will it lead to self-reliance?"[1]

The new constitution outlined social and economic policies to rectify inequities and shift power to the weaker elements. Five decades' worth of amendments and laws continued the assault against untouchability and bonded and child labor. And in a crucial way, the Indian civil service, pride of the British Empire, took on primary responsibility for translating all these new plans into reality.

In assessing the degree of success that India has achieved in meeting its founders' goals, we echo Gandhi in our central question: Who has benefited from each change—and from the lack of change? The answer in every case is instructive.

THE WAY WE ARE

We begin with the founders' aspirations and examine the extent to which social policies in each area have ameliorated poverty and inequality among the peoples of India.

Industrialization, economic growth, and poverty

A full description of all relevant economic change since 1947 is beyond our scope, but it is instructive to examine trends in Indian poverty between 1951 and 1994. The percentage of urban and rural poor[2] increased somewhat in the early 1950s (Figure 5.1) and remained more or less constant for the next twenty years, with some fluctuation. In the mid-1970s, a decline began that continued until 1991, when poverty was still high: 37 percent in rural areas and 32 percent in the cities. In 1991, economic reforms were initiated and poverty rose, especially in rural areas. It began subsiding again after 1992, but in 1994 remained slightly

---

[1] S. Mohendra Dev and Ajit Ranade, "Poverty and Public Policy: A Mixed Record," in *India Development Report 1997*, ed. K. Parikh (Delhi: Oxford University Press, 1998).

[2] The poverty line is defined as an income level that allows purchase of food providing 2,400 calories for rural residents and 2,100 calories for urban residents, plus 20 percent of that amount for other basic needs. (Ibid.)

Figure 5.1 Poverty estimates, 1951–94

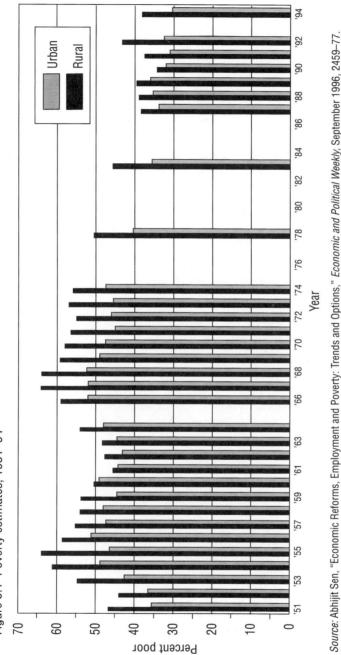

Source: Abhijit Sen, "Economic Reforms, Employment and Poverty: Trends and Options," *Economic and Political Weekly*, September 1996, 2459–77. Special Issue.

Figure 5.2 Profile of Indian poverty, 1986–87

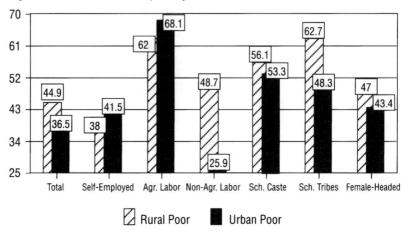

Source: Abhijit Sen, "Economic Reforms, Employment and Poverty: Trends and Options," *Economic and Political Weekly,* September 1996, 2459–77. Special Issue.

higher in rural areas and slightly lower in urban ones than it had been pre-1991.

The ultimate impact of the reforms cannot yet be assessed, and economists continue to argue over their impact. But poverty levels remain high and the long-term trend is not encouraging, despite the decline of the 1980s. Yet what is perhaps the most disheartening aspect of this phenomenon concerns the composition of the poverty population. Exactly who are the poor? (Figure 5.2.) Clearly, the burden of Indian poverty falls most heavily upon the rural population, Scheduled Castes and tribes, and urban households headed by women. Whereas rural people are 44.9 percent poor, more than 60 percent of agricultural laborers are poor, and most of those are landless. Their poverty is linked closely to the lack of nonagricultural employment in rural zones: nearly 76 percent of male workers and 86 percent of female workers there were engaged in agriculture in 1992.

As the founders hoped, government has played an important role in generating nonagricultural work. In 1987–88, nearly 60 percent of regular workers and 22 percent of casual laborers worked for the government. Yet much of this employment was either in government works

Figure 5.3 Employment patterns in India, 1992

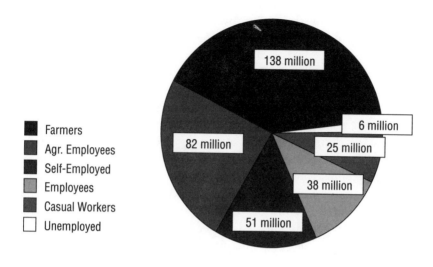

Farmers
Agr. Employees
Self-Employed
Employees
Casual Workers
Unemployed

138 million
6 million
82 million
25 million
38 million
51 million

programs or associated with public construction, sectors unlikely to grow in the current climate of fiscal austerity.

Lack of employment opportunity is also key to urban poverty. Those with regular jobs earn the highest wages, but only 39.4 percent of male and 28.8 percent of female workers are staff employees. The self-employed are 41.2 percent of male and 42.5 percent of the female workforce, and the rest are casual laborers.[3]

Reasons for this are both local and global. With India's industrialization, traditional crafts and trades have dwindled; with globalization, the textile industry has collapsed. The world's rising demand for communications and technologically skilled labor has brought some data-entry work for nimble-fingered Indian workers, but this growth has been slower than expected. India emerges as a nation of farmers, agricultural workers, and self-employed people (Figure 5.3). A relatively small proportion of the labor force holds a regular job in the formal sector.

---

[3] Note that most of the statistics in this chapter suffer from a certain degree of unreliability, but data on women's labor-force participation are the most suspect. We expect that the data on women's self-employment are highly underestimated in National Sample Surveys, and that a far greater proportion of urban women are self-employed than these figures indicate.

Modernization and the quality of life

Health. Although poverty remains widespread, the average quality of life in India has nonetheless improved tremendously in fifty years, as the founders hoped. In 1947, life expectancy was about 32 years. It rose to 61 years by 1993. Much of this reflects improvement in infant and child health: infant mortality declined from 225 per 1,000 live births in 1974 to 74 per 1,000 in 1993.

These gains are associated with broadened and stronger government health services and with the growth of private health care. Government programs of particular impact offer free childhood immunization to target six common and preventable diseases: tuberculosis, diphtheria, pertussis, tetanus, polio, and measles. The government also trained thousands of local midwives and nurses while establishing primary health-care centers nationwide in the 1960s and 1970s. By any standard, the current network is impressive: one community health worker for every 1,000 people, one subcenter per 5,000 people, one primary health center per 30,000 people, and one community health center per 100,000.[4]

Many of these institutions, however, are understaffed and deliver service of low quality. Worse, the poorest service tends to go to the poorest people and the Scheduled Caste populations. During field work, one of the authors observed a nurse practitioner whose task was to give gynecological examinations and provide prenatal care. However, she refused to enter the homes of Scheduled Caste patients because she would have to bathe afterward. Predictably, her Scheduled Caste patients suffered as a result.

Furthermore, India's gains are part of a worldwide trend and yet fall below those of other developing countries. While impressive compared to Bangladesh, India's life expectancy of 61 years is well below the 77-year average in the developed world and lower than the levels in China (69 years) and Sri Lanka (72 years).

Averages also do not tell a comprehensive story. Most of India's gains, as noted, came in infant and child mortality rates, where immunization played the primary role. Morbidity associated with gastrointestinal diseases and diseases of the upper respiratory tract (cholera, ty-

[4] Debabar Banerji, "Health Policies and Programmes in India in the Eighties," *Economic and Political Weekly*, March 21, 1992, 599–605.

phoid, tuberculosis, etc.) remains high and is far less susceptible to the quick fix of a vaccination. These diseases are primarily the recurrent ones of the poor, afflicting people who lack safe drinking water, effective sanitation systems, basic health care, and adequate nutrition. Clearly these lacks are failures of government that would distress India's founders.

Malnutrition remains at record high levels in India, where nearly 52 percent of children are classified as malnourished and 21 percent as severely malnourished. Again, the problem is much more prevalent in rural areas, where 22 percent of children are severely underfed (as compared with 15 percent of urban children), and among Scheduled Castes and tribes, where 25 percent of children are malnourished (compared to 20 percent among other groups). Yet these poor people already spend up to 80 percent of their incomes on food. Either incomes must go up or food prices must come down to deal with malnutrition among the poor.

Solving these problems will require major infrastructural investment and a genuine commitment to deliver free, basic social and health services where they are most needed. But such change is unlikely in an era of privatization, where government investment in the public sector is declining. Even more necessary—and more problematic—is fundamental change in the enduring social attitudes on caste, class, gender, region, and religion that serve to perpetuate India's inequalities.

Education. India's progress in education shows a similar pattern. The system has expanded massively since independence. The government claims male literacy has increased from 34 percent in 1961 to 64 percent in 1991, and female literacy from 13 percent to 39 percent. While striking, these gains lag behind those of other nations. India and Malaysia had comparable rates of adult literacy in 1960 (24 percent and 23 percent, respectively), for example, but Malaysia's rate in the 1990s is 78 percent while India's is only 48 percent. It is probably not coincidental that Malaysia spends 5.5 percent of its gross domestic product (GDP) on education compared to India's 3.2 percent.

Many reasons are given for this mediocre performance. Analysts tend to blame either the educational system for failing to deliver on its promises—through lack of facilities, teachers, investment, and resources—or parents for failing to send children to school—they lack interest in education or want the child's labor at home, it is said.

The National Sample Survey of 1991 found, for example, that in rural areas, 30 percent of children were not enrolled because of "lack of interest." Of those who attended but dropped out later, 16 percent were listed as failing, 26 percent as having "lack of interest," and 31 percent as having "economic reasons."

A close examination of reasons for nonenrollment suggests that the reasons are more complex than mere apathy by parents or students. About 10 percent of all villages lack schools. Where schools exist, their officials are not accountable to the community but to distant government bodies. The curriculum, therefore, may have little or no relation to local livelihood needs and will appear irrelevant to many parents and students. Teachers are overburdened with enormous classes and are often absent, so that students are never sure whether their school will be open. Many teachers discriminate against underprivileged children, and may ignore or abuse Scheduled Caste or tribal children altogether. Teachers tend to be poorly paid and often prefer wealthier students, whom they may charge extra for after-school tuition. Physical punishment is common. All these factors involve structural elements as well as social attitudes; they reduce student and parental motivation and raise dropout rates.

Moreover, many parents have begun to realize that financial returns to education are often quite low. Nonagricultural employment is lagging badly in rural districts. Sixty percent of those who do manage to graduate from secondary school in those areas continue as self-employed farmers. Rural employers even seem to prefer uneducated workers for farm labor.

Social inequality and redistribution of resources

Of the three primary goals of India's founders named at the start of this chapter, redistribution of resources remains the least accessible. The reasons—inequities of region, gender, class, caste, and religion—are the same as those that cripple progress in economic growth and in modernization, but here they cut most deeply (Tables 5.1 and 5.2).

Regional inequality. Poverty, high infant-mortality rates, and low levels of public spending and literacy in India are concentrated in the Hindi-speaking states: Uttar Pradesh, Madhya Pradesh, and Bihar. These areas exhibit India's highest fertility rates, well above the national population-replacement goal of 2.1 children per female. In the 1991 census, these states reported 292 million people, 27 percent of India's population. But prosperity and education levels are linked worldwide to declining fertility. If India is ever to achieve real economic growth, political stability, and social equity, major change must come to these areas first and comprehensively.

Gender inequality. Discrimination against girls and women is rampant in India, and, oddly enough, highest in both the poorest and the richest states. A key measure of it is sex ratio—the comparative number of boys and girls. Worldwide, about 105 boys are born for every 100 girls, but evolution has favored female survival, so grown women generally outnumber men. In the United States, for example, male life expectancy is 72 years and female is 79 years, so that the adult sex ratio is 1,050 women for every 1,000 men.[5]

In India, however, all states except Kerala have fewer women than men (Table 5.2). The gap has increased over time, from a national average of 946 women per 1,000 men in 1951 to 927 women per 1,000 men in 1991. The disparity is starkest in Uttar Pradesh and Bihar (very poor states), and in Punjab and Haryana (relatively wealthy states). What explains this?

Sex-selective abortion is practiced quietly in India, where information makes it possible. Where it does not, traditional families celebrate the birth of boys and bewail the birth of girls and often discriminate against girls in access to food and health care. Even educated families discriminate: one study found that educated mothers in Punjab were far more likely to discriminate against their daughters than were uneducated mothers. Another study argued that although educated women have fewer children, they still prefer boys to girls.

Girls are simply not valued in much of India, even by women. One obvious reason is that most parents rely upon sons to provide old-age support, so see little reason to invest in the health or education of their daughters. Under strong patriarchal norms and village exogamy in northern India, for example, girls tend to be married off young to distant districts, spending their lives under strict seclusion. Nationwide, young girls are fed less and taken to doctors less readily, so more of them die than boys. Medical attention for women is also less than for men, and

---

[5] United Nations Development Program, *Human Development Report* (New York: Oxford University Press, 1994).

Table 5.1. *Regional disparities in socioeconomic conditions for major states and union territories*

States	Infant mortality rate[a] (1990–92)	Literacy rate[b] (1991)	Total fertility rates[c] (1992–93)	Poverty rate[d] (1993–94)	Per cap. public expenditure[e] (1990–91)
South					
Andhra Pradesh	71	44.09	2.6	16.0	505.7
Karnataka	73	56.04	2.8	28.2	576.9
Kerala	17	89.79	2.0	25.9	594.4
Tamil Nadu	58	62.66	2.5	32.6	594.8
West					
Goa	20	75.51	1.9		
Gujarat	69	61.29	3.0	22.2	699.9
Maharashtra	59	64.87	3.0	38.6	702.1
Central					
Madhya Pradesh	111	44.20	3.9	40.8	447.7
Uttar Pradesh	98	41.60	4.8	42.6	428.5
East					
Bihar	72	38.48	4.0	58.0	356.1
Orissa	120	49.09	2.9	49.9	489.5
West Bengal	66	57.70	2.9	40.3	430.9
Northeast					
Arunachal Pradesh	64	41.59	4.2	—	
Assam	76	52.90	3.5	45.0	609.9
Manipur	24	59.89	2.8	—	—
Meghalaya	58	49.10	3.7	—	—
Mizoram	—	82.27	2.3	—	—
Nagaland	10	61.65	3.3	—	—
Sikkim	46	56.94	—	—	—
Tripura	51	60.44	—	—	—

North					
Himachal Pradesh	70	52.13	3.0	—	—
Jammu & Kashmir	—	—	3.1	—	—
Punjab	57	58.51	2.9	12.5	943.5
Rajasthan	84	38.55	3.6	27.5	539.2
Haryana	71	55.85	4.0	28.7	755.4
India	80	52.19	3.4	37.5	—

Note: Data not available for all items with —.

[a]per 1,000 births
[b]per 100 people
[c]children per female
[d]per 100 people
[e]Figures for public expenditure are in rupees, and relate to three-year averages centered on the years shown.

Sources: EPW Research Foundation, "Social Indicators of Development for India—II: Inter-State Disparities," *Economic and Political Weekly*, May 21, 1994, 1300–1308; Indian Institute for Population Sciences, National Family and Health Survey, 1992–93 (Bombay: IIPS, 1995).

Table 5.2. Gender inequality in India across various states

States	Gender ratio	Literacy rate, 1991		Workforce participation, 1991		% Women with hospital birth		% Women with prenatal care	
		Male	Female	Male	Female	Rural	Urban	Rural	Urban
South									
Andhra Pradesh	973	55.13	32.72	55.48	34.32	21.31	69.35	61.41	87.75
Karnataka	961	67.26	44.34	54.09	29.39	24.87	69.15	58.98	83.61
Kerala	1040	93.62	86.13	47.58	15.85	86.53	95.66	96.79	99.74
Tamil Nadu	972	73.75	51.33	56.39	29.89	49.24	90.10	71.20	91.5
West									
Goa	969	83.64	67.09	49.56	20.52	87.23	90.23	95.04	95.49
Gujarat	936	73.13	48.64	53.57	25.96	25.27	63.58	40.20	79.71
Maharashtra	935	76.56	52.32	52.16	33.11	25.26	76.38	58.21	90.88
Central									
Madhya Pradesh	932	58.42	28.85	52.26	32.68	7.67	52.25	23.97	75.39
Uttar Pradesh	881	55.73	25.31	49.68	12.32	6.38	34.50	24.46	65.33
East									
Bihar	912	52.49	22.89	47.92	14.86	7.80	39.63	22.49	59.45
Orissa	972	63.09	34.68	53.79	20.79	9.67	42.19	35.49	71.56
West Bengal	917	67.81	46.56	51.40	11.25	20.27	69.18	64.23	80.72
Northeast									
Arunachal Pradesh	861	51.45	29.69	53.76	37.49	16.43	47.89	42.49	81.69
Assam	925	61.90	43.00	49.45	21.61	8.25	51.86	45.88	80.82
Manipur	961	71.63	47.60	45.27	38.96	16.61	42.34	57.65	77.37
Meghalaya	947	53.12	44.85	50.07	34.93	18.95	76.70	43.15	86.41
Mizoram	924	85.61	78.60	53.87	43.52	31.46	68.98	82.02	94.12
Nagaland	890	67.62	54.75	46.86	37.96	4.85	10.67	34.62	54.67

Sikkim	878	65.74	46.69	51.26	30.41	—	—	—	—
Tripura	946	70.58	49.65	47.55	13.76	20.40	76.71	57.71	97.26
North									
Himachal Pradesh	996	75.36	52.13	50.64	34.82	12.70	57.88	72.47	94.26
Jammu & Kashmir	923	—	—	—	—	17.70	48.57	76.30	96.86
Punjab	888	65.66	50.41	54.22	4.40	22.64	37.68	85.06	90.85
Rajasthan	913	54.99	20.44	49.30	27.40	7.13	34.60	20.09	51.77
Haryana	874	69.10	40.47	48.51	10.76	11.63	37.80	63.91	85.17
India	929	64.20	39.19	51.55	22.25	18.62	56.90	46.13	81.25

Note: Sex ratio is calculated as females per 1000 males.
Source: EPW Research Foundation, "Social Indicators of Development for India—II: Inter-State Disparities," *Economic and Political Weekly*, May 21, 1994, 1300–1308.

maternal death in childbirth is unacceptably high: nearly 550 maternal deaths per 100,000 births in India, compared to 180 in Sri Lanka and 130 in China.

It is a vicious circle. Parents concentrate their resources on their sons. Where a patriarchal system declares that virtue and modesty are women's highest prize, parents are reluctant to send daughters to schools, especially to those that may be distant or have no female teachers. Females educated enough to be teachers are therefore scarce, especially in remote areas that may have few schools for anyone. Fewer than one-third of primary and middle-school teachers are women, and most of those are in urban areas. While the male literacy rate is 64 percent, the female rate is only 39 percent. In the poorer states like Bihar, Rajasthan, and Uttar Pradesh, only a quarter or fewer of females aged 7 or older are literate—and these figures may be too optimistic. Most high-paying jobs require higher education and so few are open to women; when girls and women do work, their wages are lower than men's, and the men in their families tend to take control of the money. Only rarely, then, is a working woman able to assist her own parents to help break the cycle of expectation.

Gender discrimination is evident in many other ways. In the hills of Uttar Pradesh where forest reserves are vanishing, women spend nearly five hours daily collecting wood for household fuel. Elsewhere they spend more time fetching water. But the government pays little attention to preserving supplies of domestic fuel-wood and local water. It provided major loans to large sugar farmers for digging bore wells in Maharashtra, for example, without noticing that those wells would drain water from common-use domestic water sources nearby. Women's burdens were thereby increased.

School enrollment of women, however, is higher in areas that have high female wages. A growing demand among better-educated men for better-educated brides may provide an incentive for some parents to educate their daughters. And groups of elite, educated women are working to raise awareness among India's women about the injustice of their status, for change will not come until more women themselves insist upon it.

Inequality in landholdings. The enduring strength of India's caste and class boundaries is seen most clearly in the pattern of rural land distribution. At independence, India's founders were vocal in advocating land

Figure 5.4 Distribution of landholdings in rural India, 1953–82

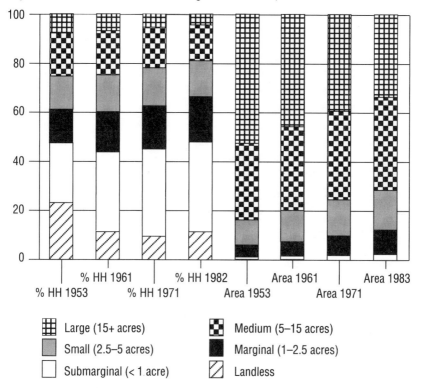

Legend:
- Large (15+ acres)
- Small (2.5–5 acres)
- Submarginal (< 1 acre)
- Medium (5–15 acres)
- Marginal (1–2.5 acres)
- Landless

Source: H. R. Sharma, "Distribution of Landholdings in Rural India, 1953–54 to 1981–82: Implications for Land Reforms," *Economic and Political Weekly,* March 26, 1994, A12–A27.

reform—reallocation of large landowners' holdings into smaller parcels that desperately poor rural sharecroppers and landless farm workers could own and live on. National and state laws were enacted to limit single-family holdings and affirm the rights of tenant farmers. Land declared surplus under those laws was supposed to be acquired by state governments and redistributed to the landless, particularly to the Scheduled Castes.

Despite these radical laws, and their often enthusiastic implementation in the 1950s and 1960s, redistribution has slowed considerably (Figure 5.4), to the point of systemwide failure. Figure 5.4 shows that between 1953 and 1982, an increasing percentage of the rural population shifted from being landless laborers to being submarginal farmers, with holdings of less than one acre.[6] However, the proportion of households a little better off, with small and medium holdings, showed only very slight change. Moreover, the total amount of land available to submarginal and marginal farmers has remained more or less constant since 1953,[7] although the number of such farmers has risen sharply. As a result, most submarginal and marginal farmers cannot make ends meet from working their too-small parcels, so they supplement their income through agricultural wage labor. Their livelihood, in other words, remains unchanged by land reform.

The main shifts in landownership have occurred at the upper end, where farmers with small to medium holdings have gained at the expense of large farmers. But some of this change is due to land fragmentation that arises when brothers in a large extended family divide up the ancestral property.

The overall picture is one of failure of land reform to achieve the founders' stated goals. The reasons are many. Much less land overall has been transferred to the poor than the founders intended—only 1 percent of India's cultivable terrain. Of areas declared surplus under land ceiling legislation, only 78 percent was acquired by the government and only 75 percent of that was redistributed—a total of less than 60 percent of what was supposed to have gone to the poor. Government bureaucrats, though sworn to uphold land reform, in fact often support large landholders by deliberately destroying land records and failing to enforce the laws. Much land that was nominally transferred was not transferred in fact, because new titles were not given, were faulty, or were not recorded. Many transfers occurred within families to avoid ceilings on individual holdings; many dispossessed landowners, still wealthy and powerful, simply took back their former land by force.

Meanwhile, the new farmers, still poor, had no funds to make investments of seed, fertilizer or equipment, so many crops failed. Where loans were given for those purposes, terms were often usurious and secured by the land, which quickly reverted to the old owners. In rural Uttar Pra-

---

[6] Some of the changes may be attributable to the National Sample Survey's shifting definition of landownership. In 1952–53, it included owned land only. In subsequent rounds, "possession" of land has been included.

[7] H. R. Sharma, "Distribution of Landholdings in Rural India, 1953–54 to 1981–82: Implications for Land Reforms," *Economic and Political Weekly*, March 26, 1994, A12–A27.

desh, fieldwork by one of the authors found Scheduled Caste families (the majority of the landless there) who complained bitterly that although they were allotted one acre of land, the upper-caste former owners did not allow them to farm it. When they reported this to government authorities, the area development officer negotiated a "peace" in which the Scheduled Caste families were allowed to farm the land they legally owned but were forced to pay half their produce as tribute to the former owners.

Caste-based and religious inequality. The role of caste and religion in Indian society, never small, has escalated sharply in the last fifteen years. Part of the implicit contract the independence movement made with untouchables (now included under the "Scheduled Caste" label) was a wholehearted commitment to reduction of caste and religious inequities. Legislation was enacted to fulfill that promise: seats in local governments were formally reserved for Scheduled Castes; jobs in the public sector were set aside for them; and they were to be preferentially admitted to competitive educational programs like medicine and engineering.

Once again, however, high-caste bureaucrats did not act against their own interests at any level. Primary and secondary schools nationwide continued to exclude Scheduled Caste children with impunity, and where they were admitted, teachers continued to ignore them. Without primary education, members of the Scheduled Castes cannot fill the higher education slots that await them, nor do representative numbers seek the allocated legislative seats. Without a real voice among policy makers and with few articulate advocates, the Scheduled Castes are still far more likely than other caste members to be poor, uneducated, and landless.

A stark illustration comes from research on programs to serve the scavenger population of rural Gujarat. Scavengers, whom Gandhi called *Harijan*, "God's beloved people," clean toilets and clear garbage, work that few highborn Hindus will do. The central government set up rehabilitation programs aimed at providing 4 million scavengers with alternative jobs.

Entrenched attitudes within the bureaucracies, however, led few states to take the law seriously. For example, although legal guidelines suggest that the state should provide Rs 20,000 per scavenger for rehabilitation—50 percent grant, 15 percent loan at 4 percent interest, and 35 percent bank loan at commercial rates—Gujarat provided an average of Rs. 7,686—7 percent grant, 12 percent loan at subsidized interest, and 81 percent bank loan at commercial rates. This effectively shifted responsibility for the program from government to banks controlled by local elites, whose general response to scavengers applying for rehabilitation has been the predictable one.

Like caste-based inequality, religion-based problems are both prevalent and so sensitive in India that they are difficult to document. However, available research suggests that the minority Muslims are worse off in several measures of well-being than the dominant Hindus, particularly in urban areas. About 25 percent of urban Hindus have a secondary school education or better, but only 15 percent of Muslims do. Rural Muslims and Hindus have roughly similar incomes (judged by monthly per capita spending), but many more Muslims than Hindus in urban areas are poor, spending only Rs 160 (about U.S.$46) per month or less—53 percent of Muslims compared to 39 percent of Hindus. In another example, Hindu police officers during the Bombay religious riots of 1992–93 were observed watching atrocities by Hindu mobs against Muslim slum residents without intervening to stop them.

Rural-urban inequality. As a result of economic decline and job shortages in rural areas, people are migrating to towns and cities, and villages are becoming semiurban. The migrants find low-paid work in the informal sector for the most part, but are forced to live—and often work—in shacks and slums or on the streets. Neither landlords nor government provides adequate water, sanitary, sewer, or other basic facilities. Women accustomed to using open fields as their latrines have no clean or private spaces. Without land rights, street and slum dwellers have no security against removal by developers or city authorities.

Inequalities in political power. Women and Scheduled Castes and tribes are beginning to occupy their reserved seats in *panchayats* (local councils) and other bodies in order to push for political power, but they cannot force change without financial resources or administrative control. They are more aware of their rights, turn out to vote, mobilize around issues, and in the name of participation are consulted on development projects, but they have little real decision-making authority.

Functioning democracies worldwide require the existence of interest groups articulating their members' needs so that government decisions may reflect those demands. Such nongovernmental organizations (NGOs) serve to monitor and enforce official policies, as well as to call attention to private and corporate abuses, proposing change and fueling debate. The louder voices tend to prevail.

In India, NGOs are proliferating in the form of self-help groups, community-based organizations, women's groups, consumers, caste groups, unions (now only 10 percent of the working population, and tied to political parties), *panchayats* (village councils), and so on. They do amplify their members' voices and have already changed power relationships in some states, but for the most part, traditional structures and divisions persist within them, so that they remain unreliable as a force for change.

India's NGOs do not always bridge existing social divisions and may even reinforce them. Some are the clones of corporations, retired government officials or party politicians, set up to seek the government aid available to NGOs. Most others are resource-poor, with little capacity in organizing, management, advocacy, leadership, attention-getting, or institution-building. With significant exceptions, they are mostly unfamiliar with modern media and communications techniques and are generally unaware of each other's existence. Most have not yet considered nationwide reach nor India-wide alliances, much less the possibility of links to international networks or allies who could buttress their pressure for change.

As a result, Indian civil society does not have the strength at the moment either to take on many of the functions of social reform and development or to wrest social initiative away from the central government. One exception is caste groups that have entered the political process and succeeded in altering some power relationships.

Success and failures: The role of the political system. After fifty years, it is clear that great progress has occurred. India has held together, an achievement many did not expect. It has become a modern industrial state with a rapidly expanding economy and middle class, and it produces enough to feed itself. As in most of the world, significant improvements in the quality of life have taken place. But great failures have also occurred. The majority of the founding fathers' promises have not been kept, despite some progress on each front. In retrospect this is not surprising, given the founders' radical vision. They underestimated the degree to which the state needed to transform itself before it could transform the country.

Themselves upper-caste, upper-class, and male, the new rulers passed laws designed to transfer power away from upper-caste, upper-class males. However, when it came to implementing these laws, they were unable or unwilling to enforce them or to implement policies and programs designed to reduce their own power. Moreover, they did not anticipate the obstacles these policies would face at the hands of the bureaucratic apparatus.

Before independence, the bureaucrats had been recruited mostly from generations of landlords educated to protect the British Empire from the Indian masses: they handled police, land records, taxes, and revenue. After independence, they simply acquired more power in elected and appointed bodies at all levels. They controlled more resources and expanded into areas like employment and management, resource distribution, and construction, where traditional relationships had long held sway. As a result, every five-year plan since 1952 set concrete steps for increasing the well-being of the poor and the marginalized, but not a single plan lived up to expectations.

The bureaucracy did carry out many programs with amazing efficiency and professionalism—child immunization and grain-crop betterment especially, among others that did not disturb the balance of power. But programs involving redistribution of resources or bestowing government largess, as in land reform and rural credit schemes, were languidly enforced at best and often sabotaged overtly. Bureaucrats who tried to carry out the law were often transferred.

In short, the new laws reinvigorated ancient frictions along the old fault lines of class, gender, caste, religion, and region, and many were crushed by those combined pressures. It was not a failure of law, but a failure of implementation. Indian society has been utterly transformed in many ways, but in other ways it is just as it always was.

THE WAY WE MIGHT BE

India is now at a pivotal juncture. The society must decide whether the goals and promises of India's founders are still worthy of attempts at achievement. As always, the key questions are those of values and priorities. Who will decide who may use which resources, and for what purposes? The alternative answers either challenge underlying social structures and power relationships or maintain the current course.

If present trends continue, the middle class will grow and so will the numbers of the impoverished millions—39 percent of all Indians now, according to the latest planning commission figures. Fully 85 percent of the population has no connection to government-sector employment or benefits. With widening global communications, their expectations are certain to keep rising, but they will have no new access to productive resources, capital markets, information and technology, or employment and educational opportunity. The weakest sections, with low productivity and stagnant wages, will have a more difficult time buying food, health care, and other necessities as costs rise.

In the absence of minimum-wage employment, families will still subsist through the work of bonded laborers, now estimated at 2.8 million in the agricultural sector alone, along with child labor and scavenging. In the absence of real transfers of power and resources to marginalized groups, resistance to change will continue in the power elite of politicians, bureaucrats, landowners, industrialists, and the new technocrats and private entrepreneurs. The ancient divisions, in short, will widen and impede growth. And meanwhile, restive political, caste, tribal, women's, secessionist, and religious fundamentalist groups will burgeon, pressing for political and social change and leading inevitably to disorder and violence.

The state now appears to have turned to the capital markets as a way of achieving its goals, assuming that individuals acting in their own interests will create an economic system of growth, productivity, efficiency, and equality. However, current research shows no intrinsic or systematic correlation between long-run aggregate growth and overall equity. Growth may ease absolute poverty, but it does not necessarily change distribution patterns and may often widen inequality. A 5 percent increase for a poor Indian means very little real change, but the same percentage increase for a wealthy landowner greatly widens the absolute gap between them.

Indian social inequalities also prevent the creation of a free market. The assumption is, for example, that the inefficient and low-quality government-run health system can be replaced by a fee-for-service system that will respond to public pressure with high-quality, efficient medical care. If all families had spare resources and made good-faith efforts to find the best health care for all family members, and if doctors were willing to live and practice in rural areas, this assumption might prove true. But in India, many families neglect the health needs of women and girls, as previously noted, and doctors are unwilling to move away from cities. Decline in government provision of health services and institution of user fees are therefore likely to result quickly in plummeting health for women and girls and in separate and unequal facilities for the poor and the wealthy, Hindus and Muslims, and so on.

Similarly, common-property resources like drinkable water and fuel-wood cannot be allocated purely on profit-making grounds. Nothing then prevents large-farm owners from sucking dry all the local water to irrigate their cash crops, while ever-shallower common wells cause water shortages for the poorer folk, with a corresponding rise in gastrointestinal disease.

Government reservation policies will not be enough for social transformation. Quotas for higher education and jobs are irrelevant for those who drop out of primary school. The women and Scheduled Castes and tribes with reserved seats in *panchayats* and other bodies cannot easily make demands upon the vested interests who control their livelihoods and most of their lives.

A promising alternative

A more optimistic scenario presumes that activist leaders might decide to restart the dreams of the founding fathers with new initiatives and firm nationwide enforcement across all divisions of caste, class, religion, region, and gender. They might recognize that neither they, the private sector, nor citizens' groups alone can successfully take on such goals and functions, but that all sectors are essential to success.

These leaders would redefine national security to include economic and social security. They would promote policies offering the poor the inputs required to increase their productivity, assets, mobility, and decision-making authority. The poor would thereby gain access to natural and financial resources, raw material and markets, job opportunities, and the methods and tools of development that the private sector takes for granted—communications, technical, and managerial skills. These leaders, in short, would facilitate rather than hinder the ability of the poor to accumulate their own resources and make productive investments allowing informal sectors access to things that the formal sector takes for granted.

For example, visionary leaders would reform banking regulations that restrict loans to the poor, encouraging viable community-based financial institutions to invest in the informal economy. The many informal institutions that now lend to the poor tend to keep them on a treadmill of rising debt. With even slightly more income, the poor have proved that they are willing and able to invest and save in ways that promote growth, and to pay for their own social needs, including health and child care.

Other visionary policies would promote full employment and creation of jobs in the rural sector, farm and nonfarm alike, and would promote investment in urban infrastructure. Slum-dwellers and more of the rural poor would be able to acquire land titles, especially where land rights are badly defined. Common property would be more equitably distributed: forest rights, for example, would go to local people, for whom they would mean employment and resources. Laws and rules would be changed to allow women and the poor equal access to property and inheritances, credit, training, or land tenure, or the ability to do business (e.g., in licensing and zoning regulations).

Such a government would draw many more of its political and administrative leaders from a nontraditional base that for the first time would actively recruit women, the poor, and the marginalized. It would raise their numbers in every decision-making body, invest heavily in educational-system reform, and launch public awareness and incentive programs to draw all children, especially girls, into the schools.

This government would demand that international donors, which now provide only 10 percent of India's budget, support the priorities they have proclaimed. It would seek to monitor and control the reach of foreign corporate involvement in India, while enacting legislation to enable NGOs and other civic organizations to organize, grow, and thrive more easily. Some NGOs would be expected to help monitor corporate and government activity at every level, to make their voices heard, and to be included in decision-makers' policy debates. The poor would have a much larger role in naming problems, designing solutions, and carrying them out than they now have. And most crucially, the government would work much more actively to close the gaps between castes, classes, regions, and religions, promoting women's roles and rights as much as men's.

Such a broad menu would of course cause new tensions and problems to arise, as change always does. But the shift is needed if India is going to grow and become a more just society. Inequities were at the root of India's troubles fifty years ago and they remain the reasons why the promises of the country's dreams at independence remain unfulfilled today. Political will and leadership will determine which road the new India now takes.

SUGGESTED READINGS

Acharya, Promesh. "Universal Elementary Education: Receding Goal," *Economic and Political Weekly*, January 1–8, 1994, 27–30.

Banerji, Debabar. "Health Policies and Programmes in India in the Eighties," *Economic and Political Weekly*, March 21, 1992, 599–605.

Das Gupta, Monica. 1987. "Selective Discrimination against Female Children in Rural Punjab, India," *Population and Development Review* 13 (1987): 77–100.

Desai, Sonalde. *Gender Inequalities and Demographic Behavior in India*. New York: Population Council, 1994.

Dreze, Jean, and Amartya Kumar Sen. *India: Economic Development and Social Opportunity*. New York: Oxford University Press, 1995.

EPW Research Foundation. "Social Indicators of Development for India—I," *Economic and Political Weekly*, May 14, 1994, 1227–40.

Jain, Devaki, and Nirmala Banerjee, eds. *Tyranny of the Household*. Delhi: Shakti Books, 1985.

National Commission on Self-Employed Women and Women in the Informal Sector. *Shramashakti*. New Delhi: Government of India, 1987.

Nehru, Jawaharlal. *The Discovery of India*. New Delhi: Oxford University Press, 1982 (first published 1946).

Radhakrishnan, P. "Land Reforms: Rhetoric and Reality," *Economic and Political Weekly*, November 21, 1990, 2617–21.

Sen, Abhijit. "Economic Reforms, Employment and Poverty: Trends and Options," *Economic and Political Weekly*, September 1996, 2459–77. Special issue.

Shariff, Abusaleh. "Socio-economic and Demographic Differences between Hindus and Muslims in India," *Economic and Political Weekly*, November 18, 1995, 2947–54.

Sharma, H. R. "Distribution of Landholdings in Rural India, 1953–54 to 1981–82: Implications for Land Reforms," *Economic and Political Weekly*, March 26, 1994, A12–A27.

Shiva, Vandana. *Ecology and the Politics of Survival: Conflicts over Natural Resources in India*. New Delhi: Sage Publications, 1991.

Vaidyanathan, A. "Employment Situation: Some Emerging Perspectives," *Economic and Political Weekly*, December 10, 1994, 3147–56.

Visaria, Pravin, and Leela Visaria. "India's Population in Transition," *Population Bulletin* 50, no. 3 (1995).

Vyas, V. S., and Pradeep Bhargava. "Public Intervention for Poverty Alleviation: An Overview," *Economic and Political Weekly*, October 14–21, 1995, 2559–72.

Weiner, Myron. *Child and the State in India*. Princeton, N.J.: Princeton University Press, 1991.

6

Pakistan: Some progress, sobering challenges

ANITA M. WEISS

It is indeed sobering to reflect on social developments that have transpired during Pakistan's first fifty years. The sociocultural ethos of the country in 1997 was substantially different from that of 1947. Far more people had access to the *tools* of development—education, capital, a political voice—than fifty years before, although the percentage of those with access had thus far consistently failed to meet targets laid out in the government's various five-year plans. The *goods* that development was to have brought—better health, prosperity, greater diversity in making vocational choices, an overall betterment in the quality of life—remained out of reach for the two-thirds of the population that still resided in rural areas, although these goods lay close enough to fuel the hopes of the throngs of Pakistanis descending on their nation's cities, causing them to grow at a rate of 4.6 percent per year. Life expectancy for a child born in 1960 was 43 years; in 1997 it was 60. Rates of children dying before the age of one plunged from a high of 162 per 1,000 in 1960 to 92 per 1,000 in 1994, but 40 percent of all children in the country under the age of five suffered from malnutrition in 1995. Although television viewing—which enables rapid sharing of information— seems nearly universal to an urban observer of Pakistani social life, less than 2 percent of the population owned a television set in 1992. Automobiles and minibuses transport people more swiftly than the tongas prevalent at independence—until, of course, one gets stuck in a traffic jam in one of the megacities, Karachi, Lahore, or Faisalabad, collectively home to nearly one-fifth of the country's population.

In an effort to articulate social development goals, members of the federal Planning Commission expressed that the ultimate aim of development should be to improve the well-being of society as a whole and to ensure that the benefits of economic progress are distributed fairly over the entire community. The alleviation of poverty, the provision of greater opportunities, the containment of excessively high incomes and the achievement of a more equitable distribution of income and wealth all contribute towards the attainment of economic justice.[1]

At the outset, Pakistan's future held great promise of achieving such goals. Independence was the culmination of what had finally become a mass-based grassroots movement, embracing partisans from a range of ethnic, class, and regional backgrounds, comprising male as well as female freedom fighters. The populist vision was of a country well worth struggling for, as seen in the actions of the hordes of migrants who left everything behind as they boarded trains for the "land of the pure," Pakistan. The havoc and social chaos that became the legacy of partition—particularly the legacy of those trains—kindled a unifying spirit among many of the inhabitants of the new state. But not among all.

Therein has lain one of Pakistan's greatest social challenges: how to create a sense of citizenry among communities that have not historically regarded each other as "a people," aside from most being adherents of the same major religion. Pakistan has also faced a range of other distinct social challenges. Various development strategies attempted in the past five decades have made minimal headway in improving the average person's life. Key social-development indicators remain among the lowest in the world: adult literacy is at a dismal 36.4 percent (female adult literacy is even worse, at 23 percent); it has a daily calorie supply per capita lower than that of Burkina Faso, one of the world's poorest countries; nearly three-quarters of the population do not have access to proper sanitation; and the country's ranking in the 1996 United Nations (UN) Human Development Index places it among other countries with far lower gross domestic product (GDP) per capita rates.

Now, at the turn of the millennium, I would argue that Pakistani society is at a pivotal juncture. It is confronting its greatest challenge with the demise of a social contract between Pakistanis while simultaneously facing the greatest possibilities with the rise of a civil society and the proliferation of nongovernmental organizations (NGOs) eager to make a difference on the social landscape. I will return to this theme toward the end of this chapter. At this point, however, I would like to

---

[1] Government of Pakistan, Planning Commission, *Seventh Five-Year Plan (1988–93) and Perspective Plan (1988–2003)* (Islamabad: Printing Corporation of Pakistan Press, 1988), 35.

frame this analysis of the transformations under way in Pakistani society
by placing divergent viewpoints and visions within a historical context.

HISTORICAL GUIDEPOSTS AND MOORINGS

Questions, debates, and mistrust of a shared social vision by its leaders
arose in Pakistan from the outset. Muhammad Ali Jinnah and other
Western-oriented professionals envisioned a multiethnic, pluralistic—
and indubitably democratic—country, free from the hegemony of any
one group. In his inaugural address to the Constituent Assembly of Pakistan three days prior to independence, in his capacity as its first president, Jinnah implored, "If we want to make this great State of Pakistan
happy and prosperous we should wholly and solely concentrate on the
well-being of the people, and especially of the masses and the poor."[2]
His vision of Pakistan was one of a profusion of groups working together for the overall well-being of the state regardless of ethnic or religious divisions, as stated very clearly later in the same speech:

[If you] work together in a spirit that every one of you, no matter to what
community he belongs, no matter what relations he had with you in the past, no
matter what is his colour, caste or creed, is first, second and last a citizen of this
State with equal rights, privileges and obligations, there will be no end to the
progress you will make. . . . You are free; you are free to go to your temples,
you are free to go to your mosques or to any other places of worship in this
State of Pakistan. You may belong to any religion or caste or creed—that has
nothing to do with the business of the State.[3]

Leaders from varying backgrounds recognized the substantive political
and economic challenges confronting the new state, and most shared the
conviction that a popular consensus existed on its necessity, viability,
and structure.

But other views also existed. Some factions initially wanted no part
of Pakistan, for diverse reasons. Supporters of the Punjab Unionist Party
placed their loyalties with the British; their successors still do, as they
educate their children in British-style schools, speak English among
themselves, and value indigenous aesthetics only as quaint historic relics.

[2] Reprinted in C. M. Naim, ed., *Iqbal, Jinnah and Pakistan: The Vision and the Reality*,
South Asian series #5 (Syracuse, N.Y.: Syracuse University Maxwell School of Citizenship and Public Affairs, 1979), 212.
[3] Ibid., 212–13.

Alternatively, many Islamist groups initially recoiled from the demand for Pakistan on the grounds that Islam could not be bounded by the borders of a nation-state. After partition, however, many with Islamist views migrated, out of necessity, to Pakistan. To them, the Pakistan of 1947 was a rough diamond: the possibilities of creating a *dar-ul-Islam*[4] were now boundless, once their message was understood by their new compatriots.

Indeed, despite the assumptions of the Two Nations theory,[5] Pakistan's formidable Muslim population came from diverse practices and heritages. These ranged from the austere Deoband school and the orthodox Berelvi school to the modernist Aligarh school among the majority Sunnis, and from the followers of the Twelve Imams, the disciples of the Aga Khan, to members of the *Dawoodi Bohra* and *Memon* communities among the minority Shi'a groups. Notwithstanding these formal divisions, Sufi teachers who had spread Islam throughout the subcontinent still had their followings, and most Bengali Muslims, accustomed to a more syncretic Islamic tradition, found little in common with the rest.

The vision of a Muslim-majority state in which religious minorities would share equally in its development came under question shortly after independence, and the debate continues amid questions of rights of Ahmediyas, issuance of identity cards denoting religious affiliation, and government intervention in the personal practice of Islam. Jinnah's pluralistic view of Pakistani society was shaken somewhat in the mid-1960s and 1970s as divisions and distinctions between different ethnic and class groupings became more conspicuous. Animosity grew between *muhajirs* (migrants from India) and Punjabis, the two most economically powerful ethnic groups in the country. The 1971 secession of East Pakistan contributed to unease because not all voices may have a place to be heard in Pakistan. Zulfikar Ali Bhutto also opened up a Pandora's box of sectarian conflict when his PPP adopted the slogan of Islamic socialism. The pluralistic perspective was definitively discarded in 1979 when

---

[4] *dar-ul-Islam*: a land where Islam would be the highest authority.
[5] The Two Nations theory, elaborated by Iqbal, argued that two separate distinct communities have historically inhabited northern South Asia, one now consisting of Hindus and the other of Muslims. For further information, see Naim, *Iqbal*. A contemporary interpretation of this from the Pakistani point of view is offered in Aitzaz Ahsan, *The Indus Saga and the Making of Pakistan* (New York: Oxford University Press, 1996).

President Muhammad Zia ul-Haq's administration left no question that some interpretations of Islam were to wield unprecedented influence in the state.

Notwithstanding the imperial loyalists and divisions within Muslim factions, there were also considerable regional cultural divides. Punjabi, Pakhtun, Sindhi, Baluchi, and Bengali orientations toward kinship, power, the role of the state, and citizenship differ substantially. The roughly seven million *muhajirs* who migrated to Pakistan after partition emerged as an additional ethnic group (manifesting later as a political group, the MQM—Muhajir Qaumi Movement—as well). The challenge had become how to create a shared sense of being Pakistani which could overcome the compelling local cultural orientations and political conflicts. In the case of Bengal, physically ensconced at the other end of the subcontinent and sharing very few sociocultural similarities with the major ethnic groups of western Pakistan, this was ultimately not possible. The remainder of Pakistan is still engaged in this task.

Religious outlook and regionally based traditions, however, were not the only demarcations of social orientation and values. In Pakistan, family traditions also have considerable bearing on what its members do and how they think. Family values influence individual members' perceptions of proper gender roles, occupational choice, whether or not to pursue an education, and alliances with others. The large extended families of the past provided ample opportunity for socialization, sustenance, protection, and regulation. However, the growing nuclearization of the family in Pakistan is substantively affecting the country's social character, as values today are imparted in schools, through the media, and on the streets. Younger generations of Pakistanis are now questioning the priorities of their elders.

ARENAS OF SOCIAL TRANSFORMATION

In trying to determine the most significant arenas in which social transformation has occurred in Pakistan in its first fifty years, I decided to group them into four discernible categories: education, literacy, and health; linguistic and ethnic identity issues; the empowerment of women and subsequent changes within the family; and population growth, urbanization, and sustainable development. Together, these issues reflect the hopes, promises, efforts, limitations, and contradictions that shape Pakistani society in 1997.

Education, literacy, and health

"Education is an indispensable ingredient of development and a fundamental right of every individual."[6] So begins the section on education in
Pakistan's Eighth Five-Year Plan, targeting the years 1993–98. But if
education is so indispensable to development—aside from being a "fundamental right of every individual"—why has Pakistan's record in this
arena been so abysmal? Why too, in a related domain, does the World
Health Organization's promise of "health for all by the year 2000" remain an inexplicable dream for two-thirds of the inhabitants of rural
areas? There is a fundamental axiom we should note here: people who
receive a solid, viable education and are in good health are then able
both to interpret and synthesize issues for themselves, as well as act upon
their knowledge in a range of circumstances (e.g., employment, health
care, participating in democracy).

I have grouped education, literacy, and health as a single category
because they are indices that can inform us (in the words of Gunnar
Myrdal) if there is a "deepening of the human potential" accompanying
development and social change.[7] The UN Development Program
(UNDP) computes adult literacy rates and life expectancy at birth with
GDP per capita in compiling the aforementioned Human Development
Index, in which Pakistan has not fared well. Some basic data reveals
Pakistan's overall education, literacy, and health status (Table 6.1). In
1994, the government of Pakistan passed the Compulsory Education Act
to achieve the goal of universal primary education, which is not close to
being met. Minimal public resources have been spent on education and
health: only 2.7 percent of GNP was spent on education in 1992; even
less, 1.8 percent, on health in 1990. Clearly, priorities have been placed
elsewhere. Military expenditures, as a percentage of combined education
and health expenditures, were 393 in 1960 and 125 in 1991. In 1989,
Pakistan held the dubious distinction of being tied for fourth place in the
world in its ratio of military expenditure to health and education expenditures: 239 to 1.

---

[6] Government of Pakistan, Planning Commission, *Eighth Five-Year Plan, 1993–98* (Islamabad: Printing Corporation of Pakistan Press, 1994), 299.
[7] Gunnar Myrdal, in *Asian Drama: An Inquiry into the Poverty of Nations* (New York:
Twentieth Century Fund, 1968), defined development as implying a material betterment
of the human condition and a deepening of the human potential, increasing access to
many goods and services, including higher literacy rates, better health-care systems, and
freedom from poverty, famine, and social injustice.

Table 6.1. *Social indicators for Pakistan, 1990s*

	Total	Males	Females
Life expectancy at birth (1993)	61.8	62.9	60.9
Percentage of adults who are literate (1993)	36.4	48.6	23.0
Number (millions) of illiterate adults (1995)	48.7	20.5	28.2
Percentage of age group enrolled in primary education (1993)	80	49	—
Infant mortality rate per 1,000 live births (1994)	92	—	—
Percentage malnutrition under age 5 (1995)	40	—	—
Percentage of low-birth-weight infants (1990)	25	—	—

Note: Data not available for all items with —.
Sources: United Nations Development Program, *Human Development Report, 1996* (New York: Oxford University Press, 1996), and World Bank, *From Plan to Market: World Development Report, 1996* (New York: Oxford University Press, 1996).

Pakistan's education system has expanded greatly since independence, although the number of schools remains insufficient. I would argue that even more important than the number of schools is the quality of what is being taught in the curriculum. Furthermore, despite Pakistan's having one of the lowest female literacy rates in the world, no systematic, nationally coordinated effort has been made to improve female primary education in the country. Whereas it was once assumed that the reasons behind such low rates in schools were cultural, research conducted by the Ministry for Women's Development and a range of international donor agencies in the 1980s revealed that *access* was the most crucial concern that parents had. Indeed, reluctance turned to enthusiasm when parents in rural Punjab and rural Baluchistan could be offered guarantees regarding their daughters' safety—and hence, their honor.

Education in the colonial era had been geared to staffing the civil service and producing an educated elite sharing the values of and loyal to the British colonizers. It was unabashedly elitist. Contemporary education—reforms and commissions on reform notwithstanding—shares the same bias. Until the late 1970s, an excessive amount of educational spending went to the middle and upper levels. The elitist nature of education was also in evidence in the glaring gap between the country's public and private schools, which were nationalized in the late 1970s in a leveling effort to increase access. While access to students from poorer class backgrounds has increased in the nationalized schools in the 1980s and 1990s, teachers and school principals alike bemoan the decline in quality education that has occurred.

Three initiatives characterized educational reform efforts in the late 1980s and early 1990s: the move to privatize schools previously nationalized in the 1970s; the move *back* to using English in the more elite of these privatized schools where Urdu had also been imposed as the language of instruction in the 1970s; and the ongoing priority of promoting Pakistan Studies and Islamic Studies in the curriculum. The government's goal in promoting the latter is to use schools as a hub for nascent nationalism. Another reform has been the increase in the number of technical schools throughout the country, including ones designated for females. Key efforts now include the construction of hostels near women's training centers, as the provision of secure housing for women was determined to be a key element in the success of such centers.

Health-care improvements in Pakistan have been relatively difficult to achieve as health remains a province-based responsibility and its structure is decentralized. Scant resources have been appropriated for health-care concerns; state spending on health has only marginally increased in the past four decades, from 0.3 percent of public expenditures in 1960 to 1.8 percent in 1990. Pakistan has come under a great deal of international criticism because of this low level of expenditure.

There are four chief threats to health in Pakistan: the extensive incidence of communicable disease; widespread malnutrition; inadequate sewage disposal and safe drinking water; and extremely high fertility rates. The leading causes of death are respiratory infections, diarrhea, congenital abnormalities, tuberculosis, malaria, and typhoid; parasitic, gastrointestinal, and respiratory ailments contribute substantially to morbidity, as well. Childhood diseases such as measles, diphtheria, and whooping cough continue to take a substantial toll among children under five, as does malnutrition. Poor nutrition is widely regarded as the most important constraint on Pakistan's achieving greater success with the programs that it has been trying to implement; nearly half of all Pakistani children today are malnourished.

Although national health planning began in the early 1960s, local governing bodies remained in charge of addressing health needs until the early 1970s. By then, the system had evolved into one based on basic rural health units designed to provide primary care for a surrounding population of 6,000 to 10,000, supported by a higher level of rural health centers, both of which were to channel critically ill patients to urban-based hospitals. While providing health care for the rural populace has been an oft-stated priority, substantial rural/urban disparities remain. In 1995, the UNDP estimated that of urban dwellers, 99 percent had access to health care, 96 percent to safe water, and 62 percent to sanitation, while of rural dwellers, only 35 percent had access to health care, 71 percent to safe water, and 19 percent to sanitation.

One area that has enjoyed appreciable success is infant inoculations. In 1981, only 5 percent of all one-year-olds had been immunized; this figure skyrocketed to 97 percent by 1990. A good network—virtually free in most places—exists in urban areas, which ensures that health workers are notified upon a child's birth; word of mouth and media attention, coupled with rural health clinics, seem to be responsible for successes in rural areas. The infant mortality rate remained unreasonably high in 1994, however, at 92 per 1,000 live births.

The present orientation of the country's medical system, including medical education, favors elite groups. In 1992, there was one doctor per every 2,127 persons, one nurse per every 6,626 persons, but only one hospital per every 131,274 persons. (Underscoring the lack of attention that has been paid to dental care—especially to preventative measures—there was only one dentist per every 67,757 persons.) There has been a marked boom in private clinics and hospitals since the late 1980s, and an unfortunate deterioration in services provided by nationalized hospitals.

Mention must be made to Pakistan's high population-growth rate. A falling death rate (from 27 per 1,000 in 1950 to 9.1 per 1,000 in 1993) unaccompanied by any significant decrease in the birth rate (40.7 per 1,000 in 1993) has been the impetus behind the country's astronomical population growth. With a 1992 fertility rate at a high 6.2 percent, the contraceptive prevalence rate is an alarmingly low 12 percent. At the current rate of growth, the UNDP estimates that Pakistan's population—roughly 133 million in 1997—will double in twenty years.

Despite varied government and nongovernmental efforts under way since 1952 (the year of the birth of the Family Planning Association of Pakistan), little headway has been made in lowering the population-growth rate substantially. The government of Pakistan embarked on a new campaign—*Abbadi Sanbhalo*—in July 1997, in which it plans to spend $300 million (with donor support) in the next two years. However, activists in the women's movement have argued that the crux of the population growth issue lies ultimately in improving the status of women. Until a woman's status is determined by something other than her reproductive capabilities—and especially by the number of sons she bears—severe limitations to lowering population-growth rates in Pakistan will persist.

Linguistic and ethnic identity issues

Separatist movements and ethnic crises have plagued Pakistan since its inception, though the nature and composition of such conflict has changed over time. At independence, there was a definable fear that Pakistan might cease to exist; East Pakistan's secession in 1971 further aggravated that anxiety. But separatist movements in the North-West Frontier Province (NWFP), Baluchistan, and Sindh have given way to demands for greater power and autonomy, and the widespread view in 1997 is that Pakistan, as a nation-state, is a long-term enterprise.

An example of this change can be seen in the NWFP, where Pakhtuns have had an uneasy relationship with the central government from the outset. Despite some Pakhtuns becoming integrated into the national infrastructure, many still regard themselves as having the right to make their own independent choices irrespective of central government dictates. While no longer fighting for a separate Pakhtunistan—the anarchy in Afghanistan has likely contributed to quelling that sentiment—the mid-1990s revolt in the Malakand region of Swat is illustrative of the irredentist attitude of ethnic Pakhtuns. The Tehrik Nifaz Shariat-i-Muhammadi (TNSM), an Islamist political group, demanded that Islamic law (*shari'ah*) become the absolute law in the country and staged violent protests to promote its implementation. In response, the central government announced a *Shariat* ordinance and established religious courts in the area, but as they were not in line with the TNSM's demands, the agitation continues.

Language remains an important marker of ethnic identity in Pakistan, where more than twenty languages are spoken. South Asian Muslims have long identified themselves through the medium of the Urdu language, although it is spoken as a native tongue by only 8 percent of Pakistanis. Today, a greater proportion of people from educated backgrounds (and who aspire for upward mobility) now speak Urdu in their homes, as opposed to a regional language, usually to facilitate their children's learning it.

The Muslim League supported elevating Urdu to be Pakistan's national language, one with which the new state could build an identity. However, since so few people actually spoke it, English was retained as the de facto national language. The adoption of Urdu as a national language, however, was not a popular decision in East Pakistan, as most of its population spoke Bengali, an important marker of Bengali ethnic identity. Language riots broke out in Dacca in the 1950s as East Pakistanis demanded to have a place—an identity—within the new state, which culminated in Bengali being elevated to the stature of a second national language until the secession of East Pakistan in 1971.

In a move to promote nationalism, President Zia ul-Haq declared the medium of instruction in government schools to be Urdu in the 1980s. His government also actively promoted other vehicles for the dissemination of Urdu to a wider population, such as through television and radio. Private schools (where many children of the elite study) could retain English, while smaller rural schools could continue to teach in provincial languages.

Nearly half of all Pakistanis (48 percent) speak the provincial language Punjabi, while over two-thirds identify themselves as ethnic Punjabis. The next-most-populous language group is Sindhi, spoken by 12 percent of Pakistanis; 13 percent identify themselves as ethnic Sindhis. Other significant language groupings include Pashto (8 percent), Urdu (8 percent), Baluchi (3 percent), Hindko (2 percent), and Brahui (1 percent). Pakhtuns make up 9 percent of the population, *muhajirs* 8 percent, and Baluchis 3 percent. Additionally, the political crisis in Afghanistan has resulted in over three million Afghan refugees settling in Pakistan. Aside from the environmental effects of populating desert areas, the social impact has been considerable.

It is widely assumed that population distribution within the country is similar to ethnic and linguistic breakdown, although not identical. However, the government of Pakistan postponed its decennial census in 1991 due to fears that holding it might heighten communal unrest by delineating which ethnic groups had increased and which had decreased in given locales. The government felt that tensions between ethnic groups were such that holding the census might provoke violent reactions from groups that felt they were undercounted. The census was finally conducted in March 1998 amid protests from a wide spectrum of groups throughout the country that their constituencies were being underenumerated. Results of the census were unavailable at the time of this writing.

An effort to integrate Pakhtuns into the larger Pakistani society can be seen in the growing number of comprehensive development projects in areas of opium-poppy cultivation, including roads and schools, as well as incentives for industrial investment. However, the government lost much credibility when it proposed in 1991 to build up the local infrastructure in the Gadoon-Amazai area of the NWFP and encourage it as a target for tax-free investment. Most people attribute local politics to the government's withdrawal of the incentive package shortly after it was proposed.

Baluchistan has also been the stage for sporadic separatist movements. The often violent antagonism with the central government that characterized provincial/national relations in the 1970s has since been replaced by an escalation of internecine conflicts between tribal leaders and between Baluch and Pakhtun political groups. The latter is due largely to changes in the province's demographic balance as ethnic Pakhtuns—many refugees from Afghanistan—have come to settle in Baluchistan in the past two decades. It is widely assumed that Pakhtuns now make up the majority of the population of Baluchistan, where they have become an important political force via the Pakhtunwha Party.

Partition caused the creation of a new ethnic community in Pakistan when a great number of migrants from India shifted to Karachi and created a new self-reference group, *muhajirs*. Although most Pakistanis remain tied, emotionally as well as politically, to a specific place in the country, *muhajirs* do not share this sentiment. The first clashes of resident Sindhis and Punjabis with *muhajirs* emerged soon after partition when the new state gave *muhajirs* replacement housing and land for what they claimed to have left behind in India. Some questioned the parity involved when those who had fought for the country but remained within it could not also be compensated with abandoned property. Over time, *muhajirs* created new institutions to care for the needs of their community members, culminating with their own political party, the MQM.

The empowerment of women and subsequent changes within the family

Every major political party contesting the February 1997 elections placed women's empowerment, in some way, at center stage of their political agenda. An unprecedented twenty-nine women contested seats in the National Assembly; five women actually won. Indeed, formal efforts to empower women in Pakistan—or at least the discourse to do so— have been part of mainstream political rhetoric for nearly a decade. However, despite the ratification by the government of Pakistan of the UN Convention on the Elimination of All Forms of Discrimination Against Women (CEDAW) in March 1996, women in Pakistan still fare poorly when compared with women globally. In the UNDP's 1996 Gender Empowerment Measure (GEM)—which ascertains the percentage of women holding seats in parliaments, managerial positions, and professional and technical positions, and the percentage of the national earned income going to women—Pakistan holds one of the lowest rankings: 101 out of 104 states.

A hundred years ago, the promotion of female education had been regarded as a first step toward empowering Muslim women, and it remains so today. The nationalist struggle incorporated this goal as it linked women's empowerment to the larger issues of nationalism and independence. In the lead-up to independence, it appeared that the state would prioritize the empowerment of women; Muhammad Ali Jinnah, in a speech in 1944, noted that "no nation can rise to the height of glory unless your women are side by side with you." He criticized the past socially sanctioned treatment of women: "It is a crime against humanity that our women are shut up within the four walls of the houses as prisoners. . . . There is no sanction anywhere for the deplorable condition in which our women have to live."[8]

Two issues—promoting women's political representation and finding some accommodation between Muslim family law and civil, democratic rights—came to define the discourse regarding women and sociolegal reform in Pakistan. The latter became particularly prominent in the eleven years of Zia's government as women's groups emerged in urban areas in response to the promulgation of an Islamization program that many feared would unduly discriminate against women. It was in the highly visible territory of law that women were best able to articulate their objections to the Islamization program, arguing that the resultant laws regard men and women as having different legal rights, and despite the rhetoric that such laws were promulgated to protect women, they

[8] Quoted in Khawar Mumtaz and Farida Shahid, *Women of Pakistan: Two Steps Forward, One Step Back?* (London and Karachi: Zed Press, 1987), 183.

were indeed constraining women's power and participation in the larger society.

Aside from religio-legal issues, another area of consideration concerns women's integration into the labor force. By 1990, women made up only 23 percent of the adult labor force. Given the dissolution of extended families concomitant with high rates of inflation, more and more urban women are engaged in working for remuneration. However, because of restrictions on women's mobility, the most common way for urban women to earn money is to engage in home-based manufacturing for a middleman. While women make such items as ready-made clothes, artificial earrings, scrub brushes, and embroidered goods, concerns over traditional notions of propriety still prevent women and their families from admitting that women are working and that a family is living off the labor of its women. Indeed, a great deal of confusion remains regarding the work that women do. On the basis of the predominant fiction that most women do not labor outside of their domestic chores, past governments have been hesitant to adopt deliberate policies increasing women's employment options and to provide for legal support for women's labor-force participation.

The past few years have witnessed a critical, bipartisan reconceptualization of priorities on the part of the state regarding the necessity of inviting women to participate in the planning process and to incorporate their concerns into its planning goals. The Seventh Plan (1988–93) initiated the process by incorporating goals to advance women throughout its cross-cutting social initiatives. In its preparations and deliberations for the Eighth Plan (1993–98), the Muslim League government enlisted representatives from women's groups for feedback on a range of important areas affecting women, resulting in the plan's support for rural democratization and community development programs, and an entire section targeting affirmative action for women. For the first time in Pakistan's planning history, the government's Social Action Programme sought to mobilize women both as participants and beneficiaries throughout the country by expanding access to basic education, primary health care, and other social services.

Concurrently, it appears that a melding of the women's movement's traditional social welfare activities with its political activism is occurring as diverse groups are supporting small-scale projects throughout the country that focus on women's empowerment. These projects have involved such activities as instituting legal-aid cells for indigent women, opposing the gendered segregation of universities, developing microcredit support programs, and condemning and publicizing the growing incidence of violence against women. Groups such as AGHS, ASR, the Aurat Foundation, Bedari, Pattan, Shirkat Gah, and Simorgh are conducting a great deal of activist research, much of which is concerned with female education, women's political participation, and the rise in domestic violence (particularly associated with rapid urbanization).

Population planning, growing numbers of educated women, and the nuclearization of previously extended families have brought about important changes in the family as an institution in Pakistan. While the family still plays an essential role, its nature is rapidly changing as Pakistan moves from a culture based on ascription to one based on achievement. Access to many opportunities is often contingent on the connections that one's family has with others. Men's power within the family, once absolute in its control over women's mobility, is declining.

The traditional concept of the gendered division of space continues to be perpetuated in the broadcast media. Women's subservience is consistently shown on television and in films, while popular television dramas raise controversial issues such as women working, seeking divorce, or even having a say in family politics. What is often depicted, however, is the image that when a woman strays from traditional norms, she faces insurmountable problems and becomes alienated from her family.

The apparent and growing loss of will to maintain the extended family seems to be an important factor in increased domestic violence. While the desire by men to control their wives has a long-standing basis, physical violence was contained by the intervention of other family members within joint families in resolving conflict. While extended family members still intervene somewhat, the absence of others physically present within the household—especially in one facing the uncertainties of having recently migrated from a village to a city—has increased the possibility of domestic violence.

Many women feel they can no longer rely on the men of their family as securely as they had in the past. They have seen men abandon their wives or go abroad to work (leaving the wife virtually on her own), and also witnessed increased drug addiction among men. Many feel that the education and work opportunities now available to women can help them take a tentative step toward independence. However, when a woman becomes the primary economic support of her household, she may gain a stronger voice in influencing important family events, but she by no means becomes an independent agent. In virtually all instances, she must still ultimately defer to men from either her natal family or her husband's when faced with major decisions, such as arranging marriages for her children.

Population growth, urbanization, and sustainable development

Although Pakistan's land area is thirty-second in size in the world, its population is the ninth largest; the UNDP estimated Pakistan's 1993 population at 132.9 million.[9] Pakistan's population growth rate of 2.8 percent is one of the world's highest. Only a few years ago, it was expected that Pakistan's population would be 150 million by the year 2000; that figure is now expected to be 161.8 million. The UNDP anticipates that Pakistan will double its population by the year 2017.

Urbanization has been occurring at an unprecedented rate. In 1960, less than a quarter of the population lived in cities; the World Bank estimates that by the turn of the century, that figure will be about 40 percent. Over half of all urban residents live in cities of over a million people; 18 percent of Pakistan's total population in 1994 lived in such megacities. Limited opportunities for economic advancement and mobility in rural areas galvanize migration to urban areas. The traditional hold—both economic and political—that local landlords enjoy in rural areas, especially in Punjab and Sindh, virtually ensures the continuation of ascribed status.

The megacities in the late 1990s have tremendous infrastructural problems. In Lahore, for example, the city has expanded so far—Defense, Iqbal Town, and Township now being commonplace residential locales—that it has lost its sense of a center. The deterioration of public-transit networks and the proliferation of automobiles and private minibuses has caused unprecedented traffic congestion, bottlenecks, and pollution. The growing usage of major thoroughfares as staging grounds for protests and demonstrations has made negotiating the megalopolis extremely difficult even under normal circumstances.

Popular concerns with sustainable, environmental growth are relatively new entrants onto Pakistan's sociopolitical landscape. For over a

---

[9] These figures are under dispute. The World Bank estimated Pakistan's mid-1994 population as 126.3 million, with a population growth rate of 2.9 percent. The government of Pakistan, in its Eighth Five-Year Plan (1993–98), estimated a mid-1993 population of 122.7 million, with a 3.1 percent growth rate.

decade, Pakistan has enjoyed two major success stories in community organizing leading to sustainable development, which have only recently attracted efforts at duplication: the Aga Khan Rural Support Program headquartered in Gilgit, and the Orangi Pilot Project located in a Karachi slum. At the outset, each of these NGOs refused much external support, careful not to compromise its goals and principles. Both include requirements for local participation in development projects, underscoring a philosophy of nonreliance on other entities to provide for community needs. In the Pakistani context, this is exceptional and in a way subversive: no longer needing to rely on people with power or access to power opens up the potential to overturn existing priorities and implement development agendas that actually seek to improve people's lives.

SOCIAL CHALLENGES TODAY AND POTENTIALS FOR THE FUTURE

As mentioned at the outset of this chapter, I view Pakistani society today as poised at a critical juncture: confronting its greatest challenge with the demise of a social contract between Pakistanis while simultaneously facing the greatest possibilities with the rise of a civil society and the proliferation of NGOs eager to make a difference on the social landscape. Let me explain this further.

An unprecedented institutional malaise appears to exist today in Pakistan, boding dire consequences for the country's future social development prospects. It makes us wonder if Pakistan ever enjoyed a "social contract" in Rousseau's sense that members of a society have unwritten expectations of each other that form a foundation for social cohesion. I would argue that most citizens of the new state shared an enthusiasm for the country's future prospects in 1947, and that the initial foundation for social cohesion revolved around a populist interpretation of Islam and a solidarity associated with the majority of the country being Muslims.

The enthusiasm that greeted the birth of Pakistan in 1947 was a far cry from the current scenario. Fifty years ago, many thought that the new country would herald a virtual renaissance for Muslims. They would build up new industry, a new ideology, engage each other in parliamentary debate, all under the umbrella of Islam; the belief was strong that they held something in common that was distinguishable, profound, and moral. But in the early 1950s, the riots in Dacca and anti-

Ahmediya protests in Punjab began to question the principle of citizenship united under the rubric of Muslim brotherhood.

In the 1970s and 1980s, governments adopted varied interpretations of a highly politicized Islam, ranging from Bhutto's Islamic socialism to Zia's appropriated Wahhabi interpretation that was not commonly adhered to in Pakistan. At the same time, personal connections dramatically supplanted expertise. Jobs, contracts, and privileges were increasingly given to those who the state felt were its allies in its contest to destroy its opposition. What could have tied disparate groups together became subordinate to the means through which they gained an identity. Kinship ties, mother tongue, and area of family origin all became overwhelming indicators not only of ascribed status, but of the potential most individuals could achieve. This insular way of constructing a social world is not conducive, under the best of circumstances, to setting aside one's own kinship identity and ties in favor of a more abstract national one based on citizenship. This is particularly true when obvious material and social advantages can be gained from clinging to the former, as increasingly became the case—and remains so—in Pakistan.

After Zia decreed his Islamization program in 1979, non-Muslim minorities began to emigrate from the country in unprecedented numbers. Shi'as marched on Islamabad in 1982 in an effort to maintain their own system of social welfare within their community. Religious schools, *deeni madaris,* sprang up throughout the country when Zia started patronizing religious groups to create a constituency for himself. Muhammad Ali Anwar, a Pakistani journalist, argues that such support factionalized communities further as it led to "the creation of sectarian hatred because each sect believes the other to be heretical," thereby pitting *madaris* against each other. He argues that while religious schools are meeting a need for education among lower-income families, that too is "because the state has abdicated its role to educate the people [and] in the process, a lot of intolerance is being spread."[10] The end result is that Islam can no longer be used as a unifying social force in Pakistan.

Social disintegration appeared to escalate in the 1980s and 1990s. The Soviet invasion into Afghanistan was a boon that the Zia government used fully, and the large arsenal of weapons dispatched to Pakistan through covert means did not always find its way into the hands of the

---

[10] Muhammad Ali Anwar, "Mushroom Growth of Deeni Madaris," *Dawn* (Internet Edition), May 24, 1997.

mujahiddin. The invasion also caused the opium pipeline from Afghanistan to the West to dry up; as Iran was also no longer a source, Pakistan became the regional focus for opium poppies. Pakistan was indeed a superior option, since many of those who held power—either traditional, bureaucratic, or military—would allow smuggling for a small percentage. As both cultivation and drug smuggling escalated in the mid-1980s, Pakistan emerged as a frontline heroin production point and transit route for the international drug trade. Along with the growth of opium-poppy cultivation came a phenomenal rise in its use within Pakistan. Whereas Pakistan had few heroin addicts in 1980, the Citizens Drug Watch Society estimates there are now three million drug addicts in Pakistan, 72 percent of whom are under the age of thirty-five. Apart from the ready availability of the drug, this dramatic increase is attributed to many things, including the breakdown of extended families in cities, leading to greater alienation; high unemployment and underemployment rates; and a powerful ethos of consumerism permeating social life.

Challenges stemming from the lack of a social contract—whether through disintegration or the surfacing reality that one had never truly existed—unfolded in myriad crises in the early 1990s. Disillusionment overflowed into the social realm in numerous ways, from the ostentatious wealth of some parading in front of the majority who are poor and disenfranchised, to how educational examinations are surreptitiously taken and passed, to the way jobs are acquired invariably through nepotism or friendship but seldom on the basis solely of skills or achievement. This social crisis was underscored in September 1992 when Pakistan experienced its worst flood in a century. Most specialists have blamed the flood on human error, arguing that the Water and Power Development Authority (WAPDA) technicians—hired through such processes—just didn't have the background or training to handle the emergency.

At the same time as it faces a social crisis, Pakistan today also faces extraordinary possibilities as greater numbers of people are participating in building a new society—invited or not. In unprecedented ways, more and more Pakistanis are taking it upon themselves to commit to a cause, which in Pakistan's history has been fairly rare outside of kinship circles. A marked proliferation of NGOs has arisen in the past decade dedicated to the various social concerns addressed earlier, as well as to others, including democratization, human rights, community organizing, and low-income housing. Independent groups are trying to make a difference on the social landscape irrespective of the ephemeral idiosyncrasies of the national government. Social activists are working together with government planners to contemplate how positive transitions can occur. A civil society is emerging in Pakistan, one engineered neither by the state nor by elite groups, but emanating from the enthusiasm, commitment, and perseverance of individuals agreeing to work together to achieve envisioned goals. It is their actions, promoting the rise of a civil society, that hold the greatest promise for Pakistan's future.

An instructive example can be seen in how different groups are cooperating together to promote women's empowerment in the country. An alliance has emerged between NGOs, donor agencies, and the state, which had relied heavily on NGO activists in developing its draft *National Report* for the UN women's conference in Beijing and in clarifying Pakistan's position on the then-proposed *Platform for Action*. The Beijing Follow-up Unit (BFU) has become a collaborative effort to maintain the energy and momentum for women's empowerment that characterized the preparatory process. NGO Consultative Committees in each of the four provinces, consisting of provincial planning ministries and local NGO representatives, are working to develop action agendas on ways to follow up on commitments made at the Beijing conference. They are the basis of a nationwide, interactive, decentralized effort under way to integrate women's concerns throughout the Ninth Five-Year Plan (1998–2003). All such proposals are to be accompanied by clear financial allocations.

Although policy changes by no means result in implementation of proposals, for Pakistan—a country that has neglected human development and has a limited history of nongovernmental social activism (especially prior to 1988)—this heralds a decisive stage. This kind of interactive, collaborative process—providing opportunities for a range of voices and opinions in Pakistan's planning strategies—holds great promise to facilitate further the rise of a civil society in the various social domains of Pakistan, to "improve the well-being of society as a whole," and, finally, to achieve the dreams that created Pakistan.

This will be possible only with political, financial, and verbal commitments. Given its track record, we can only hope that Pakistan continues to build on its emergent civil society and does not fall back into the kinds of political imbroglios that have compromised its social development in the past. The challenges are great, but so are the risks of failing. Indeed, only through groups working together, collaboratively and cooperatively, can Pakistan hope to see a new viable social contract emerge.

SUGGESTED READINGS

Amnesty International. *Women in Pakistan: Disadvantaged and Denied Their Rights*. New York: Amnesty International, 1995.

Banuri, Tariq. *People, the Environment and Responsibility: Case Studies from Rural Pakistan*. New York: Parthenon Pub. Group, 1995.

Government of Pakistan, Ministry of Women Development and Youth Affairs. *Pakistan National Report: Fourth World Conference on Women, Beijing*. Islamabad: Printing Corporation of Pakistan Press, 1995.

Kazi, Shahnaz. "Women, Development Planning and Government Policies in Pakistan," *Pakistan Development Review* 31, no. 4, part 2 (Winter 1992): 609–20.

Said Khan, Nighat, Rubina Saigol, and Afiya S. Zia, eds. *Aspects of Women and Development*. Lahore: ASR, 1995.

 Locating the Self: Perspectives on Women and Multiple Identities. Lahore: ASR, 1994.

Shaheed, Farida, and Khawar Mumtaz. *Women's Economic Participation in Pakistan: A Status Report*. Lahore: Shirkat Gah for UNICEF Pakistan, 1992.

United Nations Development Program (UNDP). *Human Development Report, 1996*. New York: Oxford University Press, 1996.

Weiss, Anita M. *Culture, Class and Development in Pakistan: The Emergence of an Industrial Bourgeoisie in Punjab*. Boulder, Colo.: Westview Press and Lahore: Vanguard Press, 1991.

 "The Slow Yet Steady Path to Women's Empowerment in Pakistan," in *Islam, Gender, and Social Change*, eds. Yvonne Yazbeck Haddad and John Esposito. New York: Oxford University Press, 1998.

 "The Society and Its Environment," in *Pakistan: A Country Study*, ed. Peter R. Blood. Washington, D.C.: Library of Congress, 1995.

Wignaraja, Ponna, Akmal Hussain, Harsh Sethi, and Ganeshan Wignaraja. *Participatory Development: Learning from South Asia*. Tokyo: United Nations University; Karachi: Oxford University Press, 1991.

World Bank. *From Plan to Market: World Development Report, 1996*. New York: Oxford University Press, 1996.

IV

Foreign and security policy

7

India: Policies, past and future

SUMIT GANGULY

The events of the 1990s have ripped the foundation from beneath Indian foreign policy. The ideas that provided its content and direction—anti-colonialism, a global redistributive justice, and nonalignment—have all lost their significance. The decolonization of the last Portuguese colonies in Africa and the overthrow of the apartheid regime in South Africa have removed the last banners of the anticolonial impulse in Indian foreign policy. In the wake of the global shift toward free-market approaches to development, India's commitment to the principles of a global transfer of resources through the use of allocative mechanisms no longer makes sense. Finally, although the mantra of nonalignment is still ritually invoked, for all practical purposes the concept is bereft of meaning.

The challenge confronting India's leadership on the fiftieth anniversary of its independence is to construct a new set of principles that can guide its foreign relations to cope with a vastly altered international system. The choices that its elites make will in large measure determine India's position in the emergent international order.

INDEPENDENCE AND AFTER

Even before India achieved its independence, Jawaharlal Nehru, one of the principal figures in the Indian nationalist movement, had devoted considerable thought to independent India's foreign policy. Nehru's interest in foreign-policy issues had an impressive lineage. He had been a delegate to the International Congress against Colonial Oppression and Imperialism held in Brussels in 1927, and his deep involvement in anti-colonial nationalism profoundly shaped his views about the importance of keeping the country free from any form of external domination. Con-

sequently, Nehru's approach was an effort to maximize India's autonomy in the conduct of foreign policy in the immediate postwar era. This
strategy, nonalignment, was intended to keep India out of the ambits of
both the Soviet bloc and the Western alliance. The strategy was not only
designed to preserve India's autonomy but was based on a realistic ap-
praisal of India's developmental needs and military weaknesses. In
Nehru's view, aligning with either superpower in the Manichaean Cold
War struggle could lead to the militarization of Indian society and divert
vital, scarce resources from economic development. The pursuit of nonalignment entailed low defense expenditures and a commitment to the
peaceful resolution of international disputes. In effect, Nehru was seeking to develop an alternative normative paradigm that challenged the
dominant power-politics approach to international relations. His strategy endowed Nehru with a moral authority on which he was able to
draw when attempting to influence the course of key international issues
and questions.

Toward this end, Nehru played an active role in promoting decolonization in Asia and also sought to limit the presence of the great powers
on the continent. Even before India became formally independent, he
supported the Indonesian nationalist struggle against Dutch colonial
rule. Nehru sharply condemned the Dutch attacks on Indonesia in 1947–
48 and called a conference on Indonesia in New Delhi in January 1949.
This conference helped focus United Nations (UN) attention on the situation in Indonesia and prepared the way for Indonesian independence
in December 1949.

Contrary to some popular assessments, Nehru had little use for the
nascent communist movements in Asia; he disdained their tactics and
disagreed with their goals. He banned the Communist Party in a number
of Indian states and directly or indirectly aided in the suppression of
communists in Burma, Malaya, and Indonesia. Nehru's vision of nonalignment, however, came under severe criticism from a number of quarters.

THE LEGACIES OF COLONIALISM:
THE FIRST KASHMIR WAR

Polemical assertions to the contrary notwithstanding, Nehru's commitment to nonalignment did not mean abjuring the use of force when
India's national security was threatened. He proved more than willing to
provide military assistance to Maharaja Hari Singh, the last monarch of

the princely state of Jammu and Kashmir, when in October 1947 a Pakistani-supported invasion threatened the latter's realm. The introduction of Indian forces stopped the invaders but not before they had occupied one-third of the state. Shortly thereafter, fighting ensued between Indian and Pakistani troops. India's referral of the dispute to the UN and a subsequent UN-sponsored cease-fire brought the conflict to a close on January 1, 1949. Despite the end of active hostilities, neither side proved willing to give much ground. India initially expressed a willingness to settle the dispute through a plebiscite, but the modalities for holding a plebiscite became the subject of controversy. By the mid-1950s India had backed away from its commitment to a plebiscite. Despite the failure of multilateral negotiations to settle the dispute, Pakistan's commitment to incorporate the state into its realm remained undiminished.[1]

THE LEGACIES OF COLONIALISM: GOA

Nehru once again proved willing to resort to the use of force when all peaceful means to induce a colonial power to relinquish its holdings on Indian territory were exhausted. Such a situation obtained in the Portuguese possessions of Goa, Daman, and Diu in western India. As early as 1949 India had opened a diplomatic mission in Lisbon specifically to negotiate a diplomatic solution to the continued Portuguese presence. The Portuguese government of President Antonio Salazar repeatedly rebuffed India's efforts to reach a settlement. As a sign of its frustration with Portuguese intransigence the Indian government closed its legation in Lisbon in June 1953. Over the remainder of the decade, Indian efforts toward a peaceful resolution of the problem were unsuccessful. Seeing little other recourse and facing criticism from domestic quarters and from Afro-Asian allies, Nehru authorized a military operation to force the Portuguese from Goa. In December 1961 the Indian army occupied the Portuguese territories with a minimal loss of life.

COPING WITH THREATS: CHINA

Although willing to resort to force against Pakistan and vestiges of European colonialism, Nehru was astute enough to realize that India lacked

[1] There is a substantial body of literature on Kashmir. For a deft defense of the Indian position, see Sisir Gupta, *Kashmir: A Study in Indo-Pakistani Relations* (New Delhi: Asia, 1966). For a pro-Pakistani account, see M. M. R. Khan, *The United Nations and Kashmir* (Groningen: J. B. Wolters, 1954).

the military strength to contend with its powerful neighbor to the north, the People's Republic of China. To this end, he supported China's bid to enter the UN, refrained from criticism of the Chinese occupation of Tibet, and readily gave up India's inherited extraterritorial privileges in Tibet.[2] Nehru's strategy had two fundamental goals: to restrain India's defense expenditures and simultaneously to bring China into the comity of nations. Through a series of unilateral concessions and gestures of friendship Nehru hoped to soften the posture of the communist regime in Beijing.

These many gestures of goodwill led to a period of seeming amity in Sino-Indian relations in the mid-1950s. Shortly thereafter, however, a series of Chinese territorial claims along the Himalayan border deflated hopes of longer-term accommodation. Worse still, sharp border clashes took place in 1958 between the Chinese People's Liberation Army and Indian forces. Despite the mounting evidence of Chinese truculence, Nehru failed to increase defense expenditures and continued his negotiations with the Chinese. After the complete breakdown of talks in 1960, the Indian government embarked on its disastrous "forward policy," which failed to meet the demands of any serious military rationale.[3] Far from making the Chinese renounce their border claims, this policy contributed to the near-complete rout of the Indian army in October 1962. Nehru's grand hope of restraining the Chinese largely through accommodation and appeasement had ended in disaster.

THE AFTERMATH OF 1962

The 1962 border war with China had profound effects on the Indian polity. To begin with, the politicomilitary debacle had devastating consequences for Nehru personally, as his towering political stature at home and abroad was sharply diminished. Many of the Western powers who had cared little for nonalignment and Nehru's moral hectoring felt that India's conceit had received a proper drubbing. Domestically, too, Nehru's position weakened. He reluctantly dismissed his cantankerous and arrogant defense minister, V. K. Krishna Menon, the *bête noire* of

---

[2] For the best account of Sino-Indian relations in the 1950s and the Sino-Indian border war, see Steven Hoffmann, *India and the China Crisis* (Berkeley: University of California Press, 1990).

[3] The "forward policy," an ill-conceived military strategy, involved sending lightly armed Indian troops into Chinese-claimed border areas.

the Western powers, and sought Western military aid. Nehru was also forced to abandon his commitment to limiting defense expenditures. To contend with the Chinese threat, India decided to raise ten new mountain divisions. New plans were rapidly drawn up for the creation of a forty-five-squadron air force equipped with supersonic aircraft. The service ceiling of the Indian army was raised to one million men. Plans were also laid for the modernization of the Indian navy.

Despite this marked shift in defense policy and military acquisitions, India did not abandon its commitment to nonalignment. Some demands to jettison the policy did emerge from the small, pro-American Swatantra Party and the jingoistic Jana Sangh (the forerunner to the Bharatiya Janata Party). The border war did invite pressures from abroad, however. After Anglo-American prodding, India agreed to hold bilateral talks with Pakistan to resolve the Kashmir issue. Six rounds of negotiations between December 1962 and May 1963 ultimately proved infructuous, as neither side was prepared to make significant territorial concessions. The failure of the talks in conjunction with other developments at international and domestic levels contributed to the 1965 Kashmir war.

THE SECOND KASHMIR WAR

By mid-1963, multilateral interest in the Kashmir issue was on the decline. Indian diplomacy had successfully stalled the issue in the UN. The failure of bilateral negotiations gave rise to Pakistani misgivings that its claim to Kashmir was steadily losing ground. Worse still, from the Pakistani standpoint, India had begun to integrate its portion of the state into the Indian union. Unless Pakistan acted promptly to reverse these trends, its leadership was convinced, their country's claim to Kashmir would be severely weakened.

An idiosyncratic event, the theft of a holy relic from the Hazratbal mosque in Srinagar, set off a series of riots and violent demonstrations in the Kashmir Valley in December 1963. The Pakistani leadership construed these incidents to be indicative of widespread Kashmiri support for merger with Pakistan. Accordingly, they worked to fashion a politicomilitary strategy to foment a rebellion in the valley and then seize it in a short, sharp incursion. Before implementing this strategy, code-named "Operation Gibraltar," the Pakistanis made a limited probe in the Rann of Kutch in the Indian state of Gujarat in early 1965. The new government of Prime Minister Lal Bahadur Shastri, on the advice of the

Indian military, decided not to respond vigorously. In fact, following British mediation, India agreed to refer the dispute to international arbitration. The fact that the Pakistani regime construed both these gestures to be signs of Indian pusillanimity strengthened its resolve to employ force to resolve the Kashmir dispute.

In the summer of 1965 lightly armed Pakistani troops slipped across the porous cease-fire line (CFL) in Kashmir, made contact with the local populace, and launched acts of arson, sabotage, and mayhem. To the surprise and dismay of the Pakistanis, however, the Kashmiris alerted the local authorities. The Indian army promptly moved to seal the border and apprehend the infiltrators. Pakistan nevertheless continued with its strategy. In mid-August, the Indian army crossed the CFL and attacked Pakistani encampments. Pakistan responded in force, and on September 6, 1965, full-scale war erupted. Set-piece battle tactics, a U.S. arms embargo, and deliberate decisions to avoid civilian casualties limited the scope of the 17-day conflict. After a UN-sponsored cease-fire and American unwillingness to mediate, the Soviet Union sponsored peace talks. Under the terms of the agreement reached at Tashkent, the two sides agreed to return to the status quo ante. The Kashmir dispute remained unresolved.[4]

DOMESTIC TURMOIL AND INDO-U.S. RELATIONS

Prime Minister Shastri died in Tashkent shortly after negotiating the agreement with Pakistan. The Congress Party chose Nehru's daughter, Indira Gandhi, to succeed Shastri. Indira Gandhi assumed office at a difficult moment. India's strategy of import-substituting industrialization, which had generated better-than-modest economic growth in its initial phases, was running out of steam. Worse still, India experienced two successive droughts in 1965 and 1966.

India, though critical of many U.S. policies, had been a major recipient of American food assistance since 1950. In November 1965, faced with the prospect of famine, India turned to the United States for increased assistance. Washington agreed to provide assistance but on the condition that India would undertake certain agricultural policy reforms.

---

[4] Sumit Ganguly, "Deterrence Failure Revisited: The Indo-Pakistani War of 1965," *Journal of Strategic Studies* 13, no. 4 (December 1990): 77–93.

In March 1966, Indira Gandhi visited the United States and President Lyndon Johnson provided his imprimatur to the food-aid agreement. Unfortunately, the goodwill of Johnson's gesture proved to be short-lived. After Mrs. Gandhi agreed to devalue the rupee under pressure from the United States and the World Bank, a highly unpopular step, she moved to mollify leftist critics. In July 1966, a joint communiqué issued after her visit to Moscow condemned, in veiled terms, the U.S. involvement in Vietnam. Johnson, who was beginning to face incipient domestic criticism for the conduct of the Vietnam War, was livid. When India faced the threat of further food shortages after the failure of the 1966 monsoon, Johnson adopted a "short tether" policy, dribbling out food shipments and insisting on full implementation of promised agricultural policy reforms. Although Johnson's approach helped bring about the Green Revolution, his tactics were resented. Indira Gandhi stepped up her criticism of the United States and particularly the U.S. conduct of the war in Vietnam. Domestically, she embarked on a series of populist measures and sought the support of leftist political parties to strengthen her parliamentary position.[5]

THE 1971 WAR

In the wake of this disillusionment with the United States, India increasingly turned toward the Soviet Union, all the while professing its commitment to nonalignment. At a domestic level, Indira Gandhi increasingly adopted populist policies and came to rely upon leftist parties for political support. Regional exigencies would soon lead India to strengthen its growing relationship with the Soviet Union.

In December 1970, Pakistan held its first democratic election. The results of the election, in which a pro-autonomy party, the Awami League, swept the polls in East Pakistan and gained an absolute majority in Parliament, were not to the liking of the Pakistani military establishment or the West Pakistani winner, Zulfikar Ali Bhutto. Negotiations for sharing power between the two wings of Pakistan quickly dead-locked and the demands for regional autonomy accentuated in the east. In March 1971, martial law was imposed in the east and the Pakistani

---

[5] See Dennis Kux, *Estranged Democracies: India and the United States, 1941–1991* (New Delhi: Sage, 1994), 240–61.

army went on a campaign of mass murder and mayhem. In the aftermath of the brutal military crackdown several million East Pakistanis took refuge in the neighboring Indian state of West Bengal.

Faced with this extraordinary refugee burden, Indian decision-makers made some preliminary efforts to obtain a political solution to the crisis in East Pakistan. The great powers, the United States in particular, evinced no great interest in exerting political and diplomatic pressure on Pakistan to reach a solution.[6] Unwilling to absorb the refugees into India's own turgid population, and desirous of delivering a significant blow to their long-standing adversary, Indian decision-makers decided to resort to war. To this end, Indira Gandhi and her closest advisers supported creation of an independent state to replace East Pakistan.

Accordingly, Indira Gandhi moved to sign a twenty-year pact of "peace, friendship, and cooperation" with the Soviet Union in August 1971. The U.S. decision to normalize relations with China played a critical role in India's seeking a treaty relationship with the Soviet Union. After returning from his dramatic trip to China, the U.S. national security adviser, Henry Kissinger, had warned the Indian ambassador to the United States, L. K. Jha, that in the event of a war with Pakistan, if China became involved on Pakistan's behalf, India could no longer count on American support.[7]

India's gamble, though it soured relations with the United States, proved to be extraordinarily advantageous in pursuit of its chosen strategy. The Indo-Soviet treaty not only protected India from American (or Western) censure at the UN but also provided a measure of security vis-à-vis China. In pursuit of its goal of creating an independent Bangladesh, India steadily organized, trained, and supported a guerrilla force in East Pakistan, the Mukti Bahini. Pakistan repeatedly warned India to desist from this course but to little avail. Unable to deter India, Pakistan formally declared war in December 1971. The war lasted about two weeks and culminated in the creation of Bangladesh.

In the aftermath of the war, India emerged as the preeminent power

---

[6] The U.S. unwillingness to bring pressure on Pakistan stemmed from Pakistan's critical role as a conduit for President Richard Nixon's opening to the People's Republic of China. For an excellent account of the negotiations between the various parties but a more sympathetic assessment of the American role, see Richard Sisson and Leo E. Rose, *War and Secession: India, Pakistan and the Creation of Bangladesh* (Berkeley: University of California Press, 1990).

[7] S. Nihal Singh, *The Yogi and the Bear: A Study of Indo-Soviet Relations* (New Delhi: Allied Publishers, 1986), 88.

on the subcontinent. In July 1972, India and Pakistan signed the Simla Accord. Under the terms of this agreement, among various other matters, the two sides agreed to abjure the use of force to resolve the Kashmir dispute. The spoils that went with victory, however, did not last long. Domestically, Indira Gandhi faced mounting problems of sluggish economic growth and social disorder. In an attempt to bolster her sagging fortunes she authorized an Indian nuclear test in the Rajasthan desert in 1974. This dramatic gesture only momentarily deflected public attention away from India's myriad socioeconomic problems. At an international level, the test marked the end of all nuclear cooperation with Canada and the United States.

THE JANATA INTERREGNUM

In 1975 Indira Gandhi declared a "state of emergency" in India to avoid a lower-court conviction on a number of minor electoral-law violations. During the Emergency, civil liberties were squelched and the Indian judiciary was rendered impotent. In an attempt to legitimize her position Mrs. Gandhi called for elections in 1977. The Indian electorate handed her a resounding defeat and brought to power an agglomeration of disparate political parties under the aegis of the Janata Dal. The new government sought to improve relations with India's neighbors and promised to restore "genuine nonalignment." Although relations with Pakistan and other neighbors improved, the coalition government fell apart after only two years in office.

THE SOVIET INVASION OF AFGHANISTAN AND AFTER

The Soviet Union invaded Afghanistan in December 1979. In India, the Janata Dal government had collapsed and Indira Gandhi had been reelected but had not yet assumed office. Upon assuming office in January 1980, she chose not to openly condemn the Soviet invasion of Afghanistan, which India had condoned in the UN General Assembly debate. Privately, however, she expressed her reservations to the Soviets.

In the United States, the Jimmy Carter administration declared Pakistan to be a "frontline" state in stemming the Soviet tide and offered it some $400 million in military and economic assistance. President Muhammad Zia ul-Haq, the military dictator of Pakistan, dismissed this offer as "peanuts." A year later, in 1981, the Reagan administration

rewarded Zia for his patience. The first tranche of U.S. economic and
military assistance to Pakistan amounted to $3.2 billion for a period of
five years. In the interim, Indian diplomatic efforts to defuse the Afghan
crisis and its effects on South Asia had yielded little. Only desultory
discussions were held with Pakistan about a "no-war" pact and a more
comprehensive peace treaty.

The American decision to supply Pakistan with substantial military
assistance led to a calculated decision on India's part: it would avoid
public criticism of the Soviet presence in Afghanistan in return for substantial countervailing military assistance from the Soviet Union. This
tacit agreement resulted in a windfall for India. The Soviets promptly
agreed to a series of arms-transfer agreements at highly concessional
rates.

During much of the 1980s, the Indo-Soviet relationship remained ce-
mented with these arms transfers. Relations with the United States, sur-
prisingly, also improved. Following another visit by Indira Gandhi in
1982, relations bettered somewhat. Nevertheless, India's close ties to
Moscow and lack of strategic or economic importance to the United
States limited the prospects of any sharp upswing in relations. Fitful
improvements continued under the next prime minister, Rajiv Gandhi,
particularly after he embarked on a strategy of limited economic liberalization.

TOWARD THE COLD WAR'S CLOSE

There was little in Rajiv Gandhi's personal or professional background
to prepare him for the demands of high political office. Not surpris-
ingly, during his term in office he failed to articulate a clear-cut vision
for India's role in South Asia and beyond. At the level of economic policy, he did try to undertake a limited program of economic liberalization. This effort proved to be short-lived. His fitful push toward liberalization was related to his personal fascination with high technology
in both civilian and military sectors. Accordingly, during his term in office, India embarked upon a significant military modernization program. India's ballistic-missile program received a significant boost, particularly with the launching of the *Agni*, an intermediate-range ballistic
missile.

In the realm of foreign policy, his regime saw a series of regional
misadventures. Specifically, India became deeply embroiled in the ethnic

conflict in Sri Lanka. Even though Rajiv Gandhi helped broker an agreement between the government of President Junius Jayawardene and the Liberation Tigers of Tamil Eelam in 1987, the accord quickly unraveled. Indian troops sent in to police the terms of the accord were rapidly drawn into the vortex of the Sri Lankan civil war. Eventually, under pressure from Jayawardene's successor, Ranasinghe Premadasa, India withdrew the Indian Peace Keeping Force in March 1991.

India's relations with Pakistan also suffered during this period. In 1987, the largest peacetime Indian military exercise, "Brasstacks," a brainchild of General Krishnaswami Sundarji, almost brought on another war with Pakistan. A series of confused signals, miscalculations, and misperceptions contributed to this crisis.[8] Despite a peaceful resolution to the Brasstacks episode, relations with Pakistan plummeted as the decade drew to a close. India repeatedly accused Pakistan of supporting the Khalistani insurgency in the Punjab.

During this period India's relations with China were initially punctuated by a border clash in 1986 at Sumdurong Chu, the trijunction of India, Nepal, and Bhutan. However, the two sides chose to settle their differences through negotiations. The general improvement in Sino-Indian relations under Rajiv Gandhi reached its apogee when he visited China in November 1988.

In 1990, another serious crisis further ruptured Indo-Pakistani relations. The crisis stemmed from India's assessment that Pakistan was deeply involved in aiding the insurgency that had broken out in Jammu and Kashmir in December 1989. Unable to stop the infiltration of insurgents across the highly permeable Line of Control in Kashmir, the Indian government drew up contingency plans to attack across the border. Knowledge of these plans alarmed the Pakistanis and raised the specter of nuclear war.[9] Seeking to head off a conflict with possible nuclear implications, Washington dispatched Deputy National Security Adviser Robert Gates to counsel restraint in both capitals. It is not entirely clear what effects Gates's message had on the two adversaries, but war did not ensue.

---

[8] For an analysis of the "Brasstacks" crisis see Stephen P. Cohen, Pervaiz Iqbal Cheema, P. R. Chari, Kanti P. Bajpai, and Sumit Ganguly, *Brasstacks and Beyond: Perception and the Management of Crisis in South Asia* (New Delhi: Manohar, 1995).

[9] The precise details of the 1990 crisis remain murky. For a sound and thoughtful analysis see Devin Hagerty, "Nuclear Deterrence in South Asia: The 1990 Indo-Pakistani Crisis," *International Security* 20, no. 3 (Winter 1995/96): 79–114.

THE COLD WAR'S END

As the Cold War drew to a close, India faced a major economic crisis. Over several decades, India's highly regulatory and welfaristic state apparatus had run up significant domestic deficits and external debts. The adverse impact of the Gulf crisis of 1990–91, precipitated by Saddam Hussein's invasion of Kuwait, turned India's situation toward disaster. The increased costs of purchasing petrochemical products, the repatriation of some 130,000 expatriate workers from the Gulf region, and the loss of their remittances cost the Indian exchequer dearly. Worse still, a number of India's loan payments to multilateral banks were on the verge of coming due.

Shortly after coming to power in the 1991 general election, Prime Minister P. V. Narasimha Rao used this crisis to embark on a strategy of economic reform. Rao's efforts at reform yielded substantial gains over the next several years,[10] as India finally broke free of its 3 percent "Hindu rate of growth." Through much of the decade India's annual rate of economic growth approached or exceeded 5 percent.

Rao also presided over a major shift in India's foreign-policy orientation as the Cold War ended. He sought to improve relations with the United States, as Russia had neither the interest in nor the capability of maintaining the prior Soviet level of closeness with India. To this end, in a signal to the United States, India voted to repeal the UN resolution in November 1991 that had equated Zionism with racism.

Despite India's willingness to improve relations with the United States, particularly to seek much-needed foreign investment and multilateral loans, important differences remained. These differences surfaced especially over questions of India's unwillingness to give up its nuclear capability and its pursuit of a ballistic-missile program. In 1996, India found itself at loggerheads with the United States over the question of the Comprehensive Test Ban Treaty (CTBT).

A REQUIEM FOR NONALIGNMENT?

In the post–Cold War era, India is still attempting to realign its foreign policy. But old habits die hard. Many of India's politicians continue to

---

[10] See Jagdish Bhagwati, *India in Transition: Freeing the Economy* (Oxford: Clarendon Press, 1993).

recite the mantra of nonalignment even though the concept no longer carries meaning. As then–Foreign Minister Inder K. Gujral put it in 1990, "Who are you going to be aligned against?"[11] Yet India's predicament is hardly unique: the United States went through several years of soul-searching at the end of the Cold War before it could identify new lodestars for the conduct of its own foreign policy.

The task facing any new regime in India will be to articulate a new set of foreign policy goals for the country as it approaches the next millennium and enters its second half-century of independence. The government of Prime Minister Inder K. Gujral made a useful start in that direction. It improved relations with India's neighbors and also sought to continue India's willingness to open its markets to foreign investment. Other hard questions facing India remain, however. For example, how will India tackle the issue of Kashmir, which has dogged relations with Pakistan since their emergence from the British Empire? What will India do about its ballistic and nuclear weapons programs? What purposes, if any, will they serve in India's "grand strategy"? Finally, what role does India intend to play within Asia and beyond?

THREE VISIONS OF THE FUTURE

Which of various pathways will India choose in pursuing a new foreign policy? One section of India's "attentive public" still appears wedded to some notion of "nonalignment." In their view, this concept can be infused with new life: nonalignment can now be given a North/South dimension. The poorer nations of the South can still make common cause and oppose the industrialized North's attempt to impose a variety of global regimes in areas ranging from intellectual property to human rights.

India's own interests would suffer were it to pursue this strategy, however. As India opens its economy to foreign investment and seeks to play a larger role in the global economy, this strategy has little to recommend for itself. More to the point, the poorer states of the South hardly constitute a monolith. Their interests vary according to the issues under discussion. An attempt to forge a common front against the North will quickly dissipate once national leaders from diverse backgrounds look beyond the rhetoric of solidarity.

[11] Interview with the author, New York City, August 1990.

A second vision suggests that India can acquire great power status through the pursuit of a muscular military posture. Those advocating this option contend that India will be taken seriously in world affairs only if it wields sufficient military prowess. To this end, advocates of this strategy contend that India needs to deal from a position of strength with its neighbors—especially its long-standing adversary, Pakistan. More specifically, they contend that India needs to acquire nuclear weapons and ballistic missiles to cope with any possible future threat from China. The votaries of this position are usually in favor of domestic economic liberalization but remain skeptical of the benefits of opening up the Indian economy to foreign investment.

It is unlikely that this strategy will yield the results that its proponents seek. India cannot achieve rapid economic growth through the pursuit of an outmoded, semiautarkic economic strategy. On the military front, India's unbridled pursuit of nuclear weapons and ballistic missiles would, without a doubt, trigger countermoves on the part of both Pakistan and China. Such efforts on India's part would also damage the incipient and fitful improvements in relations with the United States.

A third path that India may pursue can be derived from the stance of the 1997 Gujral regime. This strategy has several components. In the realm of foreign policy it would focus on efforts to improve relations with all of India's neighbors, including Pakistan. In pursuit of this end, the Gujral regime made unilateral concessions to Bangladesh and Nepal. Also, following on its predecessor's efforts, it sought to strengthen economic and political ties with the states of the Association of Southeast Asian Nations. In the economic realm, it would continue the liberalization process, which Gujral did, albeit at a slow pace. Finally, in the area of security policy it would maintain continuity, with no new or dramatic initiatives.

This strategy has much to recommend for itself. The initiatives made by the Gujral government offer much promise for the future. If successor regimes continue the steady pursuit of this new "grand strategy," India may eventually acquire the international status that it has long sought but never achieved.

SUGGESTED READINGS

Bandopadhyaya, Jayantanuja. *The Making of India's Foreign Policy*. New Delhi: Allied Publishers, 1991.

Brecher, Michael. *Nehru: A Political Biography*. London: Oxford University Press, 1959.

Chellaney, Brahma. *Nuclear Proliferation: The U.S.-Indian Conflict*. New Delhi: Orient Longman, 1993.

Cohen, Stephen P. *The Indian Army*. Berkeley: University of California Press, 1971.

Cortright, David, and Amitabh Mattoo, eds. *India and the Bomb: Public Opinion and Nuclear Options*. Notre Dame, Ind.: University of Notre Dame Press, 1996.

Ganguly, Sumit. *The Crisis in Kashmir: Portents of War, Hopes of Peace*. Cambridge: Cambridge University Press; Washington, D.C.: Woodrow Wilson Center Press, 1997.

   The Origins of War in South Asia: The Indo-Pakistani Conflicts since 1947, 2nd ed. Boulder, Colo.: Westview Press, 1994.

Hewitt, Vernon Marston. *The International Politics of South Asia*. Manchester, U.K.: Manchester University Press, 1992.

Hoffman, Steven. *India and the China Crisis*. Berkeley: University of California Press, 1990.

Horn, Robert. *Soviet-Indian Relations: Issues and Influence*. New York: Praeger, 1982.

Kux, Dennis. *Estranged Democracies: India and the United States, 1941–1991*. New Delhi: Sage, 1994.

8

○━○

Pakistan: Fifty years of insecurity

THOMAS PERRY THORNTON

THE BEGINNINGS

A half-century ago, Pakistan and India were large Asian nations facing severe problems of economic and political development. They shared a historic experience and at their birth were confronted with the task of charting a course in a fundamentally changing international system. It would thus have seemed that both countries would follow similar courses, and in fact early policy pronouncements by Pakistani leaders could almost as readily have been made by Indians.

Yet there were factors that led the two in different directions. Jawaharlal Nehru had been the brain and voice of the Congress Party in foreign affairs, and when independence came he was able to translate his ideas of nonalignment, socialist orientation, and "Asianness" into policy. The Muslim League, on the other hand, had had little foreign policy beyond support for Islam, and even after independence, "politically aware Pakistanis did have certain attitudes, of course, but these were vague and hardly constituted a basis for a foreign policy."[1]

More important was the factor of religion. The gulf that had emerged between Hindus and Muslims over the centuries had been intensified by British colonial policy and led the Muslim League to demand a separate nation. Islam would inform the foreign policy values of this new nation as a positive tie to other Muslim countries, but also in a negative sense of profound rivalry with India and fear of "Hindu domination."

Furthermore, Pakistan, like any other state, must follow a foreign

---

[1] William J. Barnds, *India, Pakistan, and the Great Powers* (New York: Praeger, 1972), 68.

170

policy that promotes values but also recognizes the security implications of geopolitics. To a great extent, the ability to do the former is determined by the latter. Being big helps, and Pakistan is big, but size is a relative thing. When Pakistan became independent in 1947 it was the world's fifth-most-populous nation, but three of the four above it— China, India, and the Soviet Union—were its nearby neighbors. Pakistanis came to think of themselves as a small country that had to shape its foreign and security policies accordingly. To make matters still worse, Pakistan came into existence split in two and lacking strategic depth; its borders were ill-defined and indefensible, dividing ethnic groups.

Pakistanis excluded the possibility of accommodation and acceptance of Indian regional leadership as a means of ensuring their own national well-being. After all, they defined their very rationale for existence as being "not-India," and the heritage of conflict had been intensified by orders of magnitude through the horrors of partition. A forthcoming approach on the part of New Delhi might conceivably have assuaged these concerns, but the Indians chose a policy of firmness. The armed conflict that immediately developed over Kashmir was seen in Pakistan as proof that India did not accept the legitimacy of the Muslim nation. Kashmir became the focus of relations between India and Pakistan—as a quarrel over territory, but even more as the symbol of the struggle between Islamic Pakistan and secular India.

Thus from its very inception, Pakistan was an "insecurity state" that perceived itself not only as small and disadvantaged but as on the defensive against a real and present threat, with its survival at stake. Constructing a force within South Asia to balance India was not feasible because India was more powerful than any combination of other states within the subsystem. Thus a central element of Pakistani policy has been to reach outside South Asia to find support that might offset Indian dominance within the system and to avoid bilateral arrangements that would put Pakistan in a one-on-one relationship with India.

Pakistan initially sought to offset geopolitics through religion: it was to be part of the universal community of believers, and as the first nation to be formed in the name of Islam felt that it should and would receive full support of the universal community of Muslims, the *ummah*. It was a matter of some convenience that most of the *ummah* lay to the west of Pakistan, lending the western part of the new nation depth vis-à-vis India.

Pakistan also saw itself in the vanguard of what would be many new nations coming to independence in the following years. Although little tangible support could be expected from that quarter for the time being, Pakistan derived satisfaction from its solidarity with Indonesia's independence struggle and with the Arabs in their resistance to the creation of Israel.

While Pakistan recognized the fact of overwhelming American predominance in an essentially unipolar world of 1947, it would be some time before Pakistan looked seriously for strategic support from a source that was so distant and unclear. The Soviet Union was not uninteresting, but in Pakistan's early days Stalin's hard-line policies offered little enticement. China was still in ill-defined chaos.[2]

Pakistan's foreign policy, buffeted from many sides, would go through a series of fairly well-defined phases over the next half-century. One element or another would be most prominent at any given time, but with little change, this menu of options would comprise the elements of the stream of Pakistan's foreign policy as it flowed over a very rocky bed defined by hostility toward a vastly stronger India.

PHASE I: FIRST STEPS

Pakistan's initial foreign attempts bore little fruit. Through skillful diplomacy it was rather successful in winning support in the United Nations (UN) for its position on Kashmir, but the key part of the disputed area remained firmly in Indian hands. India's stronger international position was also evident in Pakistan's failure to mobilize political support among the members of the Commonwealth of Nations and among the countries that achieved independence in the ensuing years. Both the United States and the Soviet Union kept Pakistan at arm's length, and such little attention as they directed toward South Asia was focused more on India.

To the west, the British had left behind a disputed border with Afghanistan, and although Pakistanis regretted that Islamic solidarity did not lay this issue to rest, they could hardly have been surprised. Much more disheartening was the attitude of the Muslims of the Middle East. Pakistan's efforts to mobilize the *ummah* through exhortation and a series of conferences in Karachi resulted ultimately in the other Muslim

---

[2] Although it was no doubt true that senior Pakistanis were hostile to the idea of communism and made much of the point in talking to Americans, it did not necessarily follow that this hostility transferred itself to communist states such as the Soviet Union and China, if these could be of use to Pakistani policy.

nations finding Pakistan too "pushy." They also had other problems and other formative political experiences that, in some cases, made India a more attractive contact.

Pakistan, therefore, stood virtually alone as the second half of the twentieth century began. When the Indians in 1950 and again in 1951 seemed to be threatening militarily, Pakistan found itself strategically naked. Its own military capabilities were almost negligible and nobody appeared to have the slightest interest in its cause. The initial approaches to policy making had been unproductive, and a rethinking of the strategic situation was urgent.

PHASE II: ALIGNMENT

Two aspects of Pakistan's foreign policy formation had to be addressed: the needs for political backing and for modern military equipment. Pakistan's last hopes for Muslim support petered out about 1952, the same year that saw the election of a Republican administration in Washington that was anxious to complete the containment ring around China and the Soviet Union. With India unwilling to cooperate, an alliance with Pakistan seemed to be an ideal match, each side meeting the immediate needs of the other. Pakistan enrolled in the Central Treaty Organization (CENTO) and the Southeast Asia Treaty Organization (SEATO), and a bilateral security agreement was signed subsequently.

For much of the next decade, economic and military assistance in the amount of $1.3 billion flowed from the United States, and the Pakistani armed forces received training and modern equipment that to some extent redressed the quantitative imbalance with India. Equally important, Pakistan now felt that it had found the much-needed source of external support. Together with impressive economic growth and a degree of domestic stability, this provided Pakistan with the strongest sense of security it would ever enjoy. This self-confidence enabled Pakistan to engage politically with India. The Nehru-Noon agreements on borders and the Indus Waters agreement were fruits of this period of relative balance. The attempts by Ayub Khan to develop a political relationship, however, came to naught, in good part because of Pakistan's continuing demands for Kashmir but also because of Nehru's disdain for any country that aligned itself with the United States.

Lacking any acceptable alternative in view of its threat perception, it can hardly be argued that Pakistan acted unwisely in aligning itself with the United States. It was, however, a problematic relationship that had strayed far from Pakistan's original preferences. Leaving aside domestic costs, the international bill was high. Pakistan found itself even further out of step with many Arabs who were influenced by Egyptian president Gamal Abdel Nasser's radicalism; the alliance provided India with a rationale for abandoning its pledge of a plebiscite in Kashmir; and it prevented Pakistan from exploring ties with the Soviet Union and China, which were becoming more open in their dealings with the emerging Third World. Although Pakistan was able to assume a significant role in the Afro-Asian movement, that grouping soon lost influence as the idea of nonalignment—which excluded Pakistan—arose to replace it. A cross-section of Pakistan's stream of foreign policy would in the mid-1950s have shown little variety; the American tie was overwhelmingly dominant.

Most costly was the fact that this almost exclusive relationship was fundamentally flawed by the divergent objectives of the parties, in particular Washington's unwillingness to enroll itself as Pakistan's ally against India. Pakistan doubtless shared some of the American concern about a Soviet threat, but this concern, much less fear of China, was never acute. Even Eisenhower considered the alliance to have been a mistake, and Ayub soon came to question its usefulness.

The U.S.-Pakistani tie ultimately fell victim to India. When, in the late 1950s, Washington saw a chance to draw India closer to itself through economic assistance and support against a growing Chinese threat, it was unwilling to let Pakistan stand in the way. Washington's protests that assistance to India—culminating in military support when the Chinese attack came in 1962—was not meant to undermine ties to Pakistan, failed to recognize the zero-sum nature of politics in the subcontinent. Pakistan's protest that it, as a friend, deserved preferential treatment went unheeded and even-handed support meant simply that the old imbalance in the subcontinent would be reconstituted. Pakistan's request for U.S. guarantees against India produced nothing more than a statement that if India committed aggression, Washington would consider what to do. Once again Pakistan had to rethink its security strategy.

PHASE III: BILATERALISM

Pakistan turned to a new approach that would diversify its relationships. As Ayub described it, "We should endeavour to set up bilateral equations with each one of them [i.e., any potential friend], with the clear understanding that the nature and complexion of the equation would be such as to promote our mutual interests without adversely affecting the interests of third parties. . . . Each equation would have to be acceptable to third parties. . . . It would be like walking on a triangular tightrope."[3] The implementation of the new policy was described as "a clever approach of caution and adventure,"[4] and that mixture probably represents the respective contributions of Ayub and his brilliant protégé Zulfikar Ali Bhutto.

First of all, they saw that deteriorating relations between India and China created an opening for Pakistan. Beijing responded in kind, and the foundation was laid for a remarkable political relationship. Ayub and Bhutto were also able to diversify ties with the Soviet Union. The U-2 incident, in which an American spy plane based in Pakistan was shot down over the Soviet Union, cast an understandable pall over already poor relations. Pakistan recovered quickly, however, and in 1961 was able to secure a grant of $30 million for oil exploration, the first step in developing a useful bilateral relationship with Moscow.

Pakistan was also able to develop new ties to the Muslim nations to the west by deemphasizing Pakistan's claims to leadership and realistically recognizing that the guiding force of other Muslim states was less Islamic nationalist than territorial. On the one side, Pakistan forged a special relationship with its non-Arab neighbors Iran and Turkey through the Regional Cooperation for Development (RCD); on the other, it found a willing associate in President Sukarno of Indonesia, who was himself at odds with India.

Amid all of these adventures, caution mandated maintaining close relations with the United States, which remained Pakistan's only substantial source of support, however unreliable. That meant, however, that Washington had to accept the bilateralist philosophy as well; specifically, that it would tolerate Pakistan's rapprochement with China. But China was still America's principal *bête noire* and during the Kennedy and Johnson administrations a distinct coolness developed. Both sides protested that their relationship was sound, but when in 1963 the United States and the United Kingdom committed themselves to major support

---

[3] Mohammed Ayub Khan, *Friends Not Masters* (Karachi: Oxford University Press, 1967), 118–19.
[4] Bhabani Sen Gupta, *The Fulcrum of Asia* (New York: Pegasus, 1970), 183.

for the Indian military, Ayub concluded that not only was the United States fundamentally unreliable, but that India would soon develop a military machine that would render hopeless any attempt by Pakistan to regain Kashmir. Guided by Bhutto, Ayub devised a highly adventurous strategy of "leaning on India," which was meant to gain Kashmir but failed and led in 1965 to a disastrous war with India.

Pakistan could take considerable satisfaction in the amount of support that it received during the war. Indonesia, Iran, Turkey, Saudi Arabia, and Jordan offered moral and token material support; even non-Muslim nonaligned nations were at least neutral in a situation where India might well have expected solace. Further testimony to Ayub's diplomatic success was evident in the enthusiastic political support he got from China and—especially surprising—the fact that the Soviet Union remained neutral in the conflict, rather than throwing its weight behind India. Yet these diplomatic successes were of little help in furthering Pakistani goals. Pakistan's worst fears were realized when the United States not only failed to back it but cut off all military supply. Without U.S. support, Pakistan was simply no match for an Indian military that had recovered from its 1962 debacle against China; kind words and even token assistance from friends could not offset India's quantitative advantage.

The policy of bilateralism had been a brilliant diplomatic success in bringing new currents into Pakistan's foreign policy stream and establishing Pakistan as an independent international player, no longer simply a client of the United States. It failed, however, when it was asked to do something beyond its capability—i.e., deliver Kashmir into Pakistani control. Ayub and Bhutto had misjudged badly, and Kashmir was farther than ever from the Pakistani grip.

PHASE IV: BILATERALISM MINUS

Bhutto quickly abandoned Ayub to try his own political fortunes, but the policies of bilateralism remained in effect; nor did they change significantly when Yahya Khan replaced Ayub in 1969. Indeed, in 1970 Yahya was able to pull off a remarkable hat trick by visiting Washington, Moscow, and Beijing—all of whom were on notably poor terms with each other.

There was, however, a big difference in the reality of the situation. The 1965 war marked the end of American interest in South Asia as such and the emergence of the Soviet Union as would-be security manager of the region. For over a decade, little military aid from the United States would be forthcoming, and China's attempts to fill the gap were inadequate for Pakistan's security needs. Moscow also showed interest in becoming a military supplier to Pakistan, but in the face of Indian opposition and later political developments, the modest program soon petered out.

Pakistan's security problems in the late 1960s, however, were only marginally related to foreign policy. With military support from India, disaffected East Pakistan broke loose in 1971 and declared itself independent. In one stroke, Pakistan was reduced to half its size and its rationale as the home for the subcontinent's Muslims was gravely undermined.

The wound had been self-inflicted. Pakistan had mismanaged its affairs badly and its handling of the revolt in the east was barbarous. Under the circumstances, the amount of international support it received was impressive. The Soviet Union, to be sure, lined up behind India, but only after it found itself incapable of averting conflict. China and the Muslim world gave Pakistan strong moral backing and the United States also gave political support. The American role did not, however, indicate renewed commitment to Pakistan as such. The conflict provided President Richard Nixon and his national security adviser Henry Kissinger with a useful way of signaling to Moscow and Beijing that Washington would act in regional conflicts in ways that supposedly lent credibility to the new policies of détente and triangular diplomacy they were then developing. In the last analysis, neither the United States nor other outside actors had effective leverage to apply; India's triumph was indisputable.

PHASE V: READJUSTING THE FRAMEWORK

Through skillful diplomacy, Pakistan rose phoenix-like from its ashes. Bhutto not only rescued Pakistan's badly battered sense of identity, he was also able rapidly to restore its international position. Immediately after taking over from the disgraced Yahya, Bhutto set off on a round of visits abroad to thank those countries that had supported Pakistan in the war. He understood, however, that his first priority was finding a modus vivendi with India. He met with Prime Minister Indira Gandhi at Simla in 1972 and made a major concession, effectively agreeing to settle Indo-

Pakistan disputes bilaterally. Although it is not clear that they reached any agreement on the future of Kashmir, there can hardly be any doubt that he was seeking to remove India from the center of Pakistan's foreign policy concerns and to take Pakistan back more to its roots—close ties with the Muslim world and with the Third World generally. Once the Indians tested a nuclear device in 1974, Bhutto decided to give additional priority to Pakistan's nuclear weapons program, as a parallel way of dealing with the problem of Indian predominance through means independent of the goodwill of others.

Bhutto was both skillful and fortunate in his approach. He was able to project himself as a Third World populist leader, a model much in vogue at the time. The withering of Pakistan's security alignment with the United States gave support to the claim that Pakistan was non-aligned. Most important, Bhutto's approach to the Muslim world came at precisely the time of the upsurge of Islamic strength, fueled by the 1973 Arab-Israeli war and the ensuing oil price increases. By hosting the 1974 Islamic summit, Bhutto put Pakistan at the center of Muslim politics for the next decade and more. In addition, Pakistan's role in Muslim politics reinforced its claim to be a leader among the Third World and nonaligned nations, who were themselves being radicalized around issues of economic redistribution that were being pressed in the UN and Group of 77 fora.

Bhutto had gotten a good number of balls into the air and was adept at keeping them moving, but his ultimate objective never became clear and he did not have the opportunity to demonstrate that his policies could actually guarantee Pakistan's security. His successor, General Muhammad Zia ul-Haq, generally hewed to the same foreign policy directions, which general-turned-foreign-minister Sahibzada Yaqub Khan described as "maneuver with flexibility on multiple fronts."[5] Careful maneuvering was crucial for Zia, who emphasized involvement in the *ummah* even more than Bhutto had but needed to tread gingerly as the Muslim world fell into conflict over the Camp David accords, the Iranian revolution and, later, the war between Iran and Iraq. Zia also encountered difficulties as he sought modern weaponry for his army. Matters had been difficult enough between Bhutto and Kissinger, but the Zia-Carter equation was unpromising to begin with and became impossible

---

[5] Cited in S. M. Burke and Lawrence Ziring, *Pakistan's Foreign Policy*, 2nd ed. (Karachi: Oxford University Press, 1990), 453.

as Pakistan pursued its nuclear program over U.S. objections. By 1979, U.S.-Pakistani relations had reached their nadir.

Zia profited from the relatively forthcoming policies of India under the leadership of Prime Minister Morarji Desai (India had removed its objections to Pakistani membership in the Non-Aligned Movement) and the sporadic generosity of some of Pakistan's oil-rich friends in the Gulf. Nonetheless, by late 1979 Zia's policies, foreign as well as domestic, seemed to be running out of steam. Relations with Iran were sour, a communist coup had taken place in Afghanistan, and a mob had burned the American embassy in Islamabad. Robert Wirsing observed, "Never before had Pakistan been quite so isolated and quite so threatened at the same time."[6]

PHASE VI: ALIGNMENT WITH A DIFFERENCE

Once again, the Cold War intervened to give Pakistani policy a new lease on life. The Soviet invasion of Afghanistan certainly presented a new threat to Pakistan, but it also catapulted Pakistan to the forefront of international attention and made it the darling of anti-Soviet forces. In a short period of time, Pakistan's relations with the United States turned around completely as the American nonproliferation priority was overwhelmed by the need to resist the Soviet advance into Afghanistan. Over the next decade, Washington would commit over $7 billion in military and economic aid to Pakistan and still more would flow from China and the Gulf states.

Pakistan's fortune was further enhanced by the fact that India seemed to be siding with the Soviet Union over Afghanistan. Because Pakistan had hosted the conference of 1974, it still chaired the Organization of Islamic States and could use this position to rally the Islamic world to support it and its clients in Afghanistan. Since the nonaligned (less India) were also aghast at the Soviet action, they allowed Pakistan to manage their Afghanistan policy in the United Nations, a task that Pakistan executed skillfully.

Shrewd Pakistani diplomacy was able to keep considerable daylight between Islamabad and Washington. Alignment with the United States was strictly in the framework of Pakistani bilateralism and was recog-

---

[6] Robert G. Wirsing, *Pakistan's Security under Zia, 1977–1988* (New York: St. Martin's Press, 1991), 10.

nized by all concerned as a limited partnership focused on Afghanistan, lacking both the commitments and the illusions of the 1950s. President Zia successfully walked a very narrow line in his dealings with the other superpower; while relations with Moscow were tense, Pakistan was never in real danger of Soviet attack beyond occasional border incursions. Zia was careful to keep the level of tension at a safe level.

Relations with India were dangerous and Indian military acquisitions more than offset the new materiel that Pakistan received from the United States. Limited fighting broke out in 1985 along the Siachen Glacier in Kashmir and a general conflict threatened when large-scale maneuvers further south became threatening. Zia recognized that India was too dangerous and expensive an enemy, and maneuvered adroitly to fend off serious conflict. The creation of the South Asian Association for Regional Cooperation (SAARC) in 1985 offered a framework within which India and Pakistan could discuss their problems, at least informally. The outcome of these contacts was meager, but India and Pakistan did agree not to attack each other's nuclear establishments, and the assumption that both sides had nuclear weapons no doubt introduced a note of mutual restraint.

This impressive display of Pakistani diplomacy produced prestige and resources. It ultimately also brought success, as the Soviet Union was unable to prevail in Afghanistan and withdrew, leaving the field largely to insurgent forces who had been given resources, refuge, and guidance by Pakistan. It appeared that even the long-standing dispute over Pakhtunistan might become a thing of the past, and Zia envisioned a friendly Afghanistan providing Pakistan with strategic depth. Even at the height of this success, however, Pakistan's involvement in Afghanistan was exacting a fearful price. Drugs, ethnic conflict, corruption, and hyperarmed violence became ubiquitous, reaching previously unheard-of levels. The impact of the Afghan adventure on the Pakistani social fabric was severe. Zia, whose domestic political position had been weak at the beginning of the Afghan war, was able to consolidate and maintain power in ways that were ultimately damaging to Pakistan's political system.

PHASE VII: THE FRAMEWORK BROKEN

Pakistan had now profited twice from the Cold War. The end of that era recast many of the premises of Pakistan's foreign policy, confronting it with difficult choices. Like every other country, Pakistan had to deal with a world that had lost its familiar shape. The United States, for instance, no longer defined its policies in terms of the bipolar confrontation with the Soviet Union and lost interest in Afghanistan once Moscow had withdrawn its forces. That, in turn, meant diminished interest in Pakistan; in 1990 Washington "discovered" that Pakistan was no longer eligible for aid because of its nuclear program. Islamic glue also began to run thin once the issue in Afghanistan was no longer a *jihad* against Soviet occupiers but a contest among factions, all Muslim of course, who in turn had a variety of Muslim backers abroad. Relations with revolutionary Iran had always been difficult and are now nearly hostile. The Gulf War illustrated how rifts within the Arab world can play back into Pakistani society. The one dividend that Pakistan had hoped to gain from the collapse of the Soviet Union was a close relationship with the Muslim successor states of the Soviet Union—at least profitable economic ties and if possible strategic depth. These new states, however, are primarily concerned with their own security and with economic growth. In those terms, Iran and even India are at least as interesting as Pakistan.

In a world in which economic strength is increasingly the criterion for prestige and recognition, Pakistan has fallen badly behind. The Pakistani economy, plagued by corruption, an excessive defense budget, the social ills attendant upon the Afghan adventure, and—hardly accidentally— abysmal social infrastructure, is in a shambles. Internal security is precarious and it remains to be seen if the second Nawaz Sharif government can meet the challenges. The record of Pakistani political leaders is not encouraging.

AN INTERIM BALANCE

Pakistan understood from the beginning that it was playing at a disadvantage and shaped its policies accordingly. The execution of these policies was generally sound, sometimes brilliant. For a nation that had no diplomatic service nor tradition fifty years ago, Pakistan has produced a series of world-class diplomats, such as Sir Zafrullah Khan, Sahibzada Yaqub Khan, Agha Shahi, and Abdul Sattar. Zulfikar Ali Bhutto was a gifted and imaginative foreign policy theorist and Ayub Khan and Zia ul-Haq were more than competent practitioners. At all levels, Pakistanis mastered the skill of not unnecessarily offending important interlocutors, whether Americans over Vietnam or Russians over Afghanistan, even when there were sharp policy divergences.

Pakistan was also playing from weakness on the military front. Its most remarkable accomplishment is, perhaps, that it has survived for half a century; that was by no means a foregone conclusion in 1947. The Pakistan military has generally given a good account of itself in the face of prohibitive odds. The nuclear program is both a remarkable technological accomplishment and a rational response to Pakistan's strategic situation. It gives Pakistan another type of "equalizer" in its relationship with India—more reliable than the political support it has sought elsewhere—and it has considerably increased Pakistan's capability of passive deterrence against India. Although Pakistan has received substantial outside support for its program, it has acted responsibly in not transferring technology, fissile material, or equipment to other nonnuclear states. It is a Pakistani, not an Islamic, bomb.

Military skills and diplomatic style, even brilliance, however, are not automatic guarantees of security; results are what matter, and the record of the past fifty years is mixed. Consider the individual components of Pakistan's policy stream:

Ties to the United States have been extremely profitable for Pakistan and were especially important in giving Pakistan a secure basis from which to operate in the 1950s. Pakistan has never been able to put together an acceptable security package that was completely independent of the United States. Ultimately, however, the U.S. tie proved frustrating when Washington found other options more attractive, or Pakistan's behavior unacceptable, and backed away. Pakistan still needs support from the United States but even if the current impediments are overcome, there is little likelihood that the United States would ever again enter into an extensive or expensive security relationship with Pakistan.

The relationship with China has been a much more steady prop to Pakistan, especially valuable in filling in gaps that the American relationship left behind and, apparently, in the nuclear and missile areas, where Chinese support has been critical. As politically and psychologically important as it has been, however, the China tie has been of limited security importance. From 1965 on it was clear that Pakistan could expect no direct military support, and the conventional weaponry provided by China was not at the highest technological level. Whatever the past, the future of the Sino-Pakistani relationship looks to be more limited. The Cold War compulsions that underlay the Chinese attachment to Pakistan are no more, and for Beijing, for the time being at least, India is more interesting as a negotiating partner than as an enemy shared with Pakistan.

Relations with the Muslim world have also brought Pakistan both rewards and disappointments. It was not until the 1960s that Pakistan was able to establish a strong relationship with Iran and Turkey, and the real rewards of working with the *ummah* came only in the 1970s. The Afghan war put Pakistan for a while at the center of Muslim politics, but in later years the concerns of the Middle East have returned to center stage and Pakistan finds it difficult to navigate those treacherous shoals. The Muslim connection continues to provide Pakistan with prized diplomatic and moral support; it is, however, only a partial contribution to Pakistan's security. The Islamic economic bloc created in June 1997 is hardly likely to make a major contribution to Pakistan's economic needs.

Attempts to play a Soviet card never really amounted to much; the Afro-Asian movement proved a rickety vehicle for Pakistan's aspirations; and aside from its leadership position on Afghanistan, Pakistan has never found a comfortable role among the nonaligned—a movement that is, after all, virtually defined by India.

In the military area, Pakistan has never been able to acquire or otherwise develop a conventional military capability that would permit it to take the offensive against India successfully. At most, it can aspire to be strong enough to make an Indian attack very costly and prevent India from becoming the unchallenged hegemon of the region. Nor does the nuclear program enable Pakistan to win a war against India or even force concessions. War is not a viable option for Pakistani policy under any foreseeable circumstances.

A nation that has been diminished by half, lost two wars, and finds itself without reliable allies is hardly a success story. Simple survival is not enough. What have been the reasons behind Pakistan's often disappointing performance in getting the most from its policy streams?

First is the simple fact that Pakistan holds very few high cards for its international dealings. It is overshadowed by India militarily and politically and has only a few assets that lend it more than regional importance. Pakistan is therefore very limited in its choices and must be extremely creative in order to maximize the assets that it does have.

Creativity can and does sometimes go awry and can even degenerate into adventurism, especially when the relationship of goals and capabilities is maladjusted.

Pakistan's mixture of ambitions, goals, and threat assessment has been out of balance. In fact, Pakistan has faced very little threat in its history. Afghanistan, Iran, China, and the Soviet Union have all posed problems but not ones that were life-threatening or, for that matter, overly preoccupied Pakistani strategists. The focus on the Indian threat was no doubt warranted at first, and the events of 1971 were painful reminders of its potential, but for a quarter-century now India has been a status quo power and its threats have mostly been in response to Pakistani activities. Preoccupation with India has led Pakistan into costly debacles such as the misbegotten 1965 war, waste of budgetary resources, and policy choices that were probably counter to its values and broader interests. Attempts at pressuring India by subversion (Kashmir in 1947, 1965, the 1980s, and the 1990s, and Punjab in the 1980s) proved costly and infructuous. Preoccupation with India puts a heavy day-to-day burden on Pakistani diplomacy, and the related nuclear program involves substantial political and economic costs in dealing with the United States and other nations dedicated to nonproliferation goals.

Third, the domestic foundation, without which no country can be successful, has been woefully wanting in Pakistan. Weak leaders have been common; strong leaders sooner or later wasted what they had gained. Even the 1971 disaster was the result of domestic failures and the nation's present-day parlous state is largely the result of poor domestic policy and political incompetence. Some of this domestic weakness is the result of the nation's preoccupation with security, but if Pakistan is indeed a "failed state" (a judgment I am by no means ready to make), it is not primarily the fault of failures on the diplomatic or military fronts.

REASSESSMENTS

In South Asia

While the world has been changing around South Asia, the dynamic of the subsystem has been depressingly constant. Pakistan's relationship with India begs for reassessment. Nuclear stalemate may seem reassuring compared to the security deficit of 1947, but it is a defensive and sterile policy. Single-minded preoccupation with its subcontinental rival overtaxes Pakistan's diplomatic and security capabilities. The economic costs are crushing.

A reassessment of the relationship with India will obviously include the painful decision to rethink policy on Kashmir and decide whether holding open the possibility of gaining it is worth the immense costs involved. The recent attempts have failed under circumstances that may have been uniquely favorable, so there is scant prospect of Pakistan gaining the disputed territory. As a value, the costs of keeping the Kashmir issue open (and thereby ensuring Indian hostility) may be acceptable to Pakistan—no outsider can judge that. The outlines of a settlement are quite unclear and it is by no means certain that India is inclined to make any concessions that would meet even the minimum expectations of Pakistan and of the Kashmiris. In any event, no Pakistani military planner could assume that India presents no security problem to Pakistan. A substantial military capability will remain necessary, perhaps even including a nuclear component.

Reducing preoccupation with India does not mean forgoing defense or pretending that Pakistan is not part of South Asia, but recognizing that new moves are required to defuse the relationship and permit Pakistan to use its scarce resources—political as well as material—in ways that will further its domestic and international interests. A more balanced involvement in South Asian affairs could bring dividends at the economic and personal levels. Pakistan has an "advantage" that can help it reassess its needs: it simply cannot afford the effort of the past decades. The current government appears to recognize this fact and recent Indian counterparts also profess an apparently sincere desire to reduce tensions.

Global

There is a close correlation between the period of the Cold War and the times when Pakistan had—or felt it had—strong external support. In the 1950s and again in the 1980s, the United States played that role, albeit with far fewer illusions on either side in the latter period. In the 1960s, Pakistan looked primarily to China as its hope. In the 1970s, it was the Muslim world that provided a framework for Pakistan. Certainly there was considerable overlap among the periods but the pattern of a strong external tie is characteristic of the years of bipolarity and the related North-South tension. Now, however, there are no clear sources of outside support. Appeals to Islam are unpredictable and the global structures that Pakistan learned to exploit—bipolarity and nonalignment—are passé. The familiar policy currents are running dry. Unlike in 1947, however, Pakistan now faces no pressing military threat to its existence, and thus it has much less need for external security support (which, in any event, proved of limited value in crises). Islamabad can now seek relationships on a bilateral basis that rely solely upon its partners' own capabilities and attractiveness, rather than the roles that they may play on the larger scene.

Conversely, of course, other powers will be interested in what Pakistan offers them in bilateral terms more than in its support of some global cause. The outside world does not judge Pakistan on India-related issues, such as the size of its armed forces, or on what its position is with regard to Kashmir. (Even China and the Muslim nations are shying away from that issue.) Pakistan will be judged by post–Cold War criteria: its ability to deal with its domestic political and economic problems and the role it can play in the global economy.

Pakistan could, of course, play for time in the hope that something will turn up as international society goes through unpredictable changes in the post–Cold War era. Perhaps some configuration of the "conflict of civilizations" will deal Islamabad a winning hand. Perhaps India may come apart. Perhaps there will be an Islamic resurgence in Central Asia that will lend Pakistan the security framework that it lacks. Perhaps Pakistan will be able to convince the United States that it is the guardian of a new international "front line" against drugs, terrorism, and extremism. These are Micawberish policies, however, and Pakistan may not have the time to wait for providential intervention before it slips into the status of a failed state.

Such an approach also runs counter to almost all the forces that are now pressing on Pakistan. The global equation, the emerging regional configuration, and, above all, the exigencies of Pakistan's domestic situation compel a redefinition of Pakistan's security concept and point in the same direction: changes domestically and in the relationship with India. Overcoming the anachronistic zero-sum politics of South Asia is of course not solely Pakistan's responsibility, for India will inevitably remain the principal determinant of Pakistani policy just as the United States is for Canada or Mexico. India's new prime minister, Atal Behari Vajpayee, has explicitly extended to Pakistan the principle of the "Gujral Doctrine" (that India would go the extra mile in dealing with its neighbors). Yet Vajpayee has also indicated that his government is not interested in discussing the central issue of Kashmir, so that Islamabad will certainly remain skeptical of a regime whose credentials are already suspect because of its strong Hindu coloration. No matter what India does, however, Pakistan cannot continue to allow its security policy choices to be dictated solely by its neighbor. It must take a larger part of its future into its own hands.

Even more than in 1947, Pakistan is an "insecurity state" because of weaknesses in its national unity, political system, social infrastructure, and economy. If Pakistan is to play an international role commensurate with its potential and the skills it has demonstrated, it must have a secure domestic platform from which to launch its diplomatic and security policies. Only then can it make itself attractive to all of its foreign constituencies, be they Muslim Central Asia or Western Europe. It is a challenge very different from that of Pakistan's first half-century, but offering more promise and better attuned to the realities of the post–Cold War world.

SUGGESTED READINGS

Ayub Khan, Mohammed. *Friends Not Masters*. Karachi: Oxford University Press, 1967.

Barnds, William J. *India, Pakistan, and the Great Powers*. New York: Praeger, 1972.

Bhutto, Zulfikar Ali. *The Myth of Independence*. Karachi: Oxford University Press, 1969.

Blood, Peter, ed. *Pakistan: A Country Study*. Washington, D.C.: Library of Congress, 1994.

Burke, S. M. *Mainsprings of Pakistan's Foreign Policy*. Minneapolis: University of Minnesota Press, 1974.

Burke, S. M., and Lawrence Ziring. *Pakistan's Foreign Policy*, 2nd ed. Karachi: Oxford University Press, 1990.

Choudhury, G. W. *India, Pakistan, Bangladesh, and the Major Powers*. New York: Free Press, 1975.

Cohen, Stephen P. *The Pakistan Army*. Berkeley: University of California Press, 1984.

Ispahani, Mahnaz. *Pakistan: The Dimensions of Insecurity*. London: Brassey's for International Institute of Strategic Studies, 1990.

Kux, Dennis. *Sometime Allies: Pakistan and the United States, 1947–1997*. Forthcoming.

Moskalenko, V. N. *Vneshnyaya Politika Pakistana*. Moscow: Nauka, 1984.

Rai, Hameed A. K. *Readings on Pakistan's Foreign Policy*. Lahore: Aziz, 1981.

Rizvi, Hasan-Askari. *Pakistan and the Geostrategic Environment*. New York: St. Martin's Press, 1993.

Sen Gupta, Bhabani. *The Fulcrum of Asia*. New York: Pegasus, 1970.

Sisson, Richard, and Leo E. Rose. *War and Secession: India, Pakistan, and the Creation of Bangladesh*. Berkeley: University of California Press, 1990.

Wirsing, Robert G. *Pakistan's Security under Zia, 1977–1988*. New York: St. Martin's Press, 1991.

Ziring, Lawrence, Ralph Braibanti, and W. Howard Wriggins, eds. *Pakistan: The Long View*. Durham, N.C.: Duke University Press, 1977.

9

The United States, India, and Pakistan:
Retrospect and prospect

STEPHEN PHILIP COHEN

It is tempting, but oversimple, to divide fifty years of U.S. relations with
India and Pakistan into two periods: the Cold War, extending from 1947
to 1989, and the post–Cold War years, from 1990 to the present. This
division is misleading for four reasons. First, American differences with
India—in the shape of the Indian nationalist movement—actually began
before independence; the two took dissimilar positions on the war
against Nazism and Japanese imperialism. This strategic divergence
helped establish patterns and habits on both sides that persist today.
Second, Washington's interest in India and Pakistan during the Cold
War waxed and waned. Long stretches of apathy alternated with inter-
mittent vigorous pursuit of non–Cold War issues (for example, President
Jimmy Carter's introduction, in the late 1970s, of nuclear nonproliferation as a central element of America's relations with both states). There
were even occasions when Cold War objectives were supplanted by other
regional issues (as from 1965 onward, when the United States and the
Soviet Union tacitly and then explicitly coordinated elements of their
respective South Asian policies—even when they were battling each
other in Afghanistan). Third, Washington's Cold War interests were
themselves complex, notably as the object of containment policy came
to include China after 1949, and then excluded it after 1970. Finally,
U.S. policy makers are bedeviled now, as they were during the entire
Cold War period, by the difficulty of formulating a policy toward either
India or Pakistan when these states appear to be locked in conflict with
each other.

I am grateful to the Alton Jones, Ford, and Rockefeller foundations and the Department
of Energy for their support for the University of Illinois's South Asia security projects.

189

BEFORE THE COLD WAR

Any survey of American relations with India and Pakistan might begin five years before the latter nations became independent, when the United States in 1942 first discovered a significant strategic stake in the Indian subcontinent. Until then, American interest in British India was diffuse but supportive of independence or greater Indian self-rule. This view stemmed from a Wilsonian belief that independence was morally appropriate and that it would help the region alleviate poverty. The limited American commercial and missionary interests in India were negligible compared with the far more substantial human and material investment in China.

The critical turning point in America's policy, which anticipated later Indian-American disputes, was precipitated by the decision in the summer of 1942 by the Indian National Congress to go to prison rather than actively support the war effort. This, plus the support given to the Axis powers by the nationalist leader Subhas Chandra Bose and the Indian National Army, forced the Franklin Roosevelt administration into a choice between an ally and a potential friend. Roosevelt ceased pressuring the British to grant independence, a choice that disillusioned many Indian nationalists—and one that prefigured later disappointments when Washington was forced to choose between other allies and a nonaligned India.

THE COLD WAR: A CLUSTER OF STRATEGIES

The onset of the Cold War brought the United States back to South Asia in search of allies (or at least friends) in a struggle against another global threat. The "loss" of China in 1949 accelerated the search, as did the discovery that the Soviet Union was catching up in the nuclear arms race and had consolidated its power in Central and Eastern Europe.

An inventory of America's Cold War involvement in South Asia from 1949 to 1989 would count at least six different themes. Over the years these sometimes weakened, often to reemerge five, ten, or twenty years later:

- The Cold War led the United States to think once again about the strategic defense of the region. South Asia had come under attack by Japan in World War II—did it face the same kind of threat from Soviet, and later

Chinese, forces? Early U.S. containment policy as implemented in South Asia was to help India and Pakistan defend against Soviet and/or Chinese forces. Although their motive was to obtain arms for their own dispute, both Indian and Pakistani officials stressed to the United States the risk that the subcontinent faced from the "bear" to the north. Pakistan received significant military and economic aid, especially from 1954 to 1965. Nonaligned India received considerably more in economic aid, purchased about $55 million in military equipment, and received $90 million in military grant assistance after the Sino-Indian war of 1962. The "second" Cold War, precipitated by the Soviet invasion of Afghanistan, revived the moribund U.S.-Pakistani military relationship. Pakistan received over $7 billion in military and economic assistance before the George Bush administration concluded (in 1990) that Pakistan's covert nuclear weapons program violated U.S. law.

- The Cold War in South Asia also had a domestic front. As the internal vulnerabilities of Pakistan and India became more evident (especially in light of the Comintern's 1949 call for revolutionary uprisings throughout the world), Washington mounted a variety of developmental, intelligence, and information programs in South Asia. The Indian communists were seen to be under the influence of the Soviet Union, and America provided huge amounts of food aid and advice on land reform, and cooperated with Indian and Pakistani governments in countering local communist parties. The logic of these programs was based on an assumed correlation between poverty and susceptibility to communism: by encouraging economic growth (and redistributive policies, such as land reform), the communists could be beaten at their own game in India and Pakistan. Although this ideological cold war peaked in the 1950s and 1960s, Washington was, as late as the mid-1980s, still actively countering Soviet disinformation programs directed at Indian journalists and politicians.

- The Cold War intermittently made India or Pakistan major prizes in their own right. Despite the poverty of the region (or perhaps because of it), many Americans argued that the "real" contest in Asia was between communist China and democratic India. Imitating Leninist logic (that the vulnerability of the metropolitan country lay in its colonies), India was seen by some U.S. officials as a pivotal battleground in the Cold War, the most important of all of the dominoes. In the 1980s, during the Soviet occupation of Afghanistan, it was frequently heard in Washington (more than in Islamabad) that Pakistan was a "frontline" state, and that if Afghanistan fell, Pakistan—and all of South Asia—would be vulnerable and the Soviets would have a clear run to the warm waters of the Indian Ocean.

Over time, the Cold War, in its South Asian manifestation, acquired other dimensions, and India and Pakistan themselves came to take advantage of the global bipolar structure:

- Although Indian diplomats were among the first to learn of the Sino-Soviet split, it was Pakistan that exploited the crack in the communist monolith by helping to arrange U.S. national security adviser Henry Kissinger's secret visit to Beijing in 1971, leading to improved ties with China.
- While at first India's role as a cofounder and leader of the Non-Aligned Movement was seen in Cold War terms (Secretary of State John Foster Dulles once criticized Indian "neutralism" as immoral), the ultimate view of all U.S. presidents from Harry Truman to Lyndon Johnson (including Dwight Eisenhower himself) was that India could be used to influence the Non-Aligned Movement and that a nonaligned India did little damage to substantive American interests.
- Finally, as the Cold War wound down, Washington's relations with New Delhi and Islamabad came to be quite permissive in regard to their movement toward China or the Soviet Union. At the height of the "second" Cold War in 1980–89, the United States did not try to punish India for its close relationship with the Soviets, but rather attempted what was termed an "opening" to New Delhi, in the hope of both luring India away from the Soviets and protecting Pakistan's southern flank. Nor did Washington worry overmuch about Islamabad's continuing diplomatic and economic links to Moscow, despite the proxy war in Afghanistan.

Thus, America's Cold War strategic engagement with India and Pakistan was varied and complex. The formal alliance with Pakistan did not even rule out a close intelligence relationship with India—whose major external intelligence agency, the Research and Analysis Wing (RAW), was begun with the advice and support of the U.S. Central Intelligence Agency (CIA).

Reciprocal fears: Overcommitment and betrayal

The most contentious issue that dogged American relations with India and Pakistan over the years was the extent of U.S. obligations to either state, and the implications for its relations with the other. This remains, today, a lively issue, transcending its Cold War roots.

Formally, the only U.S. commitments in the region were to Pakistan, should it be faced with "communist" aggression. However, informal assurances were offered, sometimes giving rise to serious miscalculation, especially when accompanied by military assistance or military gestures.

From an American perspective the greatest fear has been of being dragged into a regional crisis by India or Pakistan when no U.S. interests were at stake. The first such crisis was the Sino-Indian war in 1962, when Nehru frantically called for direct U.S. military intervention to help turn back the tide of Chinese soldiers. The U.S. response was to send the U.S.S. *Enterprise* aircraft carrier into the Bay of Bengal as a warning to the Chinese, to decline Nehru's rather frantic requests for direct military assistance, and to encourage India and Pakistan to settle the Kashmir problem. Ironically, the same carrier was in 1971 sent to the Bay of Bengal as a way of reassuring Pakistan (and China) of U.S. support and opposition to the impending occupation of East Pakistan by Indian forces. Again, the signal was only a signal: Indian forces defeated the Pakistani army, and a new state, Bangladesh, was created.

Every U.S. military assistance program in South Asia has generated vehement objections from the nonrecipient. America's initial program for Pakistan provided India with the pretext to back away from its pledge of a plebiscite in Kashmir and encouraged Delhi's move toward Moscow. Subsequent U.S. assistance to India immediately after the Sino-Indian war led Pakistan to move toward China and question the value of its ties to the United States. The revival of the U.S.-Pakistani military relationship in the 1980s propelled India toward the Soviet Union and contributed to the largest arms-buying spree in regional history.

U.S. policy makers have been confronted with the same Hobson's choice in the nuclear arena. Washington's initial reluctance to come down hard on New Delhi for its 1974 nuclear test was taken as further justification for Pakistan's own nuclear program. Conversely, when Washington looked the other way while Pakistan perfected its nuclear program in the 1980s, Indian hawks argued that an Indian nuclear test would be a fitting response.

The lessons of the Cold War

What strategic lessons can be drawn from America's pursuit of Cold War objectives in South Asia?

First, South Asia came to be seen by two generations of U.S. policy makers as a region of war and intractable conflict. The absence of co-operation between India and Pakistan made the region vulnerable to outsiders and made it hard for the United States to work with either state to pursue common strategic objectives in or out of the region.

Second, the United States came to the view that its well-intentioned offers of mediation or conflict resolution were seldom welcomed by both sides and almost never accepted except under duress. In this regard no issue was more important, and more frustrating, than that of Kashmir. From the first year of independence (and the emergence of Kashmir as the core dispute between India and Pakistan), U.S. officials, private citizens, foundations, and scholars have pressed the two states to resolve or at least suspend the conflict, so that they might better manage the joint defense of the subcontinent and stop the diversion of scarce resources away from urgent economic and development needs. An enormous amount of American political capital was expended on Kashmir with few positive results.

Third, because of the inability to put together what partition had torn apart—South Asia's strategic unity—U.S. administrations often toyed with the idea of choosing between India and Pakistan to help contain the Soviet Union or China (or both). This view held that the value of an alliance with either India or Pakistan against a third, nonregional state would be greater than the costs incurred by choosing one or the other and that the United States could reduce collateral regional political damage by compensatory economic or military aid programs. However, Washington never could bring itself to make such a choice and stick with it; any leaning to one side was usually accompanied by a compensatory movement in the other direction. Thus, U.S. economic assistance to India peaked at the very moment the U.S. military assistance program to Pakistan was in full swing; later, when U.S. military equipment began to flow to India, compensatory military hardware was supplied to Pakistan.

Fourth, even this policy lapsed from time to time. For long periods South Asia simply vanished from America's strategic map, and apathy, rather than engagement, was the norm. The United States was uninterested in South Asia very early in the Cold War. It took the victory of the Chinese communists and a threatening Stalin to tip the balance of opinion in Washington in favor of an alliance with Pakistan. But by 1964 Washington had become disillusioned with both Islamabad and New Delhi, and seized the opportunity presented by the 1965 Indo-Pakistani war to stop military aid to both countries and to yield the role of regional conflict manager to the Soviet Union. After a brief spell of activity in 1970–71, Washington again retreated from the region, only to return after the Soviet invasion of Afghanistan in December 1979.

Fifth, as far as South Asia was concerned, it took a crisis to build a policy—or at least to rouse U.S. strategic interests. Without either a threat to the region by an outsider or a threat to regional stability brought about by an Indo-Pakistani war, Washington tended to regard South Asia as a strategic sideshow. While it may have been a site of Cold War competition, it was not consistently judged to be vital territory—at least compared with the oil-rich Middle East or the industrially vital Europe and Northeast Asia.

Finally, U.S. officials and strategists came to their own understanding of the region's strategic style—the way in which Indian and Pakistani diplomats set forth their respective positions in the Cold War. The United States grew wary of Pakistan's exaggeration of the Indian threat to Western interests, and came to discount Islamabad's pronouncements of the communist threat from the north. Pakistan had been saying that "the sky was falling" for forty years, and there was, as of 1978, no evidence that it was going to happen. This fateful miscalculation gave Islamabad considerable leverage in its dealings with Washington after the Soviet Union occupied Kabul on Christmas Day in 1979. Today Pakistan is widely (if inaccurately) regarded in Congress and sections of the executive branch as a trusted and loyal U.S. ally from the Cold War. As for India, successive generations of U.S. officials have been driven to distraction by New Delhi's diplomatic style: for many years it seemed that no Indian diplomat's day was complete unless he or she had lectured an American on the evils of the Cold War and the self-evident foolishness of U.S. support for Pakistan against India. Thus, when the Cold War came to an end, Pakistan found itself with a considerable group of friends and supporters in Washington and India was widely regarded as pro-Soviet, anti-American, and having betrayed its own lofty Nehruvian-Gandhian standards on nuclear issues.

OUTSIDE THE COLD WAR: ECONOMIC, POLITICAL, AND IDEOLOGICAL CONSIDERATIONS

The U.S. strategic and military policies in South Asia described above intersected at many points with concern over the region's economic and political development. The latter may turn out to be of historically equal or greater importance. These economic and social concerns had two wellsprings: (1) a deep moral concern with South Asia's poverty, and (2) the need for economic and social reform to keep the region from slipping into the communist camp. A third U.S. economic interest is now emerging after decades of disappointment—South Asia as a prospective area for American investment and as a market for American products.

Official U.S. interest in the social and economic problems of South Asia predated the Cold War, emerging at the very moment during World War II when the region became strategically important. The first, and most extensive, American exposure to South Asia took place when thousands of impressionable American soldiers and civilians bound for the CBI (China-Burma-India) theater went to eastern India in 1943. India was then reeling under the impact of the Bengal famine and was threatened by a Japanese invasion. Many of these young Americans later contrasted their experience in India with the warm welcome they received in China, where Americans worked closely with all elements of the anti-Japanese alliance. Both countries suffered from terrible poverty, but the Chinese seemed to be more eager to cooperate militarily with their U.S. allies.

By default, India's poverty moved to the forefront of U.S. interests in South Asia. If India would not join any American-sponsored alliances, then the United States could at least help it indirectly, through economic and developmental projects. This strategy fit into mainstream American thinking. Many liberal Americans held that a high level of defense spending by poor states was immoral. It also coincided with the observation that precisely because India and Pakistan were poor, they had to resolve their disputes, and that America should help in facilitating dialogue. Furthermore, many Americans were especially attracted to India because Jawaharlal Nehru and other Indian leaders were critical of the Cold War, with its never-ending cycle of arms races and huge expenditures on nuclear and other weapons of mass destruction. (This later led to disillusionment with India among many American liberals who regarded the Indian nuclear test of 1974 as a morally appalling betrayal of once-shared values.)

Americans have generally held the view that South Asia (unlike East Asia or the Middle East, where there were real strategic stakes) was first and foremost an economic and social "project." As a result, it was difficult to take India seriously. In the 1950s and even the 1960s most Americans were telling their Indian counterparts to "grow more food and fewer children"; India might be an "emerging" power but it would not be a real power until it put its own domestic house in order.

In the 1950s and 1960s this view not only contributed to American efforts to get India and Pakistan to the bargaining table to settle the Kashmir problem, it helped build support for massive food and economic assistance to India and Pakistan. These aid programs were expanded to include the transfer of modern agricultural technology, which in turn paved the way for India's Green and White Revolutions (in grain and dairy production, respectively). It also led to the establishment of South Asian studies programs at many American universities that had developed a strong stake in India and Pakistan (most importantly, the state universities of Illinois, Kansas, Minnesota, Missouri, Texas, Washington, and Wisconsin).

These developmental programs were usually justified in Cold War terms, but they were not solely the result of realpolitik: they had humanitarian motives that resonated deeply. They were the extension of the American impulse to do good and share America's wealth with less-fortunate people. They have been derided as misguided, patronizing, or unwise, and the American scholars who found their intellectual homes in India and Pakistan have been labeled as academic imperialists, but a review of these programs—sponsored by hundreds of private groups, foundations, and universities, as well as official U.S. aid and developmental agencies—would reach a net positive assessment.

America's capability to impose economic reforms upon India and Pakistan was limited. The U.S.-brokered Indus Waters Treaty of 1960 was publicly disparaged (although privately welcomed) in both India and Pakistan. Only one U.S. president, Lyndon Johnson, tried to force India to change its economic policy by a "ship-to-mouth" strategy that only triggered a strong backlash by Indira Gandhi. President Carter did make an offer of massive aid for an Eastern-waters regional-development program, but his real priority was nonproliferation. Throughout much of the Cold War era, U.S. officials were critical of the buildup of massive, state-controlled industries in India, but were reluctant to support inefficient and "socialist" state-run enterprises, and in some cases legally prohibited from doing so.

Only since 1990 and the transformation in Indian economic policy has American private investment begun to take India seriously. This, in turn, opens up possibilities that were unimaginable ten or twenty, let alone fifty, years ago. The economic benefits of this development are obvious, but the political ones are no less important: a strong economic relationship between the United States and both South Asian states will provide an incentive to manage other issues more carefully. American corporations now actively lobby Congress for legislation favorable to the region, although they are reluctant to side with India or Pakistan on contentious issues when it means criticizing the other country—where they might have important economic interests.

NONPROLIFERATION: RIGHT ISSUE, WRONG REGION?

Timing is important in determining which issues achieve high priority and which are relegated to the back burner. The balance of American policy in South Asia was dramatically tilted in the early 1990s toward a single issue: nuclear nonproliferation.

The groundwork for the subordination of U.S. regional policy to non-proliferation concerns was established in 1974, when, stimulated by the Indian nuclear test, Americans came to believe that the world was on the edge of a rapid burst of nuclear proliferation. Carter made nonprolifer-ation the centerpiece of his foreign policy and singled out South Asia as a particularly important target. In the 1980s, nonproliferation ranks were swollen by the suspicion that the Reagan administration had failed to apply credible sanctions to Islamabad's covert nuclear program. Iron-ically, virtually no nonproliferationist was willing to provide Pakistan with the kind of iron-clad security guarantees that would have made its program unnecessary.

Finally, a series of intelligence misjudgments were made that gave the impression that South Asia had joined the company of such states as Libya, Iran, Iraq, and North Korea. After Washington underestimated the severity of the "Brasstacks"[1] crisis in 1987, the intelligence commu-nity then exaggerated the possibility of Indo-Pakistani tensions leading to conventional or nuclear war. The chain of assumptions (widely held in official circles) was that a war over Kashmir was likely, that this would lead to conventional war, and that this, in turn, could light a nuclear conflagration between India and Pakistan. There was also a strong disposition for the United States to assume the leadership role in

---

[1] In late 1986, the Indian military began South Asia's largest-ever exercise, "Brasstacks." By January 1987, it appeared to be threatening Pakistan, which in turn embarked upon significant maneuvers of its own. The crisis extended over several months, and may have led one or both states to bring their nuclear weapons programs to fruition.

heading off this chain of events by trying to contain the two South Asian nuclear programs.

This disposition was bipartisan in its ideological coloration, as was the larger focus on nonproliferation policy. Both were the offspring of a liaison between strategic conservatives (who wanted to make the world safe for American nuclear weapons) and liberals (who wanted to get rid of all nuclear weapons, and who thought that other countries would be more susceptible to pressure than the U.S. Department of Defense). The nonproliferation coalition had earlier succeeded in embedding into law many constraints on the conduct of U.S. policy. These constraints apply to all potential proliferators, even though they are less than effective in the case of states that believe their survival is dependent upon nuclear weapons or the maintenance of a nuclear option. Pakistan, for one, is not going to trade its nuclear option for five or six airplanes.

The fact that India and Pakistan were the only near-nuclear or covertly nuclear states with whom the United States could have a dialogue also explains much of the heightened interest in the region at the time. American officials could, and frequently did, travel to Islamabad and New Delhi to lecture their counterparts on the perils of nuclear weapons; they were unable or unwilling to do so in Teheran, Pyongyang, or Jerusalem. Thus, India and Pakistan received a disproportionate amount of official and unofficial attention aimed at "capping, freezing, and rolling back" the regional nuclear programs, very little of it addressed to the motives behind these nuclear programs. The unexamined assumption was that Washington knew better than India (or Pakistan) what was right in the area of nuclear disarmament. There were some within the U.S. Government and others outside who thought opportunities had been missed to work out alternative formulations that might have gained Indian and Pakistani agreement to key provisions of both the Non-Proliferation and Comprehensive Test Ban Treaties even if they did not formally subscribe to either. This was unlikely.

U.S. policymakers, with strong support in Congress, were determined not to yield on key nonproliferation policy issues. No new nuclear powers were to be added to the five that had tested by the 1960s. It was up to the existing nuclear powers to determine the pace of nuclear disarmament. No specific timetable for complete disarmament was to be discussed. Indian views on the discriminatory character of both international treaties intensified. Intellectual and political support for preserving India's nuclear options after the indefinite extension of the NPT in 1995 became even more entrenched. Compromise on nuclear testing became virtually impossible for the governments of both India and Pakistan.

ORGANIZATIONAL IMPERATIVES

Four years ago the Department of State was required by Congress to detach South Asia from the Bureau of Near Eastern and South Asian Affairs (NEA) and establish a separate bureau for the region. Historically, South Asia had been a subordinate component of NEA and was looked after by a deputy assistant secretary of state (only one past NEA assistant secretary, Phillips Talbot, was a genuine South Asia expert). The arrangement was defended in the bureaucracy on the grounds that an assistant secretary could always raise South Asian issues in meetings with higher officials when he or she went to discuss "more important" issues such as the Arab-Israeli peace process, Gulf policy, or relations with Iran. Congress anticipated that the new South Asian bureau, headed by its own assistant secretary, would raise the profile of South Asia within the government; that it would engage in long-term strategic planning; and that it would be better able to push a policy through the bureaucracy if it were headed by a more senior official.

As things turned out the new bureau was in difficulty from its birth. It received little support from the State Department bureaucracy (which had opposed its creation); it lost its chief advocate in Congress (Congressman Stephen Solarz); and most senior Clinton administration officials knew little and cared less about South Asia, seeing it only as a suitable target for the prosecution of a tough nonproliferation policy. No overall South Asia strategy was ever developed in the first Clinton administration, and nonproliferation issues dominated the U.S.–South Asian discourse. The process was filled with people who had little or no experience in the region and whose primary interest was India's and Pakistan's adherence to proliferation-related treaties.

The one bright spot was the strong interest in South Asia by the Departments of Commerce and Energy. The Department of Commerce, led by Secretary Ron Brown, identified India as one of the BEMs (Big Emerging Markets) most deserving of American attention, and encouraged visits to the region by corporate and government officials. The Department of Energy managed to work around legal restrictions on discussions with India concerning nuclear safety and pursued a wide-ranging dialogue with Indian and Pakistani counterparts on energy and environmental issues. But these departments cannot develop or formulate a national strategy; they can only function within the constraints of that strategy.

MAKING SOUTH ASIA RELEVANT

Starting over

In the past five years, while the Clinton administration seemed to be stuck on nuclear issues, there appeared a number of American studies of the future relationship between the United States and India and Pakistan. Most of these identified certain common features. They all argued that the number and importance of U.S. strategic, economic, and ideological interests embedded in South Asia were not matched by attention given to the area, especially to India. All of these reports suggested a new look at the region, and some of them offered quite specific steps that might be taken to remedy the situation. With a few exceptions, however, the more specific the proposal, the greater the disagreement among the American regional and strategic specialists who signed or wrote these reports. Any five American experts on South Asia will offer six different recommendations.

These and other differences in U.S. policies suggest a larger issue: the difficulty of formulating policies toward a region where there are genuine U.S. interests, but none of them vital. Can the United States organize itself to deal with the one-fifth of the world that is *not* a threat to U.S. security interests, that does *not* show signs of calamitous collapse, that has *not yet* (and is unlikely to) become a major economic partner, and that persists in expanding a political ideology that is *not* hostile to American values? When a country—the United States—has been engaged in a global struggle against totalitarianism for two generations—from 1942 to 1990—it is hard to mobilize U.S. policy makers, let alone Congress, around a nonthreat to strategic, political, economic, and moral interests. During the Cold War, the United States accomplished many useful things in South Asia, but the rationalization of the Cold War was always available to policy makers; a threat, real or potential, could always be conjured up in the service of an otherwise worthwhile objective. The discipline imposed by a geopolitical framework—even a flawed one—forced U.S. policy makers to treat the region as a whole. There has been no such strategic framework since 1989–90. Paradoxically, the absence today of a threat to South Asia, or to the United States from South Asia, makes it difficult to persuade the policy and legislative communities to support a policy in which real, but limited, U.S. interests are advanced.

A glimpse of the future?

A sound U.S. policy must meet several criteria. First, it must devote proportionate attention to America's diverse interests in South Asia. South Asia should not be moved to the top of the U.S. foreign policy agenda, nor should it languish as a policy backwater. Second, policy must be realistic, which means that it must be achievable with available resources. Third, such a policy must be low cost; South Asia does not need elaborate aid programs, risky military commitments, or the diversion of significant U.S. resources—except the scarcest resource of all, the serious attention of senior policy makers and Congress.

With these criteria in mind, the following cluster of policy goals seems a good place to start. They have the advantage of being internally self-reinforcing—that is, progress in one area can lead to movement in another. Indeed, U.S. policy should be seen as advancing along a broad front: pressing too hard on one issue will be detrimental to other important interests, and in the end could be self-defeating. A new U.S. policy in South Asia will have to emerge from the confluence of five different interest clusters. The first is the continuation of economic liberalization, which has provided (in the words of an Asia Society study group) a new "ballast" for U.S. relations with India and Pakistan. Market reform, tariff reduction, the elimination of state subsidies for inefficient industries, and the promotion of regional free-trade zones are all policies that are in U.S. interests—and those of India and Pakistan. India and Pakistan, however, are especially sensitive to distortions and inequalities generated by uneven economic growth. U.S. policy makers, corporations, and investors must be sensitive to the fact that growth without social justice will be politically unacceptable in lively, multiparty democracies. A rising tide lifts all boats, but in the real world some boats rise sooner than others, and no emotion is more politically explosive than envy.

Second, the United States should continue its encouragement and strengthening of democratic institutions in India and Pakistan. Quite apart from the intrinsic moral value of democratization, it has important by-products. Democratic states are less likely to go to war than nondemocracies. Over time, mature democracies develop political, cultural, and economic links that increase their interdependence and influence the gain/loss calculation regarding the use of force. No politicians in South Asia understand this better than the current Indian and Pakistani prime ministers, Atal Behari Vajpayee and Nawaz Sharif. A democratic India and a democratizing Pakistan are not only more compatible with the further movement toward market reforms, but will be sensitive to the abuses that market systems can produce. Elections are powerful ways of ensuring that economic growth will be equitable, both geographically and in terms of social class and rural/urban divisions. Democratic India and Pakistan are less likely to engage in human rights violations, and will be more sensitive to international criticism in this area.

America's third regional goal should be to promote strategic normalization between New Delhi and Islamabad. This is an old objective of the United States, but still a worthy one. Change will not come quickly, however. All unstable or weak democracies find it difficult to accommodate each other on issues as contentious as Kashmir (or even the Siachen Glacier dispute); a process of internal debate and dialogue will have to proceed in both states. Thus, the United States should not press for a quick "solution" to the Kashmir problem, but help create the conditions under which such a solution, satisfactory to a wide range of the political community in both countries, can emerge.

America's fourth regional goal is to assist India and Pakistan in managing their nuclear weapons capabilities. Strategic normalization has consequences for America's concerns over the spread of nuclear weapons in South Asia. The antiproliferationists may be correct in their assessment of the disruptive role of nuclear weapons elsewhere, but in South Asia they provide Pakistan with the confidence to deal with India, and for India they are an additional incentive to normalize its ties with Pakistan. It is unlikely that Pakistan or India will give up maintaining a nuclear capability of some sort in the foreseeable future, but a realistic goal would be to create the conditions whereby neither sees any gain in moving its program forward beyond some definable limits. Any U.S. legislation that hampers Washington's ability to address the situation needs to be reexamined—we have let the best become the enemy of the good.

A fifth foreign policy goal should be to develop a dialogue about short-term and long-term strategic cooperation with India and Pakistan. There is no such dialogue at the present. There are contingencies, immediate and distant, that might be discussed. In the short run, India and

Pakistan may be able to expand their peacekeeping roles. In the long run the emergence of China as an aggressive power could raise profound issues for all three states. Pakistan would have to decide whether its quasi-alliance with China might drag it into conflicts for which it is ill-equipped; India must decide whether it is better to attempt to wean a totalitarian, powerful China away from Pakistan or to wean a newly democratic Pakistan away from China. These are still hypothetical questions—and they may remain hypothetical—but they need to be discussed between Americans and Indians, Americans and Pakistanis, and most importantly, between Pakistanis and Indians.

How does one get from here to there? In the past, U.S. policy toward India and Pakistan was formulated and implemented from the top down in the context of a global strategic conflict. Policy could be discussed among a fairly small circle of officials, senators, members of Congress, and "old India hands." For most of the Cold War South Asia attracted neither a large lobby based on ethnic origins, nor an interested business community, nor an ideologically motivated group of academics and intellectuals (who were divided along pro-India and pro-Pakistan lines, derived largely from their initial regional exposure). Except for brief periods (during the height of the Bangladesh crisis, or during the Indian Emergency of 1975), the region never attracted the great passions associated with U.S. China policy, its actions in Central and South America, or the Southeast Asian intervention.

Now there is less interest at the top but growing activism at the grass roots. Human-rights groups find South Asia especially interesting because they can readily visit the somewhat less than perfect democracies in the region; America's business and investment communities have doubled and tripled investment in India during the past five years; there are now active, affluent lobbies of Americans of Pakistani and Indian origin, with a presence in nearly every congressional district, eager to influence votes that affect their former homelands. And of course, traditional concerns with strategic cooperation, the spread of nuclear weapons, and other "high" policy issues continue as before.

Although U.S. interests in South Asia are more diverse than during the Cold War, the policy process has not adapted to the management of this complexity. Since there can be no return to the overarching framework that characterized U.S. policy during the Cold War, the process has to begin at the other end: the development of coalitions among various groups and interests that regard South Asia as important. An objective assessment of the importance of India and Pakistan over the next decade will see it less as a threat than as a region where there is a significant opportunity to advance important, diverse, positive American interests. The immediate challenge to U.S. policy in South Asia in the post–Cold War period will be to stay ahead rather than trail behind these generally positive trends.

SUGGESTED READINGS

Asia Society. *Preventing Nuclear Proliferation in South Asia: Report of a Study Group*. New York: Asia Society, 1995.

South Asia and the United States after the Cold War: Report of a Study Mission. New York: Asia Society, 1994.

Bajpai, Kanti P., and Stephen P. Cohen, eds. *South Asia after the Cold War*. Boulder, Colo.: Westview Press, 1993.

Barnds, William. *India, Pakistan, and the Great Powers*. New York: Praeger, 1972.

Chari, P. R. *Indo-Pak Nuclear Standoff: The Role of the United States*. New Delhi: Manohar, 1995.

Council on Foreign Relations. *A New U.S. Policy toward India and Pakistan: Report of an Independent Task Force*. New York: Council on Foreign Relations, 1997.

Ganguly, Shivaji. *U.S. Policy toward South Asia*. Boulder, Colo.: Westview Press, 1990.

Ganguly, Sumit, and Harold Gould, eds. *The Hope and the Reality: U.S.-Indian Relations from Roosevelt to Reagan*. Boulder, Colo.: Westview Press, 1992.

Kux, Dennis. *Estranged Democracies, India and the United States: 1941–1991*. Washington, D.C.: National Defense University Press, 1993.

Limaye, Satu P. *U.S.-Indian Relations: The Pursuit of Accommodation*. Boulder, Colo.: Westview Press, 1993.

McMahon, Robert J. *The Cold War on the Periphery: The United States, India, and Pakistan*. New York: Columbia University Press, 1994.

Rudolph, Lloyd, and Susanne Rudolph, eds. *The Coordination of Complexity in South Asia* (studies prepared for the National Commission on the Organization of the Government for the Conduct of Foreign Policy), Appendix 5, Vol. 7. Washington, D.C.: U.S. Government Printing Office, 1975.

Schaeffer, Howard. *Chester Bowles: New Dealer in the Cold War*. Cambridge, Mass.: Harvard University Press, 1993.

Tahir-Kheli, Shirin. *India, Pakistan, and the United States: Breaking with the Past*. New York: Council on Foreign Relations, 1997.

About the authors

JOHN ADAMS has written extensively on economic development in South Asia. Among his books are *India: The Search for Unity, Democracy, and Progress* and *Exports, Politics, and Economic Development: Pakistan 1970–1982*. He held a Senior Fulbright Lectureship at Bangalore University in 1967–68, was a visiting fellow at the Institute of Development Studies, University of Sussex, in 1971, and is currently visiting scholar, Center for South Asian Studies at the University of Virginia.

PAUL R. BRASS is professor of political science and South Asian studies in the Department of Political Science and the Jackson School of International Studies at the University of Washington. Brass is a former Fellow of the Woodrow Wilson International Center for Scholars. He has published twelve books and numerous articles on comparative and South Asian politics, ethnic politics, and collective violence. His most recent books are *Theft of an Idol: Text and Context in the Representation of Collective Violence; Riots and Pogroms;* and *The Politics of India since Independence*, 2nd ed. He is currently working on a book on Hindu-Muslim communalism and collective violence in India.

STEPHEN PHILIP COHEN, until recently a faculty member at the University of Illinois, and cofounder of its Arms Control, Disarmament and International Security program, is currently a senior foreign policy staff member at the Brookings Institution. He has served as a member of the State Department's policy planning staff and was scholar-in-residence at the Ford Foundation's New Delhi office. An author or editor of eight books on South Asia, Cohen was a member of the Asia Society and Council on Foreign Relations study groups on the subcontinent.

SONALDE DESAI is associate professor of sociology and faculty associate at the Center on Population, Gender, and Social Inequality at the University of Maryland. She has conducted research on gender and social inequality in India and Pakistan. She has also written extensively on factors affecting children's and women's health in a variety of developing country contexts.

SUMIT GANGULY is professor of political science at Hunter College and the Graduate School of the City University of New York. A specialist on ethnic conflict in South and Southeast Asia, he has published articles in *Asian Affairs, Asian Survey, Current History, Foreign Affairs*, the *Journal of International Affairs, International Security*, the *Journal of Strategic Studies, Survival*, and the *Washington Quarterly*. He has received grants from the American Institute for Indian Studies, the W. Alton Jones Foundation, the Ford Foundation, and the United States Institute of Peace. He has been both a Fellow and a Guest Scholar at the Woodrow Wilson International Center for Scholars. His most recent works are *The Crisis in Kashmir: Portents of War, Hopes of Peace* and *Government Policies and Ethnic Relations in Asia and the Pacific* (coedited with Michael E. Brown). He is currently at work on a manuscript that seeks to explain political quiescence and ethnic violence in Sri Lanka and Malaysia.

SELIG S. HARRISON, a Senior Scholar at the Woodrow Wilson International Center for Scholars, has specialized in South Asian affairs and U.S. relations with South Asia for forty-six years as a foreign correspondent and a scholar. He served as Associated Press correspondent in New Delhi from 1951 to 1954, covering India, Pakistan, Afghanistan, Sri Lanka, and Nepal, and returned as South Asia bureau chief of the *Washington Post* from 1962 to 1965. As a senior fellow of the Carnegie Endowment for International Peace from 1974 to 1996, he revisited India and Pakistan every year on endowment projects. He has served as a senior fellow in charge of Asian Studies at the Brookings Institution and is an adjunct professor of Asian studies at the Elliott School of International Affairs, George Washington University. He has authored five books, including *India: The Most Dangerous Decades* and *India and America after the Cold War*.

PAUL H. KREISBERG is a Senior Scholar at the Woodrow Wilson International Center for Scholars. He is a former U.S. diplomat based in India and Pakistan and has moderated a series of fifteen "second track" diplomatic dialogues among Indians and Pakistanis since 1991.

DENNIS KUX is completing a history of U.S.-Pakistan relations as a companion to his history of U.S.-India relations, *Estranged Democracies, India and the United States, 1941–1991*. During his 39-year career in the U.S. foreign service, Ambassador Kux specialized in South Asia. He also had overseas assignments in Germany, Turkey, and the Ivory Coast, where he was the U.S. ambassador (1986–89). At the State Department, Kux served as country director for India and deputy assistant secretary of state for intelligence coordination. Kux is a former Fellow of the Woodrow Wilson International Center for Scholars. He has also received Fulbright and American Institute of Pakistan Studies grants to work on the U.S.-Pakistani relations book.

ROBERT LaPORTE., JR., is professor of public administration and political science at the Pennsylvania State University. He is the author of *Public Enterprises in Pakistan: The Hidden Crisis in Economic Development* (with Muntazar Bashir Ahmed), *Pakistan's Development Priorities: Choices for the Future* (with Shahid Javed Burki), and *Power and Privilege: Influence and Decision Making in Pakistan*. He is currently studying the changes in the governance of Pakistan.

KATHARINE F. SREEDHAR is director of the Unitarian Universalist Holdeen India Fund, which supports organizations in India that work for social change and human rights with the most disadvantaged groups: women, Scheduled Castes and tribes, ethnic and religious minorities, and landless and bonded laborers.

THOMAS PERRY THORNTON, adjunct professor of Asian studies at Georgetown and Johns Hopkins Universities, has dealt with South Asian matters in government and academia. Among other assignments, he was senior member of the policy planning staff of the State Department, and of the National Security Council staff under President Carter. He has written extensively on South Asia as well as on U.S. and Soviet foreign policy.

MARVIN G. WEINBAUM is professor of political science and the director of the Program in South Asian and Middle East Studies at the University of Illinois, Urbana-Champaign. Among his more recent books are *Afghanistan and Pakistan: Resistance and Reconstruction*, and *South Asia*

Approaches the Millennium (coedited with Chetan Kumar). A forthcoming book deals with economic and political liberalization in Pakistan, Egypt, and Turkey.

ANITA M. WEISS is associate professor of international studies at the University of Oregon. She has published extensively on social development and gender issues in Pakistan, including *Walls within Walls: Life Histories of Working Women in the Old City of Lahore* and *Culture, Class, and Development in Pakistan: The Emergence of an Industrial Bourgeoisie in Punjab*. She is currently researching how the U.N. Platform for Action is being implemented in Pakistan and in the larger arena of Islam, gender, and human rights. She has a forthcoming coedited book (with Zulfiqar Gilani) entitled *Power and Civil Society in Pakistan*.

Index

Other books in the series (*continued from page ii*)

Blair A. Ruble, *Money Sings: The Changing Politics of Urban Space in Post-Soviet Yaroslavl*

Deborah S. Davis, Richard Kraus, Barry Naughton, and Elizabeth J. Perry, editors, *Urban Spaces in Contemporary China: The Potential for Autonomy and Community in Post-Mao China*

William M. Shea and Peter A. Huff, editors, *Knowledge and Belief in America: Enlightenment Traditions and Modern Religious Thought*

W. Elliot Brownlee, editor, *Funding the Modern American State, 1941–1995: The Rise and Fall of the Era of Easy Finance*

W. Elliot Brownlee, *Federal Taxation in America: A Short History*

R. H. Taylor, editor, *The Politics of Elections in Southeast Asia*

Šumit Ganguly, *The Crisis in Kashmir: Portents of War, Hopes of Peace*

James W. Muller, editor, *Churchill as Peacemaker*

Donald R. Kelley and David Harris Sacks, editors, *The Historical Imagination in Early Modern Britain: History, Rhetoric, and Fiction, 1500–1800*

Richard Wightman Fox and Robert B. Westbrook, editors, *In Face of the Facts: Moral Inquiry in American Scholarship*

DATE DUE

GAYLORD			PRINTED IN U.S.A.